Praise for
One Child, Two Languages: A G
Childhood Educators of Children L
as a Second Language, Secon

"Relevant, timely, and practical . . . I recommend this book for teachers of young children and for anyone interested in second language learning in early childhood."
   —**Elizabeth D. Peña, Ph.D.,** Professor, Department of Communication Sciences and Disorders, The University of Texas at Austin

"This newly revised and expanded edition once again establishes it as *the* book that all early childhood students and professionals who work with young children must read . . . should be owned by all prospective and current teachers of young children."
   —**David K. Dickinson, Ed.D.,** Professor and Interim Chair, Department of Teaching and Learning, Vanderbilt University

"A comprehensive resource for educating young bilingual children . . . truly valuable."
   —**Carol Scheffner Hammer, Ph.D., CCC-SLP,** Associate Professor, Department of Communication Sciences and Disorders, The Pennsylvania State University

"Even better than the first edition. It provides innumerable practical suggestions, with back-up from research, for early childhood educators and trainers of early childhood educators on all aspects of the early education of ELLs."
   —**Fred Genesee, Ph.D.,** Professor, Department of Psychology, McGill University

"Enhanced to provide future and practicing teachers with more effective research-based practical examples . . . useful to those who work in classrooms with children who speak one language other than English as well as those in classrooms with children of many different language backgrounds."
   —**Andrea DeBruin-Parecki, Ph.D.,** Associate Professor, Early Childhood, Old Dominion University

"Comments from students are consistently positive about this text! They express appreciation for the practical approach of the author, the glimpses into real classrooms and lives of young children learning English, and strategies that work."
—**Karen Stanley, Ph.D.,** Birth–Kindergarten Coordinator,
The University of North Carolina at Pembroke

"An important contribution to the field that will provide valuable insights into how best to address the needs of linguistically and culturally diverse children and their families in the early years."
—**Sonia W. Soltero, Ph.D.,** Associate Professor and Director,
Bilingual-Bicultural Education Program, DePaul University

"A complete view of the needs of young children learning English as a second language . . . My students can easily relate the principles and strategies that Tabors presents to their own clinical learning experiences."
—**Karen A. Carrier, Ph.D.,** Associate Professor, Literacy
Education; Coordinator, Project QUILL, Northern Illinois
University

One Child, Two Languages

SECOND EDITION

One Child, Two Languages

SECOND EDITION

A Guide for
Early Childhood Educators
of Children Learning English
as a Second Language

by

Patton O. Tabors, Ed.D.
Cambridge, Massachusetts

Baltimore • London • Sydney

Paul H. Brookes Publishing Co.
Post Office Box 10624
Baltimore, Maryland 21285-0624
USA

www.brookespublishing.com

Typeset by Maryland Composition, Inc., Laurel, Maryland.
Manufactured in the United States of America
by Versa Press, Inc., East Peoria, Illinois.

·Author photography is by Richard Tabors. The photographs in Chapter 11
are courtesy of Jeanne M. De Temple. All other photographs in the book
and on the cover were taken by Patton O. Tabors.

All of the individuals in this book have been given pseudonyms to protect
their privacy.

Library of Congress Cataloging-in-Publication Data
Tabors, Patton O.
    One child, two languages : a guide for early childhood educators of children
learning English as a second language / by Patton O. Tabors. — 2nd ed.
        p. cm.
    Includes bibliographical references and index.
    ISBN-13: 978-1-55766-921-6 (pbk.)
    ISBN-10: 1-55766-921-X (pbk.)
    1. Second language acquisition. I. Title.
P118.2.T325 2008
372.652'1044—dc22   2007031425

British Library Cataloguing in Publication data are available from the British
Library.

2012   2011   2010   2009   2008
10   9   8   7   6   5   4   3   2   1

Contents

About the Author

Patton O. Tabors, Ed.D., retired in 2005 as Principal Research Associate at the Harvard Graduate School of Education. Prior to beginning her doctoral studies at the Harvard Graduate School of Education in 1981, Dr. Tabors was an elementary school teacher and a childbirth educator. Her doctoral studies focused on first- and second-language acquisition in young children. Her dissertation research described the developmental pathways of a group of young children learning English as a second language, which she later wrote about in the first edition of *One Child, Two Languages* (Paul H. Brookes Publishing Co., 1997).

From 1987 until 2003, Dr. Tabors was the research coordinator of the Home–School Study of Language and Literacy Development in collaboration with Catherine E. Snow and David K. Dickinson. She and Dr. Dickinson co-edited *Beginning Literacy with Language: Young Children Learning at Home and School* (Paul H. Brookes Publishing Co., 2001), which was based on the study's findings about the relationship between early childhood interactions and kindergarten language and literacy skills. More recently, Dr. Tabors co-authored, with Catherine E. Snow, Michelle V. Porche, and Stephanie R. Harris, *Is Literacy Enough? Pathways to Academic Success for Adolescents* (Paul H. Brookes Publishing Co., 2007), which explains factors beyond K–3 literacy that influenced students' later school success in the Home–School Study of Language and Literacy Development.

Dr. Tabors also directed research related to low-education and low-income mothers reading to their preschool-age children as part of the Manpower Development Research Corporation evaluations of two welfare-to-work projects—New Chance and JOBS—and was the director of research for the Harvard Language Diversity Project, a subproject of the New England Research Center on Head Start Quality, directed by Dr. Dickinson.

In 2000, Dr. Tabors became the principal investigator of a longitudinal project, the Early Childhood Study of Language and Literacy Development of Spanish-Speaking Children, which followed a sample of more than 300 bilingual children from preschool to second grade. With her colleagues, Dr. Mariela M. Páez and Dr. Lisa M. López, she has used the findings from this study to continue to inform the ongoing discussion about young children and second-language and -literacy acquisition.

Foreword to the Second Edition

At the time the first edition of *One Child, Two Languages* was published in 1997, the United States was in the midst of a demographic transformation that gained extraordinary momentum during the last decades of the 20th century (Suárez-Orozco & Páez, 2002). Eleven years later, the reality of our heterogeneous population is evident across the nation and especially in our schools. The population of the United States has changed from a largely white European-origin population to a diverse mix of ethnicity and origin. More than a quarter of this population is now made up of ethnically marked minorities such as African Americans, Latinos, and Asian Americans. Immigrant children and their families have played a significant role in this demographic transformation and continue to shape the character, needs, and successes of our nation. Between 1979 and 2004, the number of school-age children (ages 5–17) who spoke a language other than English at home increased from 3.8 million (or 9%) to 9.9 million (or 19%). Of the students who spoke a language other than English at home, 71% spoke Spanish (National Center for Education Statistics, 2004).

The largest and fastest-growing population of English language learners (ELLs) in the United States consists of students who immigrated before kindergarten and U.S.-born children of immigrants (Capps et al., 2005). These statistics are particularly important in today's context of expanding programs and services for young children in early childhood education, as an increasing number of children who are entering early childhood education settings, such as preschool, Head Start, and child care centers, are ELLs. There is a growing recognition that all teachers need to be prepared to address the needs of this population in order to realize the potential of every child, including those who are learning English for the first time as they enter early childhood settings. But how do children learn two languages, and how can we support their acquisition of English while valuing their home languages? What can teachers do to better understand these children and to plan effective classrooms that provide second-language learners with access to learning experiences? These are exactly the questions that the second edition of *One Child, Two Languages* tackles to help early childhood educators develop techniques to more effectively serve children who are learning English as a second language.

The author begins the book by providing information about second-language learning. The explanations go beyond stages of language acquisition to explore individual differences and factors that can influence learning a new language. In the second part of the book, the focus is on the instructional environment. Suggestions for classroom organization, communication approaches, and curriculum considerations are clearly explained and practical. Teachers will find the contents of this book to be exactly the type of information they need to make their classroom practices more accessible and inclusive of all students. The addition of a study guide enhances the content of this edition by encouraging teachers to reflect on their practice and apply some of the information and strategies presented in the book. The author's use of case studies and examples from observations in real classrooms allows individuals with different backgrounds to connect and reflect on their teaching. It does not matter if you are a beginner teacher or an experienced teacher, this book will be useful and have an impact on your teaching practices with young children.

One Child, Two Languages also provides strategies that help educators promote children's acquisition of English while valuing and supporting children's first language. This additive perspective is important and reflects current knowledge about how bilingual students learn. We know that children's first language can serve as the foundation for learning English and when parents and educators understand and facilitate this process, acquiring a new language can be successful. Current research in the field of early childhood education supports this approach, as studies have shown that using students' first language is an effective strategy in supporting children's transition to school and enhancing their social skills and learning experiences (Chang, Crawford, Early, & Bryant, 2007). In addition, a recent synthesis of the research in developing literacy in a second language concluded that oral language proficiency and literacy in the first language can be used to facilitate literacy development in English (August & Shanahan, 2006).

The new edition of this book is marked by a stronger focus on literacy, expanded information about assessment practices that are effective for second-language learners, and a new chapter on internationally adopted children. These changes reflect current developments in research and practice in early childhood education.

First, we have seen in recent years an increased attention to literacy and its connection to language learning. Early exposure to literacy and curricula activities that build on literacy-related skills such as alphabet knowledge, phonological awareness, and writing skills are critical as children learn how to read and write. For children learning English for the first time, an explicit focus on these precursor skills is necessary and facilitates literacy acquisition. The author describes these skills and provides information on how to incorporate effective literacy teaching in the early childhood classroom.

Second, the current context of high standards and accountability has increased the need for appropriate and valid assessment strategies in early childhood. A particular challenge for educators has been to develop assessment practices that are useful with bilingual students and embedded in curriculum practices. In this book, the author addresses this issue and presents practical tools and suggestions for improving assessment practices in early childhood classrooms.

Third, the chapter on internationally adopted children deals with a new and growing population of children in this nation. Educators will find the author's description of this group and its distinctive pathway to learning English both surprising and informative.

Children who are learning English as a second language will continue to increase in early childhood settings in the United States. The education they receive in these settings will shape their development and engagement in future learning experiences. Research has found that children who attend high-quality early childhood programs are better prepared for school academically, socially, and emotionally (NICHD Early Child Care Research Network, 2002). The quality of programs depends to a great degree upon the preparation of teachers and their ability to meet the needs of all learners. We need to strive for knowledge about our students and information that will make us better educators in the current demographic reality of our programs and schools. *One Child, Two Languages* represents a unique contribution for early childhood educators who are dedicated to excellence in teaching and endeavor to be highly qualified and well prepared for teaching children learning English as a second language.

Mariela M. Páez, Ed.D.
Assistant Professor
Lynch School of Education
Boston College
Chestnut Hill, Massachusetts

REFERENCES

August, D., & Shanahan, T. (Eds.). (2006). *Developing literacy in second-language learners: Report of the National Literacy Panel on language minority children and youth.* Mahwah, NJ: Lawrence Erlbaum Associates.

Capps, R., Fix, M., Murray, J., Ost, J., Passel, J., & Herwantoro, S. (2005). *The new demography of America's schools: Immigration and the No Child Left Behind Act.* Washington, DC: The Urban Institute.

Chang, F., Crawford, G., Early, D., & Bryant, D. (2007). Spanish speaking children's social and language development in pre-kindergarten classrooms. *Journal of Early Education and Development, 18*(2), 243–269.

National Center for Education Statistics. (2004). *Language minority learners and their labor market indicators—recent trends.* Washington, DC: U.S. Department of Education.

NICHD Early Child Care Research Network. (2002). Early child care and children's development prior to school entry: Results from the NICHD Study of Early Child Care. *American Educational Research Journal, 39*, 133–164.

Suárez-Orozco, M.M., & Páez, M.M. (2002). *Latinos: Remaking America.* Berkeley: University of California Press.

Foreword to the First Edition

Every June *The Boston Globe* publishes a picture and brief biography of each of the valedictorians from Boston-area high schools. This year, like all those in the recent past, the vast majority of valedictorians whose pictures were published—the students selected as the best in their schools—were immigrants to the United States. They had come here with their parents as 3-year-olds or 6-year-olds or perhaps even as 10- or 12-year-olds. These are not the immigrants we hear described by some politicians, immigrants who are exploiting American generosity or threatening the American way of life. These are immigrants whose parents have sacrificed to give their children a better chance, who have chosen educational achievement as their route to success, who have embraced the American dream, who have worked hard at their studies and often at after-school jobs as well, and who will be the doctors and scientists and engineers we need for the approaching 21st century. These valedictorians, and their many successful immigrant classmates, managed to learn English at some point on their path to academic accomplishment.

For immigrant children who arrive in the United States old enough to attend elementary school, a variety of programs exist to receive them and to help them adjust to a new culture and a new language. Since the mid-1960s, educators have had experience with bilingual education and with teaching English as a second language to school-age children; consequently, there is now a solid body of practical experience and research evidence available to inform good practice.

Immigrant children who arrive before the age of 6 have, until now, been largely ignored. One of the most widespread and harmful myths in our society is that very young children will learn a second language automatically, quickly, and easily—with no special attention to their needs for an optimal learning environment. Thus, as a society we have hardly considered ways to help these preschool children learn English; nor have we thought much about how to help them maintain their home language. The preschool and Head Start teachers whose classes are increasingly populated by non–English-speaking children have been constructing their responses to these new challenges with little help and sometimes with considerable puzzlement.

One Child, Two Languages is designed to inform, stimulate, and help anyone serving young second-language learners. It draws on observations of classrooms where such children are learning English, on interviews with experienced teachers of English-learning children, and on research about second-language acquisition and bilingualism. By describing a variety of children learning English in different classroom settings, it invites preschool classroom teachers to be reflective about the impact of their practices on non–English-speaking children. This book offers practical tools such as suggestions for interviews with parents and for appropriate assessments of young children, but, more important, it makes accessible the information that reflective practitioners need in order to improve their own practice.

In this book the author defines the double-bind that second-language learners face; that is, they cannot learn the new language unless they can engage in social interaction with those who speak the new language, but they have limited social access to those individuals until they learn the new language. This society faces a similar double-bind—one in which fear of the different prevents contact that would dissolve the fear. We are unable to benefit from the rich cultural and linguistic diversity of this nation as long as we view the immigrants who bring that diversity as threatening and troublesome. We cannot get to know what we fear, and we cannot reduce the fear without knowledge. Suzette Haden Elgin, a linguist and novelist, described in her trilogy *Native Tongue* (Elgin, S.H. [1994]. Bergenfield, NJ: New American Library/New York: Daw Books) a future world in which communication between Terrans and the many races of aliens in contact with the planet Terra is made possible by the existence of a caste of Linguists—specialists in the alien languages. Linguist children in Elgin's world learn the alien languages by spending several hours a day in specially designed interfaces, together with alien young, for the first several years of their lives. These children subsequently grow up to assume positions of great power and responsibility, which they obtain because of their capacities as translators and interpreters. We might think of North American preschools as low-tech interfaces where children sharing experiences at the water table, during circle time, and as they have snack come to enjoy mutual understanding and effective communication across linguistic boundaries. In the best preschool classrooms, this is happening right now. In others, it may take only minor adjustments to ensure optimal communication and optimal language learning. Such adjustments may be our best hope of devising our own effective interfaces, thus creating a society (in the next generation, if not this one) that embraces diversity and celebrates multilingualism as well as one in which all children have access to the power and benefits derived from speaking English well.

Catherine E. Snow, Ph.D.
Henry Lee Shattuck Professor of Education
Graduate School of Education
Harvard University
Cambridge, Massachusetts

Preface

The title of this book—*One Child, Two Languages: A Guide for Early Childhood Educators of Children Learning English as a Second Language*—reflects its dual focus on children as language and literacy learners and teachers as facilitators of children's language and literacy learning. The main portion of the book is divided into two parts. The first part details the second-language–learning child's task and the second part discusses the role that the teacher can play in helping children during the second-language– and literacy–learning process. The third part of the book details new information about a contrasting group of second-language learners: internationally adopted children.

Furthermore, the title is meant to convey that young children can and do learn two (or more) languages and that this process involves adding a second language to a first language rather than replacing the first language with a second. For the purposes of this book, the language being discussed as the second language is English. The information presented in this book about learning English as a second language, however, would be the same no matter what second language an individual child was learning. Although the second-language–learning process is the topic of this book, this is not meant to imply that a child's home-language and -literacy development should not also be supported and developed. For this reason, strategies that can help educators and parents continue to support first-language acquisition are included in the book as well.

This book is written primarily for early childhood educators, as the children who were involved in the research presented here were, for the most part, 3–5 years old. However, the developmental sequence of second-language– and literacy–learning and the techniques for support and facilitation of the processes that are discussed in the book are also applicable throughout the early childhood period. The recommendations in this book, on the whole, therefore, can be implemented within the context of any developmental classroom, making it possible for early childhood educators to take advantage of them without major organizational or curricular changes.

Planning early childhood education programs for second-language–learning children will require additional information beyond what early childhood educators already know about child development. Information about the importance of the cultural and linguistic backgrounds of second-language–learning children, the course that second-language learning is likely to take in young children (including internationally adopted children), the supportive techniques that teachers can use in their classrooms, and the part that second-language learners' families' plans may play in linguistic and educational decisions will need to be integrated into their basic knowledge of child development. The main goal of this book is to provide this information so that early childhood education teachers and administrators can develop effective programs for young second-language learners in the context of planning for all children.

Acknowledgments

I wish to thank the colleagues who have discussed the material in this book with me, the early childhood education administrators who have given me access to their programs, the teachers whose classrooms I have visited and whose wisdom I have tapped in workshops and interviews, and the children who have accepted me into their world and let me eavesdrop on their very important conversations.

Chapter One

Introduction

Three-year-old Chantal lives in a small city in Massachusetts with her 5-year-old brother, her 20-year-old half-sister, and her mother and father. Chantal and her brother were born in Massachusetts, but their parents and their half-sister immigrated to the United States during a time of political strife in Haiti. Chantal's father works at a hospital as an orderly, and her half-sister takes English as a Second Language classes at the community college and has a job as a housekeeper at a local hotel. Chantal speaks Haitian Creole at home with her family.

This year Chantal has been enrolled in a Head Start classroom near her home. When she first came to the classroom, she did not speak any English, but during the course of the school year, she has begun to use some English during interactions with the English-speaking teachers and children. When Chantal's mother comes to pick up Chantal at school each day, she nods and smiles at the teachers but is unable to carry on any conversation with them about Chantal's activities. After helping to clear one of the tables used for the children's lunch, Chantal's mother collects Chantal and leaves the classroom. When the teachers want to schedule a home visit with Chantal's mother, they ask a social services worker who speaks Haitian Creole to make the appointment and to accompany them on the visit to translate for them.

Chantal's family is just one of many families that have immigrated to the United States in recent years, increasing the population of nonnative English speakers. The U.S. Census Bureau reports that 20% of the people older than 5 years of age who participated in the American Community Survey of 2005 reported speaking a language other than

English. The languages represented in this population were as follows: Spanish, 62%; Indo-European languages, 19.1%; Asian/Pacific Islander, 15%; and others (including Native American, Arabic, Hebrew, and African languages), 4% (U.S. Census Bureau, 2005).

Not surprisingly, the arrival of large numbers of immigrant families has had an effect on early childhood education. For example, Head Start classrooms such as the one Chantal attended have experienced a sharp increase in the enrollment of children from other than English-speaking homes. In 2002, the English Language Learners Focus Group Report stated that

> approximately 27% of the children served by Head Start speak a language other than English at home and more than 140 languages are represented in Head Start programs nationwide. The linguistic representation of English language learners enrolled in Head Start programs is predominantly Spanish-speaking. The 2000–2001 Head Start Program Information Report (PIR) data on 900,000 children by dominant language indicated that 201,486 were Spanish language speakers; . . . 13,419 were speakers of Asian languages; 2,416 were enrolled as Native American language speakers; and 26,827 were speakers of other languages. (p. 3)

Children such as Chantal now make up a considerable proportion of the children in many early childhood programs of all types. It can be anticipated that a large percentage of these young children are native Spanish speakers but that a myriad of other languages are represented as well. Although early childhood programs in certain areas of the United States are most heavily affected, almost all early childhood programs are affected in some way. Planning ways to serve these young children effectively is now a major challenge for early childhood educators.

EARLY CHILDHOOD EDUCATION SETTINGS FOR ENGLISH LANGUAGE LEARNERS

Early childhood education programs, from small family child care programs to private or public programs or child care facilities to federally funded Head Start programs, have responded to the arrival of English-language–learning children by developing programs that deal with the linguistic needs of these children in different ways. One useful way to categorize these programs is related to how language is used in the classroom.

Early childhood education settings can be divided into three major categories related to language use (see Table 1). In the following paragraphs, each type of setting is described, and an example is presented

Table 1.   Types of early childhood education settings for children from other than English-speaking homes in the United States

	First-language classroom	Bilingual classroom	English-language classroom
Teachers	Native speakers of L1[a]	Bilingual in L1 and English or native speaker of L1 paired with native speaker of English	Native speakers of English
Children	Native speakers of L1	All native speakers of L1 or mixture of L1 and English speakers	Native speakers of L1 or native speakers of different L1s or either of above and English speakers
Classroom organization	All interaction in L1	Interaction split between L1 and English	All interaction in English
Language outcomes	Development of L1; no development of English	Maintenance or development of L1, while also developing English	Development of English; no maintenance or development of L1

[a]L1 any specific native language that is not English.

from a series of ethnographies completed as part of a research project at the Harvard Graduate School of Education (Tabors, Aceves, Bartolomé, Páez, & Wolf, 2000).

The first type of setting is one in which the home or first language of the child is the primary language of the classroom. For Spanish-speaking children, this means that the teachers must be native speakers of Spanish; for Arabic speakers, this means that the teachers must be native speakers of Arabic. This kind of classroom is a first-language classroom.

Advocates of first-language classrooms for children from other than English-speaking homes (e.g., Wong Fillmore, 1991b) emphasize the importance of the development of the first language as a necessary basis for later literacy and, consequently, for later school success. These advocates are particularly concerned that young children are highly susceptible to losing their first language if the first language is not strongly maintained during the early childhood years. Their conclusion, therefore, is that children should attend first-language early childhood education settings and should not be exposed to a second-language setting before elementary school. Even then, they believe, there should be a strong developmental first-language program throughout the early elementary years to establish literacy in the first language.

This attitude was strongly supported by the teachers in the Spanish-language Head Start classroom for 3-year-olds that was established as part of the previously mentioned research project. In this classroom, the teachers, both of whom were native speakers of Spanish, were encouraged to use Spanish for the first time in their teaching careers. The children came from homes in which Spanish was at least one of the languages being spoken. One of the teachers, Sara, talked about the benefits of Spanish-language instruction for the children: "I saw it right at the beginning of the year. . . . The kids understand and respond. . . . Sometimes we do a lot more than what I used to do with my other classes . . ." (Tabors, Aceves, Bartolomé, et al., 2000, p. 431). Alicia, the second teacher in the classroom,

> argued that second-language learning would be greatly facilitated once the bilingual children had a strong home-language foundation, "[l]o importante es enseñar su primer idioma . . . no van a tener problemas en aprender inglés—pero vamos a darle una buena base para que ellos sigan construyendo encima de su base." [*What is important is to teach them their native language . . . they won't have problems learning English—but let's give them a good base on which to construct meaning.*] (Tabors, Aceves, Bartolomé, et al., 2000, p. 431)

A second type of early childhood education setting is one in which there are individual teachers who are themselves bilingual or in which there are two teachers who have different language backgrounds. For instance, in a classroom that serves Mandarin-speaking children, one teacher in the classroom may be English speaking and the other may speak Mandarin; or in a classroom that serves children who have recently come to the United States from Haiti, the teacher may be bilingual in Haitian Creole and English. In these situations, language choice becomes an issue: Which language is being spoken to whom, by whom, and under what circumstances? This type of classroom is a bilingual classroom.

Bilingual early childhood education settings may take a variety of forms. In some settings, all of the children come from one particular other than English language background, and only the teacher or teachers communicate with the children in English. At the other end of the spectrum are two-way bilingual or dual language programs, in which approximately half of the children in any given classroom are from the same other than English-speaking backgrounds and the other half are from English-speaking backgrounds. In these programs, instruction is scheduled so that both languages are used in meaningful ways during the day or during the week. In this situation, each child's first language is supported while a second language is added and children have second-language input from other children, not just from their teacher.

The bilingual classroom that was visited for the research project was led by Brenda, a proficient English-Spanish bilingual. A second teacher, María, was Spanish dominant. All but two of the children had some Spanish-language proficiency at the beginning of the school year. In this classroom, Spanish and English were spoken alternately during the day by both the teachers and the children. "In an interview, Brenda stated she strongly believed children should have the choice of speaking their home language at school. . . . 'In my classroom, everything is done in English and Spanish—this is how children learn'" (Tabors, Aceves, Bartolomé, et al., 2000, p. 422). The two teachers told us that they made decisions about which language to use with the children based on their assessment of the children's preferences and proficiencies. However, interestingly enough, although Brenda often spoke Spanish with the Spanish-speaking children during individual or small-group activities, she always conducted large-group activities, such as book reading and circle time, in English. In this way, she turned group time into an English-language–learning opportunity.

The third type of early childhood education setting is one in which the primary language is English, even though there are children in the classroom whose home language is not English. In this situation, the teachers may have little or no proficiency in a language other than

English, and their classroom may include children from only one language group or from many different language groups. This type of classroom is an English-language classroom.

In an English-language classroom, the teacher or teachers use English for almost all interactions; therefore, in such a classroom, a child whose home language is not English will not have his or her language supported, although there may be other children from the same language background with whom to talk and play. These classrooms can be a more or less welcoming location for a child whose home language is not English, depending on how multicultural the curriculum is and on what efforts the teachers make to bring parents and other cultural representatives into the classroom.

The two teachers in the English-language classroom in the research study were both native speakers of English, and the children came from five different first-language backgrounds (Haitian Creole, Barbadian Creole, Spanish, Japanese, and English). In this classroom, the teachers relied on English to get their messages across, often augmenting their words with gestures. Early in the year, the head teacher, Robert, "explained that he believes that immersion in an exclusively English-language classroom helps children learn the language more quickly and easily. He believes their progress is slowed down when they can rely on their home language to communicate at school" (Tabors, Aceves, Bartolomé, et al., 2000, p. 414). Interestingly, however, when a Spanish-speaking student teacher came to the classroom in the spring, Robert mentioned that he was still thinking through his ideas about native language use and did not discourage her from using Spanish with the Spanish-speaking children.

In the real world, of course, it is sometimes difficult to categorize actual programs. Therefore, these categories are meant merely as guidelines under which teachers and administrators of early childhood education settings can locate their programs in relation to a set of features that have been found to be consistent across a variety of settings.

These categories are also useful when thinking about the material in this book. Because much of the research and most of the examples in this book come from an English-language early childhood education setting, it is this setting that serves as a baseline for discussing second-language learning in young children. In addition, discussions of how language acquisition processes would differ in a bilingual classroom are included. Because second-language acquisition is not a goal of first-language classrooms, such classrooms are not a topic of this book except when they are discussed with regard to supplementary settings, such as special-purpose Saturday or Sunday schools.

FIRST- AND SECOND-LANGUAGE DEVELOPMENT

When young children such as Chantal are enrolled in an English-language or bilingual early childhood education setting, they begin the process of second-language acquisition. To start the process of thinking about second-language acquisition, it is useful first to review how children learn a first language and then use that process as a contrast to second-language learning.

First-Language Acquisition

All typically developing children learn a first language, whichever language that may be. This process, which occurs in the context of social interaction within the child's family structure, begins with the production of recognizable sounds around the age of 1 year and continues intensively throughout early childhood. In fact, although most of the basic skills of oral language are acquired by the time a child is about 5 years old, more advanced uses of language (e.g., debating, lecturing) may continue to be acquired well into adulthood, and vocabulary acquisition is a lifelong process.

Acquiring a first language is a monumental task. To understand what a large task this is, one might think of the language system as a puzzle with a variety of interlocking pieces, all of which must fit together for the puzzle to be complete. There are five pieces of this puzzle:

1. *Phonology*, or the sounds of the language

2. *Vocabulary*, or the words of the language

3. *Grammar*, or how the words are put together to make sentences in the language

4. *Discourse*, or how sentences are put together to, for example, tell stories, make an argument, or explain how something works

5. *Pragmatics*, or the rules about how to use the language

For children to be considered native speakers of a language, they must have control over all of these aspects of the language system. Developing this control is a major undertaking of the first 5 years of a child's life. In the following discussion, the first language acquisition process is discussed using English as the example language, but the same discussion could apply to other languages just as well.

The process of language development begins with a baby's babbling. At first, babies babble a wide variety of sounds; over time, they begin to restrict their babbling to sounds they hear in words spoken by those around them. When infants being raised in an English-speaking environment are 5–8 months old, they start producing syllables such as *ba*, *ma*, and *ga* in the course of their babbling. Open syllables such as these are relatively easy to pronounce and thus form the basis for many "baby talk" words such as *mama*, *booboo*, and *peepee*. Words that contain closed syllables, those with a consonant at the end, are harder to pronounce, especially if quite different consonants need to be articulated within one syllable. Thus, young children learning English often say "goggie" for *doggie* or "guck" for *truck*, because they simply cannot yet pronounce two different sounds such as /g/ and /d/ or /t/ in one syllable.

Between 12 and 18 months of age, most babies produce their first word or words, having made the connection between certain groups of sounds and objects or certain groups of sounds and "getting things done." A baby's first 50 words usually contain a mix of different types of words: names for important people such as *daddy*, object names such as *cookie*, functional words such as *up*, and social words such as *bye-bye*.

After acquiring a number of words, children begin demonstrating an understanding of the grammatical requirements of language by combining first two and then more words, thus developing the ability to express more complex relationships with their words. At first a child will say "kitty" to represent everything from "there's a cat" to "I'm scared of that cat," and it will be necessary for an adult to interpret the full meaning. Soon, however, the child will combine "kitty" with an attribute such as "pretty," an action such as "bite," or a location such as "outside," thus beginning the process of building the grammatical units that are sentences.

Throughout this period, children are also learning the proper ways to use their words. *Hi* and *bye-bye* are words that are acquired early, perhaps because parents in American culture work hard to get their babies to produce these words at the proper times to show that they are being socialized correctly. At the same time, babies also learn the turn-taking rules of conversation, often before they have anything to contribute to the conversation. In exchanges between mothers and infants, mothers even consider burps as appropriate turn-taking moves by babies.

The process of learning the culturally appropriate way to use language continues throughout the early childhood years as children learn the rules of politeness and the "ins and outs" of what can appropriately be said where, when, under what conditions, and to whom. Because these rules are complicated and subtle, young children often violate

ROSE IS ROSE ® by Pat Brady

ROSE IS ROSE reprinted by permission of United Feature Syndicate, Inc.

them, giving the authors of cartoons a wealth of material (see, e.g., *Rose Is Rose* comic strip).

During the early childhood years, children engage in extended oral language development. Building on the earlier development of sounds, children begin work on rhyming and identifying initial sounds in words, often showing endless fascination with this type of word play. At the same time, they acquire a staggering 6–10 new words daily while also broadening their understanding of the meanings of the words they already know.

Children also begin to acquire the more complicated forms of grammar during this time period; in English, these are past tenses, embedded clauses, and passive constructions. This process frequently results in creative mistakes such as "My mom breakeded the plate," which show that children are noticing consistent patterns and applying them to the language system as they understand it.

A distinctive accomplishment of this period is the development of the ability to construct discourse. Young children begin to participate in the construction of explanations, the development of arguments, and the telling of narratives. In American culture, these efforts begin by being co-constructed with an older sibling or adult. In this process, the sibling or adult asks appropriate questions ("What did you do at school today?") and the child responds ("I climbed to the top of the structure!"). Gradually the child takes on more of the burden of the telling until he or she can produce the type of discourse independently (see Figure 1).

During this time, children also learn to modify what they are saying depending on the audience. A child learns, for example, that he has to give Aunt Sarah, who does not know all of his friends, a lot more background information about *who, why,* and *where* before launching into a story about a disaster at the playground.

Of course, in addition to providing children with the means to

Brad:	I want to go to the ice cream store.
Mother:	**Well, you can't. It's raining.**
Brad:	Did you see the ice cream store man go home?
Mother:	I don't know. I don't know what time they close. Maybe we could put on our rain coats.
Brad:	Do you got a rain coat?
Mother:	No, but I'll wear something.
Grandmother:	I'll let Mommy use my umbrella.
Brad:	If she has . . . (Thunder cracks outside.). Thunder.
Mother:	Thunder.
Grandmother:	Mmhm.
Brad:	*We can run to the ice cream store. Then we can run back home. And so the thunder won't get us, right?*
Mother:	Right.
Grandmother:	**You know what the thunder is?**
Brad:	**Yeah. Thunder and lightning.**
Grandmother:	**Yeah. And the thunder is when the angels are upstairs bowling. And that's one of them just got a spare.**
Mother:	Brad should get out his Berenstain Bear. I'm going to have to let Ma read it and that'll tell her what thunder is, huh? (laughing)
Grandmother:	Mmhm.
Mother:	Tells all about thunder and . . .
Grandfather:	**That's the energy. Thunder is caused by energy in the clouds.**
Brad:	*Yeah, but one day I was sleeping in my bed for a long long time and thunder and lightning came from outside and I was trying to find something that was yellow outside in the dark all by itself. And it came out. And it was thunder and lightning and I hided from it.*
Grandfather:	*And you hided from it?*
Brad:	*Yeah.*
Grandfather:	*Where'd you hide? Under your blankets?*
Brad:	*No, under my covers. Like when I was sleeping.*
Grandfather:	Do you always pull the covers up over your head? Yeah?

Figure 1. A mealtime conversation showing explanations (distinguished in bold) and narratives (distinguished in italic) between Brad (3½ years old) and his mother, grandmother, and grandfather. (From Beals, D., & Snow, C. [1994]. "Thunder is when the angels are upstairs bowling": Narratives and explanations at the dinner table. *Journal of Narrative and Life History,* 4[4], 341–343; reprinted by permission.)

communicate with others, these skills in oral language have been closely linked to literacy development in young children (Snow, Burns, & Griffin, 1998). A longitudinal study of English-speaking children from low-income backgrounds showed that early language input at home and in early childhood education settings is predictive of literacy abilities in kindergarten (Dickinson & Tabors, 2001) and that kindergarten abilities are highly predictive of fourth-grade reading comprehension (Snow, Porche, Tabors, & Harris, 2007). Therefore, starting off well in a first language has been shown to have a direct link to later school success.

Second-Language Acquisition

Some young children develop language skills in not only a first language but also in a second language. When this happens, the child is considered to be involved in a process of second-language acquisition.

There are two types of second-language acquisition among young children: simultaneous and sequential acquisition. Simultaneous acquisition of two languages occurs when children are exposed to both languages from a very early age, sometimes as a result of each parent speaking a separate language with the child or both parents speaking one language and a caregiver speaking another language with the child. Sequential acquisition occurs when a child begins to learn a second language after the first language is at least partly established.

Simultaneous Acquisition   When young children are exposed to two languages from birth, there is often an initial period of acquiring words in one or the other of the languages. Children will quickly demonstrate a capacity to keep their two languages separate, however, and often display an early developing understanding of when one or the other of their languages should be used (for case studies, see Fantini, 1985; Saunders, 1988; and Taeschner, 1983).

Taeschner (1983), for example, wrote about raising her two daughters as German-Italian bilinguals living in Rome. Although she is a German-Italian bilingual herself, Taeschner spoke only German with her children, and her husband, a native speaker of Italian, spoke only Italian with the girls. By the time the older daughter, Lisa, was 1½ years old, her vocabulary consisted of 18 words: 6 in German, 6 in Italian, and 6 that would work in either language (e.g., *mama*). Lisa was using 100 words 5 months later: 46 were Italian, 34 were German, and 20 (many of which were names for people) would work in either language. In the intervening time, Lisa had had more contact with Italian speakers because she had spent time with an Italian grandparent and aunt as well as with an Italian-speaking caregiver. As Taeschner remarked,

> It is clear that there is a close relationship between the amount of contact with each language and the child's linguistic output; the quantity of contact the child had with each language determined the quantity

of words she learned. When Lisa had more opportunities of speaking Italian, her output increased, and the same was true of German. (1983, p. 194)

Although some parents and educators worry about the possibility of language confusion in situations in which children are exposed to two languages from birth (see Meisel, 1989, for evidence against language confusion), researchers think that, far from being a problem, the process of acquiring two languages from an early age has cognitive as well as social benefits (Hakuta, 1986).

Sequential Acquisition   Other children acquire a second language after the basis for their first language has been established. This sequential acquisition of a second language occurs, for instance, when a young child such as Chantal enters an early childhood setting in which her home language is not the language used in the classroom. It is this type of second-language acquisition that is the topic of this book.

If a child learns two languages simultaneously, and if those two languages are developed equally during childhood, then the language development process is expected to be the same for both languages. In any sequential second-language acquisition situation, however, there are a number of factors that make the two processes different.

First, second-language learners, even young ones, already have prior knowledge of language and its uses. In the process of learning a first language, they have determined what communication is all about and, furthermore, what particular systems and styles of communication work in their immediate environment. For these children, then, second-language acquisition is not a process of discovering what language *is* but, rather, of discovering what *this* language is.

Second, unlike first-language acquisition, which is a feature of a specific developmental period in a child's life, second-language acquisition can be undertaken at any age. There are two variables related to second-language acquisition and age: cognitive capacity and cognitive demand. The older a child is when facing any cognitive challenge, the greater the child's cognitive capacity will be to take on that challenge. A high school student obviously has many more intellectual skills to bring to bear in any learning situation than does a student in kindergarten. The cognitive demands of the tasks that a high school student faces, however, are also much greater than those a kindergarten student faces. The idea that young children are facile, even magically rapid, language learners is no doubt derived from how little language ability they need to possess to impress someone with their language abilities.

Third, whereas learning a first language is a relatively unproblematic endeavor for typically developing children, second-language acquisition is a much riskier business in which individual characteristics may well play a large part. The following factors have all been proposed as making a difference in second-language acquisition:

1. *An aptitude factor:* Some people are more talented than others as second-language learners.

2. *A social factor*: Some people are more outgoing and more willing than others to take risks as second-language learners.

3. *A psychological factor:* Some people are more motivated than others because they want to become like the people who speak the language they are trying to learn.

In assessing the progress that an individual child is making in a second language, it may be necessary to take some or all of these factors into consideration.

What about the literacy development process when a child is a second-language learner? Given that research has established the link between oral language development and literacy, what happens to this sequence when a second language is introduced? Clearly, if children maintain their home-language development and are placed in learning-to-read situations that capitalize on that home language, then the same developmental sequence can occur. In fact, this is the process supported by bilingual education, in which children are taught to read in their first language while gaining proficiency in English, and then literacy skills are expected to transfer from their first language to English. However, as mentioned previously, there is concern about young children not developing their first language completely once they are exposed to a second language, thus making them inappropriate candidates for bilingual education. All of these issues remain the subject of research and are of great concern to early childhood educators.

WHAT EARLY CHILDHOOD EDUCATORS NEED TO KNOW ABOUT SECOND-LANGUAGE LEARNING

Given what is known about first-language development and about the differences between first- and second-language acquisition, what do early childhood educators need to know to be able to meet the challenge of making the early childhood education experience as optimal as possible for second-language–learning children? The goal of this book is to answer the following questions.

1. *What are the social and linguistic factors that affect a child whose home language is not English when that child comes to an early childhood classroom in which English is used?* When children from homes in which English is not the home language begin attending an early childhood classroom in which English is one of the languages used, they need to adjust to a new social and linguistic situation. Chapter 2 discusses what this means for these children in terms of social and linguistic constraints.

2. *What is the likely path of development for a young child learning a second language?* There is a different developmental path taken by young second-language learners than that for first-language learners. Early childhood educators need to know what this developmental path is to be able to observe, plan, assess, and serve second-language learning children. Chapters 3 and 4 discuss this developmental path, and Chapter 5 discusses individual differences among young second-language learners.

3. *What is the teacher's role, and what can be done in the classroom for second-language–learning children?* The teacher's role in the early childhood classroom that includes second-language–learning children needs to be broadened to include ways of communicating with these children as well as ways to adjust the curriculum to be as responsive as possible to their needs. Chapters 6 and 7 discuss classroom-based strategies for working with second-language–learning children.

4. *What can teachers tell parents about what parents can do to help?* Parents of second-language–learning children will have many questions about their child's developmental progress in language as well as in all other areas. They may have questions about their child's social isolation in the classroom, the possibility of first-language loss, the perceived need to learn English rapidly, the next stage of their children's education, and myriad other concerns. Chapter 8 provides strategies for helping parents to understand the importance of these issues and for mapping out ways to help parents make decisions that will benefit their children.

5. *How can early childhood educators tell when intervention is necessary with a second-language–learning child?* Early childhood educators are often called upon to assess whether a child's behavior warrants further investigation for intervention. Because communicative factors related to language affect children's social behavior, it is often difficult for early childhood educators to know whether certain behaviors in second-language–learning children are indicative of true developmental delay or are merely due to the pressures of the new social environment to which the children are being exposed. Chapter 9 discusses the ways in which teachers and administrators can assess the needs of these children.

6. *What does this information about the second-language–learning process for young children mean for effective early childhood programs?* Chapter 10 discusses the ways in which this information fits with the recommendations of the National Association for the Education of Young Children (NAEYC) concerning responses to linguistic and cultural diversity.

7. *What about children who are adopted from other countries? Do these children follow the same pathway for second-language acquisition as bilingual children? What can early childhood educators do to help these children?* It is important to know that children adopted from other countries early in their lives are likely to follow a different linguistic acquisition pattern than the pathway of second language acquisition described in this book. Research results with this special group of children and recommendations for how early childhood educators can work with these children and their families are presented in Chapter 11.

SOURCES OF INFORMATION ABOUT SECOND-LANGUAGE–LEARNING CHILDREN

A variety of sources of information are used in answering these questions, including previous studies by other researchers and classroom observations and interviews with teachers, parents, and administrators conducted by the author. One of the primary sources of information about what occurs in a classroom with young second-language learners is a study I conducted during 2 years in an English-language classroom (Tabors, 1984, 1987; Tabors & Snow, 1994). The following brief description of the classroom, the teachers, the children, and my role in the classroom provides context for the discussion of much of the information in the book.

The Classroom Setting

The setting for the study was an English-language early childhood classroom located on the second floor of a high-rise apartment building at a local university. The apartment building was used by the university for married graduate student housing, and many families from outside the United States lived in the building and sent their children to the center. All of the families whose children attended the center had some affiliation with the university.

The Teachers

The teachers in the classroom during the study were Marion, the head teacher; Rosa, the assistant teacher during the first year; and Joanne, the assistant teacher during the second year. Marion was an experienced early childhood educator. In an interview, Marion mentioned that she considered her way of running a classroom to be halfway between the extremes of very open and very structured. From my observations, I would say that she was a confident teacher with a highly verbal style who related well to the students on an adult level. She was a native speaker of English and rarely attempted to use words from the home languages of the children who were English language learners.

Rosa, the assistant teacher during the first year of the study, was a native Spanish speaker who came to the United States from Cuba when she was 11 years old. However, she spoke English in the classroom because there were no Spanish speakers among the children. Her interactions with the children were relaxed and playful. She was a frequent leader of circle time, and she was clever at getting and holding the children's attention.

Joanne, the assistant teacher during the second year of the study, was also a native speaker of English. She was very involved in the children's activities and was a frequent participant in their play. She often adopted a lightly teasing or playful technique with the children, which delighted the children and made her very popular in the classroom.

The Children

There were 15 children in the classroom at any one time. The children ranged from 2 years, 9 months to 5 years of age at the beginning of the school year. The children from the study classroom who are described in this book are listed in Table 2.

As shown in Table 2, the children who were learning English as a second language came from a variety of countries and home-language backgrounds. Because of this variety, it was unusual to hear children using their home languages in the classroom, although it was certainly not discouraged by the teachers. Except for the Korean girls, who did form their own play group on occasion, most of the children found playmates and activities that placed them in circumstances in which English was the primary language used.

Table 2. Children in the English-language study classroom during the 2-year study

Name[a]	Sex	Place of origin	Home language
Akemi	F	Japan	Japanese
Andrew	M	United States	English
Byong-sun	M	Korea	Korean
Elena	F	USSR	Russian
James	M	United States	English
Jennifer	F	United States	English
Jessica	F	United States	English
Kaori	F	Japan	Japanese
Kumiko	F	Japan	Japanese
Leandro	M	Brazil	Portuguese
Ling Ling	F	Taiwan	Taiwanese
Matthew	M	United States	English
Miguel	M	Puerto Rico	Spanish
Myong	F	Korea	Korean
Naoshi	M	Japan	Japanese
Natalie	F	United States	English
Pierre	M	France	French
Poram	F	Korea	Korean
Rebecca	F	United States	English
Sally	F	United States	English
Sook-whan	F	Korea	Korean
Supat	M	Thailand	Thai
Taro	M	Japan	Japanese

[a]The children's names have been changed.

Inside the Classroom

The study classroom was a large room with windows all along one side overlooking the playground. The room was divided into several areas that served different purposes. The block area was located in one corner of the room along the side with the windows. It was a carpeted area used for all group activities as well as a building area for blocks. The blocks were kept in the bookcases that divided the block area from the house area. Also available in the block area were toy trains and tracks, large toy trucks and buses, people figures, and plastic toy animals.

The house area occupied the other corner of the room along the window side. This area contained a large wooden structure that served as a playhouse underneath and a loft area above that was reached by climbing a ladder. The playhouse was furnished with child-size kitchen equipment and a table and chairs; the loft was furnished with pillows and books. Also available in this area were a full-length mirror and a large collection of dress-up clothes.

Opposite the house, attached to a central column that divided the room in half, were a bed area and a storage area for more books. Along one wall of the playhouse was a carpeted bench. Near the bench was a large round table that was often used for puzzles or other, similar manipulative activities. Along the wall behind the puzzle table were shelves where puzzles, LEGO pieces, and other games were stored.

There were two other rectangular tables in the classroom that were used for art or other projects during the free play period and for snack and lunch later in the morning. Typical activities at these tables included playing with playdough, drawing, and painting. Along the inside wall of the classroom was the water/sand table that could be used for play when filled with water or sand but acted as a storage surface when not otherwise in use.

The overall feeling of the room was of a bright, pleasant environment decorated primarily with the children's own artwork and set up in a fashion similar to many other early childhood classrooms.

Organization of Classroom Time

The first $1\frac{1}{2}$ hours in the morning was a free play period. During this time, children were typically offered a group of activity options from which to choose. Several projects might be put out on the activity tables, such as LEGO pieces, playdough, or drawing equipment, or a special project (e.g., pizza making) might be organized by one of the teachers. Children also had free access to the block and house areas during the free play periods and could develop their own play activities. Most of the children moved freely around the room, choosing first one kind of activity and then another, depending on what interested them at the moment. The teachers guided children in their choices if they seemed to be undecided and made sure that all of the children had completed a project if it was meant as an all class project.

A brief cleanup period followed free play. Cleanup time was heralded with a cleanup song, and the teachers helped children put away toys and other activities that had been used during the free play period. This was followed by circle time.

For circle time, all the children gathered on the carpet in the block area. Circle time usually began with the children joining hands and singing a song together. After this song, they sat down on the rug and followed the lead of the teacher in singing songs, playing games, or naming colors and shapes as a group. After circle time, the children washed their hands and sat down for snack, choosing their own location at one of the three tables. When children completed their snacks, they went to the cubby area and got ready to go outside to the playground.

Out on the playground, there was a variety of activities from which to choose. There were swings to swing on, structures to climb on, and bikes to ride.

After coming back inside, the children again came to the carpeted area for storytime. During this time, one of the teachers would read aloud from a book, alternately reading and displaying the pictures from the book to the group and frequently asking questions about the story as she read. When the book reading was completed, the children were dismissed from the area to collect their lunchboxes and settle down at one of the three tables for lunch.

After lunch, the children either went back outside or remained in the classroom to play until they were picked up to go home.

Participant Observation

To develop a complete picture of how young children go about the process of acquiring a second language, I spent several mornings each week for 2 years in this classroom, observing, taking notes, and audiotaping the children's and teachers' interactions. My role in the classroom was that of a participant observer; that is, I was someone who was slightly apart from the everyday life of the classroom but still functioned as a member of the group. Interestingly, the children seemed to accept my role without much question. When I separated myself from the children and concentrated on taking notes, they did not interrupt me and would proceed in their play as if I were not in the room. When I made myself available by putting down my notebook, the children would approach me for help or conversation much as they would the teachers in the classroom.

Occasionally, a child would ask what I was doing when I was taking notes. Leandro was one of the few children who asked me a direct question about my notetaking. I was taking notes during a conversation I was having with Leandro one day, and he asked, "What you are writing?" I said, "I'm writing what you are saying." Then he looked out the window and said, "Police car." Then he looked at me and said, "You write police car?" I said, "Yes." This type of direct questioning was quite unusual, however. On the whole, I found that it was very easy to move back and forth between interactions with the children and teachers (participant) and notetaking (observer) without jeopardizing either role. By being a participant, I came to know all of the children and the teachers; by being an observer, I was able to record interactions that might have otherwise gone unnoticed. At the end of each day of observation, I typed my notes and my personal interpretations of what I had observed. In this way, I developed an extensive record of the activities in the classroom. Much of the information about and most of the examples of second-language learning in an early childhood educational setting described in this book come from this record.

Part One

The Second-Language–Learning Child's Task

Two Portraits

Juliana and Byong-sun

When young children from other than English-speaking homes first arrive in an early childhood education setting in which English is used, they must cope with a variety of social and linguistic demands that children from English-speaking homes do not have to face. The first section of this chapter presents a portrait of an English-speaking child during a free play period in her early childhood classroom and draws attention to the social and linguistic competencies that she displays in her interactions with her classmates. The second section follows a child newly arrived from Korea during a similar period in his English-language classroom and illustrates the social and linguistic constraints on his interactions with his classmates. The final section relates the social and linguistic constraints that second-language–learning children face to a particular theory of social dominance.

PORTRAIT OF JULIANA

I visited Juliana's classroom in a large midwestern city one afternoon in October. Juliana and her classmates were 4 years of age, and their classroom was similar to the English-language classroom I had previously studied. The classroom was a large room partitioned into areas with structures and bookcases, with an entire wall of glass looking out over the playground. A lengthy free play period occurred during the afternoon, and Juliana agreed to wear a small Minnie Mouse backpack with an audiotape recorder inside as she played. After a few minutes, Juliana appeared to have forgotten she was wearing the backpack on her back and unhesitatingly entered into the play with the other children. I followed Juliana and took field notes as she played with her friends.

Juliana at Play

Although this was a free play period, it followed a brief lesson that the student teacher, Wendy, had presented to the children as part of a unit on airplanes. This lesson had included a short film about stunt pilots and their tricks, and props such as a pilot's hat, gloves, and goggles were available in the classroom from previous lessons during the week. During the free play period, Wendy encouraged the children to build an airplane out of large wooden blocks and to take the airplane on a trip.

As free play began, however, Juliana was most interested in being in the dress-up area. She and her friend Ellen began to negotiate over the roles they would play. First, Juliana informed Ellen, "I don't want to be the kitty." So Ellen offered, "I will." Then Juliana announced, "And I'll be the mommy." Ellen replied, "I'll be the m . . ., I'll be the big sister." Then Susan came into the dress-up area and entered the negotiations as well. "I'll be the mommy, too," she offered.

Having sorted out their roles and collected some baby dolls from the dress-up corner, the three girls walked over to the block area, where Wendy was organizing the building of the airplane with large wooden blocks for seats. Susan suggested to Juliana, "You be the pilot, okay?" But Juliana demurred, "No-o-o-o." Wendy asked, "What would you like to be, Juliana?" "I don't want to be the pilot," she replied. Wendy persisted, "You don't want to be the pilot? Do you want to be a passenger?" Juliana shook her head "no." Then Ellen offered, "I want to be a passenger," and Wendy quickly agreed, "Okay." Then Juliana decided, "I want to sit on one of these seats." "Okay," said Wendy, "and let's put the seats in the plane." "Can I sit on that too?" asked Ellen. "Yes," replied Wendy, and then she reiterated, "and let's put the seats on the plane."

Having arranged a few blocks for seats, Ellen and Juliana climbed into the airplane. Ellen suggested, "Juliana, let's sit next to each other back here." But Juliana wanted to sit closer to the front of the plane, so she announced, "I'm going to sit here." Then Ellen changed her mind and joined Juliana, saying, "I have to sit next to you. You know why? 'Cuz you're coming to my house."

Meanwhile, Wendy was talking with Susan. "Where are we going to go visit on our trip? Do you remember what city you drew on your map yesterday?" After further discussion about their destination, Wendy asked Ellen and Juliana, "You guys, you want to go visit Florida with Susan and me?" They enthusiastically agreed.

It was soon clear, however, that the flight was not yet ready to get off the ground. Susan hopped out of the plane, saying, "I'm going to get some dishes," and Ellen followed her, announcing, "I'm going to get the drinkies." After both Ellen and Susan returned to the plane with the dishes and cups, Wendy asked, "We've got to get some seat belts, don't we?" Ellen answered, "Oh, we forgot to get them on." Juliana reached out to take a seat belt from Wendy, who was pulling them out of a box near the plane. "That's going to be mine," Juliana said. Then she and Ellen spent a few minutes arranging dishes, cups, and seat belts near their seats on the upturned blocks. Ellen handed Juliana a cup. Juliana replied, "Thank you." Then Ellen decided that she did not need a seat belt. She announced, "I don't need one." Juliana followed suit, "I don't need one either."

Ellen then announced, "My baby needs a bottle," and exited the plane in search of a bottle from the dress-up area. Wendy offered a seat belt to Susan, but she picked up one of the rejected seat belts that Ellen and Juliana had dropped on the floor. Then Juliana decided that her baby should not be left unprotected and announced three times, "My baby needs a seat belt," until Wendy heard her and handed her a new one, saying, "Here you go."

Ellen returned to the plane and upon seeing that Juliana's baby had a seat belt, requested one for her baby from Wendy, who handed her one and then asked, "Do we have everything we need?" Ellen replied, "Yeah," but Susan contradicted her, "Not ye-e-e-t." Wendy queried her, "Not yet?" Susan replied, "My baby needs a seat belt, too." Wendy answered, "She does?" But Juliana suggested, "Let her sit with my baby, all right?" Susan rejected this idea, "No." Juliana tried again, "I'll be really friendly." Wendy intervened and suggested, "Maybe she can sit with her a little bit later. How's that?" "When we get back, she can sit with me and my little baby, all right?" decided Juliana.

Then Juliana announced to Ellen that they needed to go back to the dress-up area. They returned to the plane in high-heeled shoes, and Juliana announced, "I have my pretty shoes on. These are my shoes." After climbing back into the plane, Juliana suggested, "Ellen, let's pretend these are my shoes, okay?" Ellen then proposed an identity switch. "And then let's pretend my name's Juliana and your name's Ellen." Then Susan chimed in, "And pretend my name's . . ." "Dorothy," supplied Juliana. Susan echoed, "Dorothy."

Juliana and Ellen announced their new identities to Wendy. Ellen told her, "I'm Juliana," and Juliana told her, "I'm Ellen, and these are my shoes. And she's Juliana, so she's wearing those shoes." Playing along with this switch, Wendy asked, "Ellen, how did your hair get so light?" "I don't know why," answered Juliana. Then Juliana, while pointing to Ellen, told Wendy, "She's Juliana." Wendy obligingly said, "Juliana, your hair got so dark. Are you wearing a wig? No?"

Then Juliana announced some bad news to Ellen, "I can't go. My baby's sick." Then she told Wendy, "I can't go. Know why? 'Cuz my baby has some allergies. She has a fever. So she can't go to Florida." Susan, still intent on the trip to Florida, said, "My baby can go to Florida." But Juliana reiterated, "Because my baby has some allergies, and she has a fever." So Ellen suggested, "We need to drop off our babies, right?" Juliana agreed, "Right." Wendy asked, "How are they going to get all better?" Juliana replied, "We have to give them some medicine." Susan then decided that her baby was also sick. And Juliana graciously conceded, "Yeah, you can come with us. But first you have to take your seat belt off." As the girls began to leave the plane, Wendy asked, "And they're not going to go to Florida with us?" Juliana replied, "No, my baby can't come, but when she takes her temperature, she can come."

Then Ellen and Juliana adopted baby voices and announced, "I'm not sick anymore . . . I'm not sick anymore." Juliana told Wendy, "She's not sick anymore, so now she can go." Wendy replied, "Oh, great. Should I open up the door?" "Yeah," said Ellen and Juliana and they climbed back into the plane. Ellen announced, "Juliana and I are going to be in the way back." Then Wendy said, "I guess I should get on, huh?"

Susan asked, "How long is it going to take?" Wendy replied, "I don't know. How long does the flight to Florida take?" Susan suggested, "A day." Ellen suggested, "Ten minutes." Susan decided, "Forty-five minutes. My watch says forty-five minutes. One, two, three, four, BLAST OFF!" But Juliana was not ready. "No! My baby needs to go back. My baby has a temperature now." Wendy announced, "Oh no. We've got to have an emergency landing. Everybody fasten their seat belts for an emergency landing!" Juliana then ran from the plane, instructing, "Don't do the plane until we're back!" Wendy replied, "We'll keep it warming up." Returning to the plane, Juliana announced, "My baby's better." Wendy answered, "She's better? Are we going to go on our flight?" Juliana conceded, "Yup."

But now it was time for a few last-minute provisions. Susan brought a bag of chips. Then Ellen mentioned that they needed flowers and went and got some from another part of the room. Then Juliana said, "Wait! Everybody needs hats," and went off to get some from the dress-up area. Wendy decided to wear the pilot's hat, saying, "I want this one. If I'm going to be the pilot I want my hat back on. I need my gloves too, don't I?" Then everyone settled into their seats again and looked for their seat belts. Wendy asked again, "Are we about ready for takeoff?" Everyone chorused, "Yeah!" Susan again announced, "Forty-five minutes." And Wendy reiterated, "Forty-five minutes to Florida." Finally Susan announced, "All right, we're there!"

Soon after arrival in Florida, the free play period ended and the travelers busily dismantled the plane and put the blocks away.

Social and Linguistic Aspects of Juliana's Play

During this free play period, Juliana demonstrated a variety of linguistic and social competencies that made her an active participant. At the very beginning, she was able to enter into negotiations concerning roles. Then she indicated her willingness to be part of the sociodramatic play by declaring where she wanted to sit, although she rejected the starring role of pilot and even the lesser role of passenger. This independent move resulted in a concession on Ellen's part as she moved to sit with Juliana, after Juliana rejected Ellen's suggestion to sit with her.

A period of constant flow of talk and suggestions among Wendy, Susan, Ellen, and Juliana followed as they developed the airplane theme. During this time, Juliana had to make the same bid three times to get the seat belt she believed was needed for her baby, but she persisted until Wendy heard her and fulfilled her request.

Juliana was then involved in an unsuccessful exchange with Susan during which she tried to persuade Susan to have their babies sit together. Eventually, Wendy intervened with a suggestion to put off a decision, and Juliana proposed a final solution for "when we get back."

After the identity switch incident, Juliana twice took control of the direction of the play, first by announcing that her baby was sick and then by forcing an emergency landing when the baby's illness recurred. Both of these suggestions were powerful moves on her part that were taken up by the other participants as vital elements in the play. She was even able to keep everyone waiting until she declared that her baby was better and the flight could proceed.

During this free play episode, then, it can be readily seen how Juliana used linguistic and social strategies that established and maintained her position as a full-fledged participant in the ongoing play. She used language to negotiate, reject, persuade, bid for attention, and make suggestions, all within the flow of the play activity. Although not all of her bids or suggestions were successful, she was clearly a major player in the developing scenario and was able to use her skills to be heard and to help fashion the direction of the play.

PORTRAIT OF BYONG-SUN

Byong-sun was a 4-year-old Korean boy who began attending the English-language classroom in the second year of my study. One November morning, I followed Byong-sun everywhere he went during the free play period at the beginning of the day and wrote field notes about his activities.

Byong-sun at Play

When Byong-sun arrived in the classroom, he immediately went to the circle table and sat down where LEGOs were available in boxes that were open but not emptied out. He started to remove some pieces from the boxes. Jessica approached the circle table with her mother. She sat down and began manipulating a few pieces that were on the table. Byong-sun did not pay any attention and kept playing, humming to himself. Jessica's mother reached in front of Byong-sun to get a few more pieces for Jessica. Byong-sun protested mildly by making a noise that sounded like "Un-hunh." Then Jessica's mother moved the whole box closer to Jessica. But Jessica was not particularly interested in playing with the LEGOs, and she soon got up and left, followed by her mother. This left Byong-sun alone at the table. He continued his play, taking some more pieces out of the box and singing aloud.

As he played with the LEGOs, Byong-sun occasionally looked over at the next table, where a group of children were playing with play-dough. Eventually, he got up from the table and went over to the sink area, where there was a box full of playdough implements, including molds and knives. He knelt down on the floor and started rummaging through the box. He picked a knife out of the collection and held it in his left hand while he continued to explore the contents of the box with his right hand. At this point, he looked over at the table where the other children were playing with the playdough and then started to get up, stopped, knelt down again, and resumed his search in the box.

Next, Byong-sun looked up at me and made a requesting noise (a whining tone with rising intonation). I did not respond, but Marion, who had spotted Byong-sun on the floor, did respond. She came over and asked him a series of questions. "What are you looking for, Byong-sun? What is it that you need? You have a knife. What else are you looking for? Are you looking for a rolling pin?" "Yeah," answered Byong-sun. "It looks to me like all the rolling pins are out. We'll have to get some more so we don't have to share," she concluded. Then Marion left with a child who wanted her help in another part of the room.

Byong-sun took the knife he had gotten out of the box and went over to the playdough table, sitting down at an empty seat where there was a large glob of playdough and a roller. He began to roll out the playdough with the roller. The other children at the table, Sally, Re-becca, and Ling Ling, were making birthday cakes, talking about what they were doing as they played. Byong-sun did not join in their conver-sation and looked down as he rolled out the playdough in front of him. Then he looked up and listened to the other children at the table as they talked, holding a ball of playdough in his hand.

Next, Byong-sun looked over at the sand table, where Naoshi, An-drew, Myong, and James were playing. He got up from the table, went to the sink, washed his hands, took a paper towel to dry his hands, threw the paper towel in the garbage can, and went to the sand table.

When he arrived at the sand table, Byong-sun tried to establish himself next to James, but James protested, blocking Byong-sun's access to the table. Andrew told James that it would be all right to let Byong-sun have a place. Rebecca also arrived at the table and pushed her way into the group. Byong-sun took up a position at the end of the table, picked up a long-handled spoon, and began filling up and dumping out a small frying pan with sand.

Andrew said, "Let's make a road." Naoshi, Andrew, and James be-came involved in working on the sand at their end of the table. Byong-sun brushed some sand off his hand, patted the sand in front of him, and sang a bit to himself. Next, Byong-sun took the frying pan full of sand and threw some sand into the middle of the table while looking at James. This did not get a response. He did it again. Still his action received no response. Byong-sun banged his spoon on an orange juice container near James. James did not notice. Then Byong-sun filled an orange juice container that Naoshi had been using. Naoshi also did not notice.

James and Rebecca then started working on the sand mound to form a birthday cake as Rebecca talked about today being Ling Ling's birthday. Then James sang "Happy Birthday to You" quietly. Byong-sun dumped out the sand in the frying pan and started scooping again. Then he held up the frying pan toward Rebecca but did not say anything. She did not respond in any way. Andrew came back to the table and said to Rebecca, "Be nice to Ling Ling today, right?"

At this point, Matthew came in with his mother. His mother tried to get Matthew interested in the sand activity by picking up the long-handled spoon. Byong-sun immediately protested very clearly, "No,

Byong-sun's." Matthew's mom put the spoon down and tried to mediate a dispute between Matthew and Myong who did not want him
on her side of the table. Byong-sun alternated between watching this
drama and working on the sand in front of him.

Byong-sun picked up the long-handled spoon and put the handle
through a funnel. Then he withdrew it and patted the sand mound
with it. At this point, Rebecca reached for the spoon and said, "I need
this, okay?" and took it away from Byong-sun, who did not protest.
Next, Myong took the funnel that Byong-sun had been playing with
and added that to the sand mound; then Myong grabbed the frying
pan from him and added that to the "cake." This left Byong-sun with
nothing to play with. He put his thumb between his front teeth and
watched the other children as they continued to work on the sand
mound.

Myong called to Marion to show off their accomplishment. She
came and commented that it was great, except for the fact that it was
beginning to spill over the edge. At this moment, Rebecca reached over
to collect the sand from in front of Byong-sun to put it on the mound.
Byong-sun said, "Get out!" and gave Rebecca a good push with his hip.
Rebecca turned to Marion to complain, "He said, 'Get out.' " Marion
interpreted this to mean that Byong-sun wanted to get out from behind
the table, so she told Rebecca to just let him by. But when Rebecca
moved aside and Marion encouraged Byong-sun to come out, he did
not move. Then Marion realized that Byong-sun did not have any more
sand to play with, and she encouraged the other children to spread the
sand out again so everyone could share.

Marion then went to get one of the guinea pigs out of his cage
so that the children could take turns holding him. Byong-sun followed
the group that moved over to the chairs set up in front of the guinea
pig cages. Marion saw that Byong-sun had joined the group and
asked, "Byong-sun, would you like a turn, too?" He nodded his
head "yes." Then Marion said, "Byong-sun, would you like to sit
and watch?" He sat down opposite Matthew, who was already
holding the guinea pig, and he smiled at Matthew as he did so.
Marion gave Byong-sun a piece of carrot for the guinea pig. Matthew
reached out and took the carrot away from Byong-sun and gave it
to the guinea pig. Then Byong-sun knelt down and petted the guinea
pig on Matthew's lap.

Then Marion announced, "Now it's Byong-sun's turn." She sat
down next to Byong-sun and helped lift the guinea pig off Matthew's
lap and onto Byong-sun's, but Byong-sun was not happy with the
guinea pig on his lap, so Marion took it on her lap and let Byong-sun

pet him. When the guinea pig shook himself, Byong-sun laughed. Marion remarked, "He likes gentle petting." Byong-sun said, "No." Marion replied, "Yes, he does." After some more petting, Marion said to Byong-sun, "You could go and see if Rebecca wanted a turn," but Byong-sun made no move to leave.

Then Sally came over to the group to hold the guinea pig. Byong-sun stayed seated on a chair nearby. A piece of carrot was on the floor. Sally leaned toward it but could not reach. She looked up at Byong-sun, who picked it up and handed it to her. She said, "Thank you." A minute later I asked Sally if she had had enough holding, and she said she had, so I took the guinea pig, let Byong-sun say good-bye to him, and then put him in the cage.

Once the guinea pig was back in his cage, Byong-sun went to the block area, where Rebecca, Ling Ling, Sally, Leandro, and Andrew were playing. When Byong-sun came to the block area, Andrew was playing with the pop-push toy (a push toy with balls inside that pop up). As Byong-sun arrived, Andrew dropped the toy and left. Byong-sun picked it up and began pushing it around in an area where the other children were not playing. Byong-sun pushed the toy over to me and pointed at one of the animals inside the plastic top, saying something I was unable to understand. I said, "What's that?" He answered, "It's a bear." Then he pushed the toy out of the block area and around to the house area. Here he found Taro alone with the busy box (a toy with figures that pop up when released from a trap door).

Taro looked up from the busy box as Byong-sun came near and said something to him. Byong-sun replied "No" as he sat down near the busy box. Taro tried to play with the busy box, but Byong-sun said "No" again. Then Byong-sun turned the box so that it was facing him, and he began playing with it as Taro sat and watched. Then Byong-sun started to pop up the different creatures that appear out of the box. He turned and verbalized to Taro, but when Taro moved nearer, Byong-sun put up his arm and said, "No!" Taro stopped and sat behind Byong-sun, watching him play. After popping up one of the figures, Byong-sun looked up at me and said, "Look at the bear." Then he popped up another and asked, "What's that?" I said, "Dog?" He said, "Yeah." Then he identified the "mommy" and "daddy" figures. Then he exclaimed over the "doggie" and said "Look at the bear" again. Then Byong-sun noticed the numbers written along the bottom of the box. He counted aloud in English from 1 to 5 as he followed the numbers on the box. The next time he popped up the bear, he turned to Taro and made claws and growled at him. Then he turned back to the box and played for awhile longer with Taro still sitting behind, watching.

Then Taro picked up the pop-push toy and went away. Byong-sun continued with the busy box until cleanup time was announced.

Social and Linguistic Constraints in Byong-sun's Play

In this description of how Byong-sun spent his time during the free play period, it is apparent that he was quite socially isolated from the rest of his classmates. For part of the free play period, he worked alone with LEGO pieces that had been left on a table where he could use them without having to ask for help. When he chose to join a group, he found a seat that was unoccupied at the playdough table or, with some difficulty, worked himself into a location that was available at the sand table. When he tried to get the attention of the other children, he was mostly ignored. He rarely protested when he was being taken advantage of. Only three times during the free play period did he defend himself, twice with adults and a third time when an adult was nearby to mediate. The only child who accorded him any deference was Taro, who was also a second-language learner and considerably younger than Byong-sun. On the whole, Byong-sun was being treated as a socially irrelevant member of the class.

In the portrait of Byong-sun, it is also possible to see the linguistic constraints he must face. Because he is a second-language learner, Byong-sun has an extremely limited repertoire from which to choose in communicative situations. When he was unable to find what he was looking for in the box under the sink, he used a generic whine to indicate to me that he needed help. But when a helpful adult arrived, he was unable to tell her what it was that he wanted, and she had to try to guess. In one of the situations in which he protested being taken advantage of, he used a phrase ("Get out") that he probably had heard other children use and applied it to his situation, although it was not quite right and therefore was misinterpreted. Several other times, when he did try to communicate verbally, he was not understood.

There were times, however, when Byong-sun was able to show his competence in English, such as when he named the figures and counted the numbers on the busy box. In this situation, he was in charge and was setting the communication agenda, showing off what he knew and even turning my "What's that?" question around to have me identify one of the figures on the box. It was in this low-pressure situation that Byong-sun demonstrated the greatest proficiency in his new language.

This portrait of Byong-sun demonstrates the classic double bind that anyone who is learning a new language faces: To learn this new language, Byong-sun must be socially accepted by those who speak the language; but to be socially accepted, he must already have some proficiency in the new language. In other words, in any language-learning situation in natural circumstances, communicative competence and social competence are inextricably interrelated; the double bind is that each is necessary for the development of the other.

OMEGA CHILDREN

Classrooms constitute a particular social setting, and the social setting in the classroom is not just the background context for the second-language–learning children's language-learning experience but is instead an integral part of that experience. In fact, as detailed in the previous portrait, Byong-sun's behavior and the reaction of the other children to Byong-sun can be seen as strongly related to a social dominance theory that was developed by Garnica (1983). This theory explores the possibility that some children—omega children—are socially ineffective because they lack communicative as well as social competence.

Garnica's (1983) study focused on six kindergarten children who were identified sociometrically as being at the bottom of the social hierarchy in their classrooms. These children were compared with six other children in the same classrooms selected at random and matched for sex. The social interactions of these children were recorded in the classroom context, and three 20-minute samples were analyzed for each of the 12 children using a variety of comparison measures. The results, all of which were statistically significant, were as follows:

> The omega children were observed to engage in fewer child–child conversations with different partners and to produce fewer conversational turns . . . The differences were so marked for the omega/non-omega groups that the distributions for the two groups did not even overlap in these comparisons. The same lack of overlap in group comparisons held for measures of the number of conversation initiations that were directed to the target child and the frequency with which the child's name was used by the other children . . . during the play periods observed. Thus, the omega child does not seem to participate in verbal interactions with many other children in the group and even those exchanges that do occur are of short duration.
>
> Furthermore, the omega children are hardly ever addressed by other children . . . The range is 0–2 times for the omega children as opposed to 9–16 times for non-omega [children], which may partly explain why the omega child's name is heard considerably less frequently in the course of the verbal chatter in child–child conversations. The amount of private speech exhibited by the omega children is much greater than that exhibited by the non-omega children. (Garnica, 1983, pp. 240–241)

In her discussion concerning these children, Garnica commented:

> The emerging picture of the omega child seems to be one of a verbally neglected individual. Hardly any of the other children appear intentionally to engage the omega child in conversations and the omega child only infrequently initiates verbal exchanges with other children. The conversational partner network of the omega child is drastically limited and thus the amount of speech that the child produces in productive, interactive social exchanges with other children is highly attenuated.
>
> Interestingly, the omega child is not often silent. S/he produces a variety of verbalizations but these verbalizations consist of long self-directed narratives or conversations with pretend conversational partners and are ignored by the other children.
>
> All of these features present the omega child as a verbally neglected and isolated member of the group. . . . In light of these circumstances the omega child appears totally unrepresented in the verbal activity. This child produces vocalizations that are clearly not intended for anyone other than self. (Garnica, 1983, p. 241)

The overall picture of the omega child, then, is of one who is ignored by his or her peers and is socially ineffective in interaction situations. But how does this situation arise in the first place?

Garnica (1983) did not attempt to answer this question in her analysis, but she did present evidence of interactions with omega and non-omega children that suggested that communicative competence or, in this case, communicative incompetence may be a contributing factor in how the omega children are treated by their peers. In a discussion of an interaction sequence in which an omega child attempted to procure a pink Magic Marker from another child, Garnica mentioned that, although the omega child used the same "bidding" system as non-omega children in this situation, the omega child was not forceful (she hinted rather than requested) and did not use nonverbal communication (i.e., raising her hand) in conjunction with her bid. In other words, her communicative competence (doing it correctly both verbally and nonverbally) in this situation was not sufficiently developed to achieve the desired end: use of the pink Magic Marker.

But, commented Garnica (1983), what if she had "done it right"? Would she have gotten the pink Magic Marker? The answer here is apparently also no, this time because of the child's status as a socially incompetent individual. The rule seems to be that if an omega child does not behave forcefully, she will not get what she wants; however, if she does behave forcefully, she will be ridiculed or teased by the other members of the social group and still will not get what she wants. It seems evident, then, that communicative competence and social competence are so closely related for these omega children that it is not possible to sort out primary from secondary factors. If a child is not a good communicator, people will ignore him or her, and if people ignore the child, it is hard for the child to enter into social situations in which he or she could become a better communicator.

This, of course, is precisely the situation in which children whose home language is other than English find themselves during the first few months in early childhood education settings in which English is used. Automatically, because of their lack of language proficiency, they are extensively ignored by the English-speaking children in the classroom, who treat them as if they are invisible, do not initiate communications with them, and often ignore their attempts at initiating interactions, just as the children in the study classroom did with Byong-sun. Second-language–learning children are relegated to the bottom of the social heap right from the start.

Because of this situation, second-language–learning children such as Byong-sun are left alone much of the time at first. They may spend their time playing alone silently or humming, singing, or talking to themselves—very much the portrait of the omega children. In interaction situations, these children wait for the other person to be the initiator, and they rarely presume to try to get one of the other children to do something for them. If there is something they want, they do it themselves or they do without. These features also make second-language–learning children look a lot like the description of the omega children. In fact, for at least the first few months in an early childhood education setting, second-language–learning children are indeed omega children. Fortunately, most of them do not remain omega children. What makes it possible for second-language–learning children to eventually escape this double bind? Chapters 3 and 4 discuss the process of second-language acquisition for these young children and show how it is possible for second-language learners to gain enough facility with their new language to become social members of the group and to use their social skills to get into group situations in which they will be able to hear, understand, and then begin to use their new language as well.

Chapter Three

Getting Started in a Second Language

W hen young children whose home language is not English first arrive in a classroom in which English is one of the languages used, they are at the starting point of a new developmental pathway, a pathway that leads to the development of skills in a second language. Although there will be differences in the way that children pursue learning a second language, researchers have noted a consistent developmental sequence for young children:

1. There may be a period when children continue to use their home language in the second-language situation.

2. When they discover that their home language does not work in the second-language situation, children enter a nonverbal period. During this time, they gain understanding of the new language and perhaps spend some time in sound experimentation.

3. Children begin to go public, using individual words and phrases in the new language.

4. Children begin to develop productive use of the second language, communicating with phrases and then sentences that they construct themselves.

This chapter discusses the first two periods in this developmental sequence. Chapter 4 discusses the second two periods, and individual differences in this developmental process is the topic of Chapter 5.

HOME-LANGUAGE USE

When young children find themselves in a social situation in which those around them speak a different language, there are really only two options: They can continue to speak the language they already know, or they can stop talking altogether.

Some children initially pursue the first of these options. In my study, I observed a Brazilian boy, Leandro, during his first day in the English-language classroom, in which no one else spoke Portuguese, his home language. At lunch, Leandro tried some yogurt and then pushed it away, telling me something in Portuguese that must have involved an explanation for why he was not going to eat it. After lunch, he asked Joanna a definite question in Portuguese. She shook her head and said she did not understand. Later he asked me a question in Portuguese. I also said I did not understand. He did not seem distressed, but he did not get an answer either.

Naoshi, a Japanese child in the same classroom, limited his efforts to communicating with the other Asian children. During the first few days in class, he tried to speak Japanese to Ling Ling, who was Taiwanese, and Byong-sun, who was Korean; neither of them could respond to him in Japanese. In both Leandro's and Naoshi's cases, unsuccessful initial efforts apparently convinced these children that they would not be understood if they used their home language, and therefore each discontinued the attempt to speak it in the classroom.

Some children, however, have been observed to persist in the use of their home language for a considerably longer period in second-language situations. In a study involving 40 second-language–learning children ranging in age from 18 months to 12 years, Saville-Troike (1987) found that 3- to 7-year-old children were willing to engage in what she termed *dilingual discourse* for some time after arriving in a setting in which their home language was not spoken. By dilingual discourse, Saville-Troike meant that the children continued to speak their home language as if those around them could understand them. In fact, those around them often did answer them, using, of course, the language that the children could not understand. Saville-Troike reported that this form of communication

> was generally effective for achieving desired ends when the children were involved in play, especially when there were objects to be manipulated. When context alone did not suffice for meaning to be inferred, however, the response to an unintelligible verbalization was frequently a blank look. (1987, pp. 84–85)

The older children in Saville-Troike's (1987) study came to the realization quite quickly that this form of communication would not work;

however, two younger Chinese brothers (one 3 years old and one 4 years old) continued to use their home language for several months when communicating with anyone in their English-language early childhood classroom. For example, when a teacher (T) was working with a small group of children that included the older of the Chinese brothers (G) and an English-speaking boy (M), the following dialogue occurred (G's utterances are printed in upper-case letters and represent English glosses of what was actually spoken in Chinese):

T: Do you know what that is?

M: Egg.

T: This is an egg. An egg. And what do we do with an egg?

M: You crack it. In a bowl.

T: You crack it. In the bowl.

G: WE EAT THAT.

T: Right. And we call this an egg.

G: IF WE DON'T USE A REFRIGERATOR, THERE WILL BE A LIT-
    TLE BIRD COMING OUT.

T: Right. That's an egg. (1987, p. 88)

In this case, the teacher responded to G's comments, even though she could not understand what he had said. Saville-Troike (1987) reported that this sort of exchange occurred most frequently with teachers; successful dilingual discourse was not a common feature of child–child communication.

The younger of the Chinese brothers continued to use dilingual discourse for 4 more months, but he began to include more and more English in his utterances. The older brother, however, entered a period during which he did not use either language. When he was asked by a Chinese interviewer why he had stopped using Chinese in the classroom after 2 months of dilingual discourse, he replied that he "knew that they could not understand him, and he realized that they were not going to learn Chinese. He said that since he was learning English, he would use that language instead" (1987, p. 103).

THE NONVERBAL PERIOD

Sooner or later, then, children who face a social situation in which their home language is not useful abandon attempts to communicate in their home language with people who do not understand them. In an English-language classroom, this means that the children enter a period when they do not talk at all. In a bilingual classroom, it means that children attempt to talk only with those who speak their home language and no longer try to talk with those who do not. This period has been observed by a number of previous researchers who termed it the silent or mute period.

When I conducted a case study of a young Greek boy, Panos, who had been brought to the United States when he was 2 years old, his parents told me that he had attended an English-language child care program five mornings a week for $1\frac{1}{2}$ years before he began to use any English at all. Throughout this time, his Greek was developing normally at home, and his teachers reported that he was actively involved in all aspects of the classroom, although he did not use any English. Finally, in the spring of his second year of child care, he began to use some English in the classroom. By the time I visited Panos at his child care center when he was $4\frac{3}{4}$ years old, his English, although a bit sing-song in intonation, was well advanced, and he was having no difficulties in communicating with everyone in the classroom (Tabors, 1982).

In a case study of another young child, Itoh and Hatch (1978) observed a $2\frac{1}{2}$-year-old Japanese child, Takahiro, who was not only silent in his English-language early childhood setting but also chose to be socially isolated. During his first 3 months at the school, he spent most of his time on a tricycle as far away as possible from the other children. Itoh and Hatch called this a *rejection period* for Takahiro.

Hakuta (1978) also observed a young Japanese girl during a mute period. Although he was eager to begin collecting data about her second-language acquisition, it took from October, when she arrived in the United States, until the following April for her to begin to speak English. During the intervening time, she attended kindergarten and played with neighborhood English-speaking friends, but she did not produce any English.

Finally, in Ervin-Tripp's (1974) study of American children learning French in Geneva, Switzerland, the researcher found that many of the children "said nothing for many months" and that her own children, ages 5 and $6\frac{1}{2}$, "began speaking after six and eight weeks of immersion in the school setting" (p. 115).

This mute or silent period, then, seems to be a consistent feature of many young children's experience in second-language situations. There seems to be an age component to the length of time that children spend in this period: The younger children in the case studies maintained their muteness for lengthier periods than the older children. This difference is investigated further in Chapter 5.

Nonverbal Communication

For all of these children, the realization that they could not communicate with those around them in their home language meant that they stopped talking. But this did not necessarily mean that they stopped communicating. Except for Takahiro, who isolated himself from his classmates, most of the young children who were studied in these circumstances found alternative ways of trying to communicate with those around them. I am therefore calling this the *nonverbal,* rather than the silent, period, because although children may not produce utterances during this time, most engage in various forms of nonverbal communication with those who do not speak their home language.

I found that the use of nonverbal tactics by the second-language learners in my study was most common in the first few months in the English-language classroom. For example, one day a dispute arose between Ling Ling and Matthew, who were working with a set of plastic straws and stars at one of the tables. As I turned around, Ling Ling mutely appealed to me by turning her face up to me and looking anxious. My interpretation was that Matthew was trying to take something away from her that she wanted to keep. I moved over to their table, explaining to Matthew that there were plenty of straws and stars for everyone. Then I sat down at the table and began to make a figure out of the straws and stars. When Ling Ling had a problem with what she was building, she handed me the pieces. I put them together for her and handed them back. She was pleased with the result and walked her figure over toward me. I asked, "What's that?" but she shrugged her shoulders. When I asked her if she wanted to take the figure apart, she shook her head vigorously "no." Slightly later, Ling Ling was playing with the structure I had built and got it caught on her arm. She extended her arm toward me to show me the problem, and I took it off for her. Next she again handed me a straw and a star. I asked, "You want it on there?" and put it together for her. After this, she picked up a large number of straws, put them in an empty box, and left the table to go into the playhouse.

In this sequence, Ling Ling used some of the methods of nonverbal communication that were common among the second-language–learning children in the English-language classroom. She used the expression on her face to tell me that she needed help when Matthew was trying to take something away from her. Several times she handed me something that she wanted fixed. She advanced an object toward me, probably as a prompt for a comment from me. In addition, she was able to respond nonverbally when I asked her questions.

I had similar experiences with other children. One day, Leandro and Naoshi were working with LEGOs and a set of cards with LEGO structures illustrated on them. Leandro was building a police car using the card as his guide. At one point, he showed me the card and pointed to a black LEGO piece on the card. The piece he needed had been used by Naoshi in a fire truck, but the fire truck was now partially disassembled. I showed Naoshi the card and asked him if Leandro could use that piece for his police car. Naoshi immediately removed the piece and gave it to Leandro.

Here Leandro and Naoshi, like Ling Ling, used a combination of nonverbal techniques to get a task accomplished or to respond to requests. In all of these examples, the nonverbal communication that the children used allowed them to participate successfully in interactions in a way that would not be possible if these techniques were not used. In other words, the use of nonverbal communication makes it possible for second-language–learning children to be communicative even before they can use the verbal forms appropriate for these situations.

Although nonverbal communication can be effective, it can be used in only a limited set of situations. In the study classroom, second-language–learning children used nonverbal behavior most often to accomplish one of the following: 1) attention getting, 2) requesting, 3) protesting, or 4) joking.

Attention Getting   One of the most typical attention getters used by the second-language–learning children in the classroom involved holding up or showing an object to another person. For example, one day Ling Ling was at a table where there were some piles of different color clay and Popsicle sticks. Joanna was sitting at the table working on a poster for the wall. Rebecca and Matthew were also there playing with the clay. Ling Ling picked up a piece of clay and put it on the end of a Popsicle stick. She held it out in front of Joanna. Joanna took it saying, "Oh, for me?" and pretended to eat it. Ling Ling smiled as she watched, having successfully used a nonverbal attention getter to initiate an interaction with Joanna.

Another morning, at circle time, we were singing the song "Wheels on the Bus." Naoshi got up from the circle, got the toy bus from the shelf, and brought it to show to everyone, demonstrating nonverbally that he knew exactly what the song was all about.

Not all nonverbal attempts at attention getting, however, were successful. Frequently, particularly when nonverbal attention getters were used with other children, there was no recognition from the person whose attention was being sought. For example, one day Ling Ling was working at one of the tables on a building project. To get some more wooden pegs for her project, she had to stand on a chair and reach into the middle of the table. In the same container with the pegs were some pieces of paper with colored dots. Ling Ling picked up one of these and waved it in front of Jessica. When there was no response, she put it back in the container. Another day, Naoshi was playing at the sand table. He was using a funnel to cover up a dinosaur toy with sand. As he did this, he looked over at Supat, but Supat was busy with his own play. Then Naoshi laughed out loud and pointed to the dinosaur toy that was buried up to its eyes with sand. Again, he looked at Supat, but Supat did not respond.

In each of these instances, it is not particularly surprising that the nonverbal effort by the second-language–learning child did not receive a response, because each effort was quite ambiguous in its meaning, and may, indeed, not have been interpretable from the other child's point of view.

Requesting   There were many times during the course of the school day when the second-language–learning children needed help with something they were doing or with a problem they were having with another child. Again, as with attention getting, some of the nonverbal techniques that they used in these circumstances were successful and some were not. For example, one day Byong-sun wanted to play at the water table, but he knew he would need a smock. He walked over to the smocks, looking toward Marion, but she was busy with Naoshi. Then he stood near the smocks for a time, touching one of them. Finally, he took the smock off its peg and brought it over to Marion, who obligingly began to help him get organized for play at the water table.

On another occasion, Andrew and Supat were sitting at one of the art tables with a pan filled with cornstarch and water. When I sat down, Andrew said to me, "Look at the cornstarch. It's making a pattern." At this point, Ling Ling, who was also at the table, whimpered, looked toward Joanna, and then looked toward me when I asked her if she needed help. She then held up her arms to me so that I could roll up her sleeves so she would not get them wet with the cornstarch mixture.

In each of these instances, it is up to the adult in the situation to know what is being requested, because the amount of information provided by the second-language–learning child is extremely minimal.

If the kind of help that a second-language–learning child needs is not available, the child has only two choices: Try to do it without help or forget about it. Both of these strategies were illustrated one day at the water table in the study classroom. First, Byong-sun wanted something from the other end of the water table. He looked at me and then held his hand straight out. I did not respond, so he left his spot and walked around to the other end, where Taro was playing. Upon arrival, he reached into the water and retrieved a plastic bottle and returned to his end of the table. In this case, Byong-sun realized that if he wanted the plastic bottle, he was going to have to go get it himself.

Sometimes it is not possible for a child to solve a problem so easily. Playing near Byong-sun at the water table, Leandro picked up a pump. He tried to make it work, but without much luck. Looking around for help, he saw Joanna at the next table, but she was busy, so he merely put the pump down and picked up a funnel. In this case, Leandro seemed to decide that it would be more trouble than it was worth to let someone else know that he needed help with the pump, so he decided to forget about it.

Protesting   During the course of the day, it was also necessary for the second-language–learning children to let other people know that they were not happy with a particular situation. Examples of children looking upset or whimpering in these circumstances have already been discussed. Another technique, protesting, is revealed in the following two examples.

One day Andrew and Taro were playing with the toy cars at one of the tables. Andrew picked up the car that Taro had left on the table. Taro shrieked. Andrew put the car back and left. On another occasion, Naoshi and Leandro were playing with LEGOs. Each boy had a pile of LEGOs in front of him. At one point, Naoshi reached over and touched one of the pieces in Leandro's pile. Leandro gave a squeak of protest and took Naoshi's hand away from the piece. Naoshi returned to his own pile of LEGOs.

In these two cases, the protest is understood and the situation is changed, but, just as with attention getting and requesting, sometimes a protest is not interpretable, and it is difficult for those around to help.

Joking   It was also possible for second-language–learning children to communicate nonverbally by doing funny things that other people would find amusing. For example, one day Byong-sun was inside the playhouse by himself looking out the window at the end, near the bench where Taro happened to be. When Taro spotted Byong-sun in the window, he started to giggle. Then they both giggled and laughed at each other. A little later Taro stuck his head in the window. When Byong-sun saw him, he came back to the window, sticking his hand through again and giggling. Then Leandro came to the end of the house and stuck his head out the window. Taro, who was still on the bench, laughed at Leandro, and then stuck his head in the window.

In this sequence, three second-language–learning children developed a joking game that let them play together without the use of any language. In fact, this kind of activity was so successful that it had a tendency to become a continuing saga with the children and helped them get into contact with each other and other members of the classroom.

Imitating Nonverbal Behavior

Interestingly, nonverbal communication was so pervasive at the beginning of the school year in this classroom—in which more than half of the students were from homes where English was not the primary language—that even one English-speaking child seemed to adopt the behavior. During snack one day, Jessica came over to Joanna and started mugging and miming and pointing toward the table where a bowl of grated cheese was located. During this mugging, she wrinkled up her face into a grimace/smile while closing her eyes and gesturing strongly with her arm. Joanna refused to play the game of guessing what Jessica wanted. Rebecca kindly interpreted that Jessica wanted cheese. Joanna explained that there was already cheese on the pizza. Several more times during snack, Jessica mimed a request, but Joanna ignored her, seeming a bit perplexed by the behavior. Later, at lunchtime, Jessica used the same helpless act with me, needing extra encouragement to get her lunch and pull in her chair.

After this one day, however, Jessica ceased producing this kind of behavior, perhaps because it did not receive the kind of deference she had hoped it would. Nonetheless, it seems likely that the exaggerated gesturing and facial expressions were an overdramatized version of behaviors that Jessica had seen around her among the second-language–learning children, behaviors that received, in her mind, special attention from the adults in the classroom.

Trying to get a message across nonverbally is an appropriate early strategy in second-language settings; most young children in these circumstances seem to be able to call this strategy into play unselfconsciously when necessary. The limitations of this behavior are obvious, however. If there is not a helpful and perceptive person available to interpret nonverbal cues, the message may not be received at all.

Social Consequences of Nonverbal Communication

As detailed in the portrait of Byong-sun in Chapter 2, there are also social consequences to continuing to use nonverbal behaviors. As long as the second-language–learning children in the study classroom remained predominantly nonverbal, they were treated like infants by the English-speaking children or ignored as if they were invisible. For instance, one child, Taro, remained predominantly nonverbal during the entire year (see Chapter 9 for a case study of Taro). Andrew, who wanted to be everybody's friend, tried everything he could to communicate with Taro. Andrew's activities included kissing Taro, sticking his tongue out at him, flapping his lips at him, spinning himself around in front of him, chasing and wrestling with him, lifting him up from behind, handing play objects to him, tickling him, and pulling the hood up on his sweatshirt. This behavior on Andrew's part seemed most strongly reminiscent of how an older child might play with a much younger baby.

Furthermore, on at least one occasion, Andrew modified his speech as if he were talking to an infant as he helped get Ling Ling ready for lunch. First, he began to talk to her in a very high-pitched voice. He said, "I'll open your lunchbox." Then he discovered that one of the teachers had already helped her and said, "Oh, it's empty already." Then one of the children pointed out that some of Ling Ling's milk had spilled on the floor. Andrew walked around to check it out, and when Ling Ling looked like she might start to cry, he said, "Me fix," and went to get a paper towel. When Joanna came to see what was wrong, he assured her, "Me wipe it."

In this sequence, Andrew showed two types of modifications that adults often use when communicating with very young first-

language–learning children: a high-pitched voice and linguistically reduced forms ("me fix" and "me wipe it"). By using these modifications,
Andrew showed his sensitivity to Ling Ling's communicative difficulties, adjusting his speech as if he were speaking with a very young
child.

An example of how the English-speaking children regarded a
slightly older child who was linguistically different occurred at the end
of the school year, when a new student, Pierre, came into the classroom.
Pierre came to the classroom speaking French; he did not know any
English. He was extensively ignored by the other children, although
he did make attempts to join in the run-and-chase games that were
sometimes played in the classroom because these required no verbal
ability.

When one of the teachers took a series of slides of the children
in the classroom and then showed them during circle time, a routine
developed of naming all the children shown in each slide. Whenever
a slide was shown that included a picture of Pierre, all of the other
children's names were called out, but never Pierre's. This occurred even
though his name was used daily in the classroom by the teachers and
therefore was known to the other children. Because he had not developed enough English to become a social member of the group, Pierre
was apparently invisible to the rest of the children.

Obviously, to truly join in classroom activities as social equals,
then, second-language–learning children need to begin to start using
the new language.

Gathering Data

During the nonverbal period, children not only devise ways of communicating nonverbally but also begin to gather information about the
new language spoken around them. This data-gathering operation consists of two strategies: spectating and rehearsing.

Spectating   *Spectating* refers to active observations by second-
language–learning children when they are in proximity to English
speakers and are focusing on the language that is being used. In the
study classroom, these behaviors frequently occurred during joint activities in which second-language learners and English speakers
worked or played side by side or were involved in group activities that
involved the whole class.

For example, on the morning when Ling Ling had initiated a play
sequence with Joanna by using a piece of clay and a Popsicle stick to
make an ice cream cone, Joanna extended the play to the other children

at the table—Matthew, Leandro, and Rebecca—by taking their Popsicle stick creations and pretending to eat them as well. After that, she made a snake from clay and turned it into a letter *S*. Then she asked which other letters they could make. Andrew came by and suggested "*O* for ostrich." During this entire time, Ling Ling was holding her Popsicle stick with a ball of clay on it, listening to and watching what was going on with the other children and Joanna.

Later, at circle time, all of the children were singing songs and playing games together. Leandro, who was new to the classroom at that time, was standing across from me, watching my face intently during the songs. He was slow to copy what the other children were doing at first but began to get involved near the end.

In these instances, Ling Ling and Leandro seemed to be concentrating on watching and listening to begin to collect data about the new language to which they were being exposed. What set this spectating behavior apart from simple, noninvolved listening behavior is the intensity with which it was carried out.

Rehearsing   *Rehearsing* refers to verbalization by the second-language learners that did not appear to be communicative but indicated these children were working on producing English. Much of the rehearsing was done extremely quietly as the children played near

English speakers and therefore was difficult to hear. Sometimes it was possible, however, to tune in to the rehearsal as it occurred.

For example, one day when Byong-sun and some other children were working with playdough at one of the tables, Joanna came by and remarked, "Look at that nice playdough," and Byong-sun echoed after her, "Playdough." On another occasion at the water table, Andrew said something that contained the phrase "have to," and Byong-sun, who had been watching Andrew intently, mouthed the words "have to." In these instances, Byong-sun was not trying to communicate with Joanna or Andrew; instead, he was rehearsing the sounds that he had just heard by repeating them out loud. Interestingly, in the second example, Byong-sun was combining spectating behavior (i.e., watching Andrew intently) and rehearsing behavior (i.e., repeating something Andrew just said).

The nature of this rehearsing process was more extensively revealed in Saville-Troike's (1988) study because she used directional microphones to capture and record the vocalizations of the young second-language learners. Saville-Troike noted that much of this vocalization was at such a low volume that even those near the children could not hear what they were saying. Apparently, they were not yet ready to go public with their talk this early in the second-language–learning process.

Similar to the previous examples of Byong-sun's behavior, Saville-Troike (1988) found that the second-language–learning children used repetition as part of the rehearsing process; the younger children usually repeated the end of an utterance that they heard near them, but the older children sometimes repeated more extensive phrases. For example, a 4-year-old Chinese boy (S2) was playing with his back to a group of English-speaking children, but he repeated to himself what they were saying:

Child 1:   Pooty.

   S2:   Pooty.

Child 2:   Pooty?

   S2:   Pooty?

Child 3:   Hey, look.

   S2:   Hey, look.

Child 2:   What are you doing?

   S2:   What are you doing? (pp. 578–579)

Saville-Troike (1988) found that the children also had other uses for this type of private speech, including connecting English words with appropriate objects, actions, or situations or incorporating English in dual-language utterances as if they were explaining the meanings to themselves.

Sometimes, the children just seemed to be playing with the sounds of the new language, as in this example:

S2:   Yucky. Yucky scoop. Scoop scoop yucky scoop. Yucky yucky yuck-yucky (Saville-Troike, 1988, p. 583).

Furthermore, some of the children used this rehearsal time to begin to construct pattern drills for themselves in their new language. For example, a 5-year-old Japanese boy constructed the following:

> I finished.
>
> I have finished.
>
> I am finished.
>
> I'm finished.

and

> I want.
>
> I paper. Paper. Paper.
>
> I want paper. (p. 585)

During this nonverbal period, then, the young second-language learners were beginning to quietly unravel the patterns of the new language in their environment. As a result of these efforts, the children began to develop receptive abilities in English, understanding what words sounded like and what they meant, even before they had developed the ability to use the words themselves.

Sound Experimentation

Just as babies must develop control over the sounds of their first language, young second-language learners must develop phonological control over their second language as well. As the previous section shows, some of the rehearsing behavior observed by Saville-Troike (1988) included practice with the different sounds of the new language as well as practice with vocabulary and grammar.

It is well known that young children are particularly sensitive to the sounds of language. In fact, the only feature of second-language acquisition that has been shown to be age sensitive is accent. Young children acquiring a second language are likely to attain native-like pronunciation in the new language, whereas older learners may attain fluency in the language but are less likely to have a native-like accent, even after years of contact with the second language (Snow & Hoefna-gel-Hohle, 1977).

A colleague and I were made aware of young children's abilities to concentrate on the sounds of a new language when working on a study of a young Korean child learning English in a book-reading situation (Yim, 1984). In this study, I was the English-language model for Young-joo, a 3-year-old girl who had had very little contact with English speakers prior to the study. For the project, I met with Young-joo on a weekly basis and read a book with her in English. Most of our interactions involving the book consisted of my naming objects and Young-joo repeating names (e.g., I said, "This is a moose," and Young-joo repeated, "Moose") or of Young-joo answering questions about objects (e.g., I asked, "Who's that?" and Young-joo answered, "Baby bunny."). On occasion, however, Young-joo would insert invented words into her responses. These invented words were not intelligible as English words, but they were not Korean words either. In fact, my colleague, who was a native speaker of Korean and bilingual in English, reported that Young-joo was using sounds and intonation features that are not present in Korean but are present in English. In using these invented sequences, it seemed as if Young-joo was practicing the tune—the sounds and intonation patterns of English—before learning all the words of the new song.

Saville-Troike (1988) found the same phenomenon with the two Chinese brothers in her study. She reported that these boys

> Focused extensively on the sounds of the second language, and seemed to relate to the kinaesthetics of pronouncing certain words. High-frequency private vocabulary for them included *butter pecan, parking lot, skyscraper,* and *cookie monster.* Both children also demonstrated their attention to sound by creating new words with English phonological structure, including *otraberver, goch, treer,* and *trumble*—impossible sequences in their native Mandarin Chinese. (p. 583)

Other observers have noticed this phenomenon as well. The mother of one of the English-speaking children in the study reported that her daughter had spent the previous summer in a camp situation with many Spanish-speaking children. When she came home from camp, Rebecca would "speak Spanish" for her mother. Her mother reported that although what Rebecca was saying sounded like Spanish, it did not, in fact, consist of any Spanish vocabulary. Rebecca had begun to acquire the sound and intonation system in Spanish, and perhaps with longer exposure, she would have begun to acquire some vocabulary as well.

The second-language–learning children in the study classroom also showed a growing understanding of the sounds and intonation of English. In the first few months in the classroom, there were numerous instances of children talking but without saying anything that could be understood. On occasion, these unintelligible utterances might have been home-language use, but after the few instances reported previously, I do not believe that the children were using their home language in the classroom. In fact, I believe that these unintelligible utterances may well have been the type of sound experimentation that Young-joo was using in the book-reading study.

At the time that these strings of sounds were being used by the children, they did not have enough English to express the full idea in their new language, so they used what they had. For example, one morning Byong-sun and Naoshi were playing together at the water table. Because these two boys were from different language backgrounds, they would have to speak English to understand each other. The interaction proceeded as follows: Byong-sun held out a cup to Naoshi, accompanying this gesture with an utterance that I could not understand. Naoshi looked over and answered Byong-sun with an utterance that had a questioning intonation. Byong-sun then made another utterance with something that sounded like *nice* in the middle, but again I could not understand the whole sentence. After this, they continued their play silently. This "conversation," one would think, would be considered unsatisfactory, because neither of the participants could have understood the other, but it was not my impression that Byong-sun and Naoshi considered this communication unsatisfactory.

On another occasion, when all of the children were getting ready to go outside to play, a group of children began fooling around near the door. This upset Ling Ling, who came running in to report the children to the teachers. Although what Ling Ling was saying sounded like English, none of the sentences that she was using could be understood in English. Still, it was clear from the situation what her concern was, and it was quickly addressed.

Early in the second-language–learning process, then, children may be able to use this ability to mimic the sounds of a new language in a variety of ways. At first, they might structure entire sentences that do not, in fact, contain any English words. Later, they might use these sounds in combination with one or two English words or eventually fill in missing slots in a mostly English-language sentence. For example, one day at the water table Ling Ling had been waiting a long time for one of the pumps, both of which were being used by Byong-sun and

Naoshi. Finally, I tried to procure a pump for her by making a request of Byong-sun that ended in "please." Byong-sun gestured to Naoshi and uttered an unintelligible phrase that also ended in "please"—the suggestion being, no doubt, "take his."

On another day in the block area, Leandro had carefully constructed a fenced-in area and supplied it with large plastic farm animals. Naoshi, Supat, and Andrew all came rushing into the area to see what Leandro had done, jumping over the fence. This brought a protest from Leandro. "Don't! [unintelligible] my farm!" Naoshi, Supat, and Andrew climbed out of the fenced-in area and left, leaving Leandro alone in the middle of his farm. Although not all of the words in the sentence were intelligible, it was clear that Leandro's intention was in protecting his property, and it is possible even to imagine the words that Leandro might have been trying to utter: "Get out of my farm!" or "Be careful of my farm!" By filling the missing slot with sound, Leandro was able to develop a lengthier utterance, which certainly got the desired result.

CONCLUSION

During the nonverbal period, although second-language–learning children are not yet communicating to others in the language that is being used in the environment around them, they are nevertheless beginning to collect data about that new language. Although the children use nonverbal means to communicate their needs, they also use spectating and rehearsing techniques to tune into the new language, demonstrating receptive abilities. Once they feel sufficiently comfortable and competent in this new setting, second-language–learning children begin going public with what they have learned.

Chapter Four

Speaking a Second Language

As the previous chapter illustrates, young children who face a second-language situation sometimes begin by continuing to use the language that they know, even with people who do not understand their language. For these children, it takes a little time before they realize that this new language is different from the one that they know and that at least some of the people who speak this new language do not understand them when they speak their own language. In a bilingual setting, of course, there may be some people who do and some people who do not understand them, and that takes time to sort out as well. In other words, young children must work through a series of revelations: 1) not everyone understands or speaks their language; 2) the people who do not understand and speak their language understand and speak a *different* language; and 3) if they want to communicate with these people, they need to learn this new and different language.

Having worked through these revelations, most young children enter a phase of data gathering about the new language before beginning to try to use it. Eventually, sometimes after a lengthy nonverbal period, most young children are ready to try out what they have discovered about the new language in communicative situations.

TELEGRAPHIC AND FORMULAIC SPEECH

When young second-language learners begin to use their new language, observers have noted two consistent features: the use of telegraphic speech and formulaic speech.

Telegraphic Speech

Telegraphic speech refers to the use of a few content words as an entire utterance; this type of speech is also typical of a period of language acquisition by very young children learning their first language. Much of the telegraphic speech in the classroom during the first months of my study revolved around the identification and naming of objects in English. An almost ritualized form was used in soliciting and providing this information. The most basic version of this form involved an adult asking a child, "What's this/that?" and then, if the answer was not readily available, supplying the noun herself. So, for instance, when Ling Ling imitated Joanna by building a bridge out of playdough one day, I asked her, "What's that?" She apparently did not know the name in English, so she shrugged. I then supplied the word for her by saying, "Bridge." She repeated, "Bridge," then paused and said it again. In this way, it was very easy for Ling Ling to connect the name of the object with the object that she had just made.

If the child was able to answer the "What's this/that?" question, then the next step in this process involved an elaboration or extension by the adult, adding new vocabulary to go with what was already known. For instance, when Leandro was playing in the block area, he brought a car over to me and held it up near my face. I said, "What's that?" He answered, "Car." I elaborated for him, "A racing car."

Quite quickly, the children began to answer the question before it was even asked, showing off and confirming what they already knew how to say. For example, one day at snack time, Naoshi pointed to a basket full of crackers and said, "Crackers," then indicated which ones he had selected for himself and said, "Three," and then showed me his juice and announced, "Apple juice." Each time, he received a confirmation from me.

Using these strategies, the second-language–learning children in this classroom began to develop a vocabulary of object names in English that they could use in their interactions with the English speakers around them. Other early accomplishments included counting, naming the ABCs, and identifying colors in English—all basic skills that the English-speaking children in the classroom were also working on at the same time.

Formulaic Speech

The use of formulaic speech has also been documented by researchers studying young second-language learners. This strategy, most extensively detailed by Wong Fillmore (1976, 1979), consists of young children using unanalyzed chunks or formulaic phrases in situations in which others have been observed to use them. These formulas often help children to get into play situations and get their ideas across with a minimum of language.

For example, one day at the water table, Naoshi and Byong-sun were playing side by side building a structure out of two bottles with a tube running between them. At one point, the tube flipped out of one of the bottles, and Naoshi started to help Byong-sun put it back together. But as he lifted one of the bottles, Byong-sun protested, "Stop! Stop!" and when Naoshi did not stop, Byong-sun took the tube out of the bottle himself. Then Naoshi picked up the tube and tried to insert it in the bottle. Byong-sun started to help him, asking, "Okay?" When the structure collapsed again, Byong-sun said, "Uh-oh." As they continued their play, Byong-sun called Naoshi's attention to what he was doing by saying, "Hey." Naoshi replied, "Okay, okay, okay, okay, okay."

In this sequence, the two second-language learners had to use all of the useful language they knew to communicate with each other. Even though the language available to them was very basic, it is obvious that it made it possible for the two boys to continue to play together and let each other know how the play was going. Even phrases as minimal as "uh-oh" and "okay" give the communicative partner information about how the play is going, information that would not be conveyed by silence.

On another occasion, Naoshi and Leandro had a similar conversation while playing with cars in the block area. As Naoshi ran his car down the radiator, he called to Leandro, "Lookit this! Lookit this!" Then he made his car fly up into the air and again said, "Lookit this, Leandro." Leandro finally turned to watch what Naoshi was doing and said in turn, "Lookit" as he showed off what *his* flying car could do, adding engine noises ("zhoooom") as well. Then the two boys traded "Lookit this" and "Lookit that" back and forth five times, until Leandro ended the sequence with "Hey!"

Other phrases that were commonly used by the second-language learners early in the acquisition process were *yes, no, hi, bye-bye, excuse me,* and *I don't know.* These high-utility words were extremely helpful in getting the second-language learners into and out of social situations in the classroom.

In Wong Fillmore's (1979) study of five first- and second-grade children who had recently arrived from Mexico, it was found that these older children were able to memorize even more extensive phrases. She reported,

> All five [of the children in the study] acquired repertoires of expressions which they knew how to use more or less appropriately, and put them to immediate and frequent use. The phrases they learned were those they found most useful—expressions which helped them appear to know what was going on (e.g. *Oh yeah? Hey, what's going on here? So what? No fighting, now.*), to participate in games and play activities (e.g. *You wanna play? It's my turn. Me first. No fair!*), and to request information, confirmation, and clarification from their friends (e.g. *How you do this? What's happening? Is this one all right? What did you say?* and *I don't understand.*). (p. 211)

The way that children figure out what the meaning of a word or phrase might be and how it might be used became obvious when Leandro acquired the use of the phrase *be careful* during the course of a week. The acquisition process began one day at lunch when Leandro stood up on his chair, and I admonished him to "be careful" while motioning for him to get down. He immediately repeated the phrase. Later that same day, Matthew and Rebecca had built a tall tower in the block area, and Leandro told them to "be careful." A week later, another tower was being built in the block area. This time Byong-sun, Supat, and Leandro were the builders. Having built the tower too high, the whole structure came crashing down. I said, "Be careful." All three boys repeated after me, "Be careful!" Slightly later that same day, Byong-sun built a tall tower and knocked it down on purpose, shrieking happily and falling into the debris. Leandro, who was sitting at a nearby table working on an art project, said, "Be careful."

Another interaction shows how Naoshi acquired an even longer phrase when playing with Andrew in the block area. Naoshi was working on a block structure when Andrew came into the area. Andrew came over to the block structure and said to Naoshi, "Hey, I've a good idea." Then as they tried to add blocks to the structure, Andrew said, "Oh, I'm, I'm, oh, I've got some . . .," and Naoshi said, "I'm a good idea," putting together Andrew's two previous statements into a new phrase. For the rest of the time they played together in the block area, Naoshi prefaced every move with this new phrase, "I'm a good idea," signaling to Andrew that he was an active participant in their mutual play.

Of course, the children were not always right when they guessed about the meaning of a phrase, which sometimes could cause problems. I observed such an incident one day when Byong-sun was on the ladder to the loft and, meaning to invite Andrew to come up and join him, confidently directed, "Shut up!" Andrew looked surprised and then rather hurt and backed down off the ladder instead of continuing his play with Byong-sun. In this case, Byong-sun was taking the chance that a phrase he had often heard in the classroom, which contained the word *up*, would work in this situation; unfortunately, this time he was wrong.

In general, however, the second-language learners were usually quite quick in their acquisition of at least a limited range of telegraphic and formulaic phrases that helped them socially in the classroom, and they were usually right about the situations in which the phrases could be used. At first, these phrases were used most often in communication with the adults and the other second-language learners in the classroom, but as the interaction between Andrew and Naoshi illustrates, they also provided the first opportunities for the second-language learners to begin communicating with the English speakers in the classroom.

PRODUCTIVE LANGUAGE USE

Once second-language–learning children acquire a number of vocabulary items and useful phrases, they can begin the process of productive language use, which means that they can begin building their own sentences, not just continuing to repeat formulaic phrases or names for people and things. During this process, second-language–learning children must analyze the language being used around them and begin to make guesses about how the language is constructed. Typically, they use everything they already know about their new language, and, not surprisingly, make many mistakes as they work their way through the process of acquiring the more complicated aspects of English.

Some of the earliest productive phrases in the English-language study classroom were ones that had their origin in the building blocks of telegraphic and formulaic language. For instance, the ever-present *lookit* was often combined with the name of an object, as it was one morning when Ling Ling, Rebecca, and Byong-sun were playing with playdough. Having rolled the playdough into a doughnut shape, Byong-sun presented the results to Rebecca saying, "Lookit Dunkin' Donut."

By combining all purpose phrases such as *lookit, I do, I want,* and *I got* with nouns, pronouns, and adjectives, it was possible for the children to generate a variety of creatively constructed phrases, as in the following examples:

Akemi, Natalie, Andrew, and Ling Ling were playing with Popsicle sticks and clay. Ling Ling held up a stick with a ball of clay on top and said, *"I do a ice cream."*

§

I sat down next to Akemi at one of the tables. She said to me, "Heart," pointing to the heart-shaped dough she had created with the cookie cutter. She followed this with, "Big. *I got a big."* In fact, the heart-shaped cutter was bigger than all of the others.

§

One day when Leandro was playing "the baby," his "mother," Jessica, went out of the house area, leaving Leandro alone. Leandro complained, *"I want my mommy.* Mommy!"

§

Byong-sun was sitting at the table where other children were playing with playdough, but he did not have any. When there was a pause in other talk, Byong-sun spoke up, first very quietly, but then in increasingly louder tones: *"I want . . . want a playdough. I want a playdough. I WANT A PLAYDOUGH!"*

This "frames and slots" approach was typical of the early productive use of constructed phrases by the second-language–learning children and continued to be a consistent feature of their communications for the remainder of the school year.

Another feature of this period, when the children were beginning to use English productively, was demonstrated most often by Naoshi, who enjoyed word play in his new language. One day, when demonstrating his ability to count in English, he apparently found the usual sequence of 21, 22, 23, 24, and so forth too boring and, therefore, varied it by inventing 20-house, 20-car, 20-light, 20-book.

Another example occurred one day when Naoshi and I were looking at some Styrofoam cups that had been filled with soil, planted with bean seeds, marked with children's names, and put in the sun on the windowsill to grow. As he picked up each cup, Naoshi tried to read the name written on the cup. Several cups, however, did not have names. When he got to a cup without a name he showed me the blank cup and I said, "Nobody." The next cup appeared to be unmarked as well. He held it up to me and said, "Nobody." But then he turned it slightly and discovered a name. He quickly changed his "Nobody" to "Yesbody." In both of these cases, Naoshi is showing his ability to analyze the structure of English words and vary them in a useful or amusing way.

In Wong Fillmore's (1979) study, the researcher noticed that the children used their longer phrases to begin the process of comparison that would lead them to an understanding of the structure of English. For example, one of the children, Nora, began with the phrase "How you do dese?" Then she began adding other material to the end of the sentence to get "How you do dese little tortillas?" and "How you do dese in English?" She then realized that other verbs besides *do* could be used in this construction and came up with "How do you make the flower?" and "How do you gonna make dese?" Next, she acquired the form *how did you* so that she could make a phrase like "How did you make it?" Next Nora began to vary what came after *How did* or *How do* to get "How did dese work?" and "How do cut it?" Finally, Nora realized that *how* could be used as a question word like *what* and *why* and produced phrases such as "How you make it?" and "How will take off paste?" As Wong Fillmore commented,

> Looking at this data without the time periods specified, we might have guessed that the developmental course went the opposite direction—from the less well-formed versions to the well-formed ones . . . Indeed, this would have been the case if the acquisitional procedure had been a gradual sorting out of the rules whereby the learner was able to structure the utterances herself. Instead, the procedure was one which might be described as "speak now, learn later." (1979, p. 215)

It was often possible to observe this acquisition process as the children in my study adopted and adapted the language that other speakers were using. For example, during a play situation with LEGOs, Leandro neatly piggybacked his usage on another child's production. As Sally played with the LEGOs, she said to me, "I want to make a tower." Leandro immediately said, "I want to make this," showing me the card with the police car, substituting the generic *this* for the noun in Sally's sentence. I said, "Police car." And he said, "I want to make police." Naoshi asked, "Police?" And Leandro replied, "Yes, I want to make."

Similarly, on another occasion, Akemi and Matthew were watching Marion clean out the guinea pig's cage when Matthew asked, "Marion, can I hold the guinea pig? Can I hold the guinea pig?" After Marion demurred, "I don't remember making that promise to you," Akemi immediately chimed in, "Marion! Marion! Marion! Can I [have] the guinea pig to hold it, the guinea pig?" After Marion demurred again, Akemi persisted, "I want a guinea pig, hold a guinea pig." Then, when it did not look as if Marion was going to relent, "No-o-o-o, I, I, I, guinea PIG ... Hold the guinea pig ... [loudly] I WANT TO HOLD THE GUINEA PIG!" Having demonstrated her language flexibility to its fullest extent, Akemi got the guinea pig to hold.

Leandro was the child who made the most progress in productive language use during his time in the English-language study classroom. Because I was not concentrating on Leandro alone, I do not have an extensive record of the period when Leandro's productive language use in English really began to take form. There are suggestions, however, of how Leandro began to break out of the telegraphic and formulaic forms of usage that he adopted in his early months in the classroom and how he began to develop productive use of English.

Like Nora, there were times when it seemed that Leandro's skills in English were deteriorating. For instance, in December, Leandro, who had always used "I" as the first-person subject of his sentences—but probably in unanalyzed combinations—began to struggle with the I/me distinction that is typical of young children's acquisition of English as a first language.

On December 7, Leandro, who had been in the study classroom for approximately 3 months, was working on a puzzle at one of the tables. As soon as he was finished, Leandro moved away from the puzzle to a spot on the other side of the table where there were rubber pieces that could be put together as a train. He held up a piece and said to me, "Pat. Me make. With my poppy." This comment by Leandro has the aspect of being a vertical construction, using "me" as the first-person subject of the construction.

One week later, Leandro used both "I" and "me" as first-person pronouns in adjacent utterances when he was playing in the playhouse with Supat. Leandro was languishing in bed with Supat nearby on the floor with a cup and teapot. Leandro said to Supat, "I want a drink. Me sick, me sick." Here the *I want* + noun frame is used for the first statement, but apparently the second statement is constructed from *me* (referring to self) + adjective. On the same day, Leandro also used the constructions "Me's doctor" (which leads one to wonder if "me sick" might not be "me's sick") and "I'm a friend" (most likely a formulaic phrase). By January, however, Leandro had resolved this conflict and no longer used "me" as a first-person subject pronoun. On January 30, he told me, "I can see 'cuz I have cat's eyes."

The same kind of pattern can be seen in Leandro's development of negatives. His earliest negatives were formulaic: "Don't do that!" and "No more." Then they were broken down into components:

At circle, Leandro said to Supat (in protest over something Supat had done), *"Don't do that."* Then, after a moment's reflection, he reversed himself by saying, "Yes, that."

§

When the police car seemed finished, I said, "Good work." Leandro replied, *"No more."* Then, after checking the picture one last time, he realized he had missed a piece and said to me, "Yes more" as he pointed to the piece in the picture. "Oh, you're right," I said.

The next step in this process was for Leandro to use *no* as a negative insert into a sentence:

At this point, Rebecca brought Leandro some "milk" and some "medicine" in containers from the play kitchen. Leandro reiterated to her, *"You no my mommy."*

By January, Leandro had abandoned the negative insert strategy and was able to produce a fully correct negative sentence:

Leandro displayed the wallet to me and said, *"I don't have any money in here."*

In this same period, Leandro was also working on questions and past tense. In October, he asked me, "Your name is what?" but by January he was able to frame a question to Ling Ling as follows, "What you putting in here?" showing that the *what* placement had been regularized but that the auxiliary verb was still missing. In play with Jessica and Andrew, Leandro, who had been pretending to be sick, hopped out of bed as Jessica approached and fled up the ladder to the loft announcing, "You don't gotted me," demonstrating that he had noticed that English verbs in the past tense are usually constructed by adding *-ed* but that he had not noticed that this irregular verb was already in the past tense.

THE DEVELOPMENTAL SEQUENCE: A CUMULATIVE PROCESS

In presenting the information about young children's acquisition of a second language, the developmental sequence has been outlined as consisting of four periods: 1) home-language use, 2) nonverbal period,

3) telegraphic and formulaic use, and 4) productive use. In discussing each of these periods, examples have been presented to illustrate the type of interactions that are typical of these periods. It is important to realize, however, that children learning a second language do not move discretely from one period to the next; in fact, except for home-language use, which is usually eliminated when speaking to those who do not understand it, young children add skills to their repertoire from the next level of language use but maintain the previous techniques as well. In this way, they can bring a range of communicative possibilities to any situation, giving them the best possible chance of getting their meaning across.

The following transcript excerpts illustrate this point. These excerpts are taken from an audiotaped conversation that Leandro and I had one day in April, after Leandro had been in the English-language study classroom for 7 months. We were building with some blocks that could be put together to make a house. During this conversation, Leandro demonstrated the variety of levels of competence that he had developed in English by this time. (In the following transcript L = Leandro, P = Author, and ———— = unintelligible material.)

L: I need help.

P: Okay. What do you need help with?

L: To ——— to building a house.

P: Gonna build a house? [consulting the booklet that came with the building blocks] Which one you gonna build? Which one?

L: This one. Here.

P: Oh, wow.

In the preceding sequence, Leandro uses a few basic phrases to get my attention, using contextual cues to get his message across.

L: Now we have to make it apart.

P: You want a whole big house.

L: Yeah.

P: Well, I have to start with a wall.

L: I make them apart.

P: You're making a what?

L: Part.

P: Apart? You're going to *take* them apart. Okay.

In the preceding sequence, there was a classic miscommunication about the word *apart*, but we managed to resolve it using appropriate feedback techniques.

P: Let's see, Leandro. You taking them all apart? Let's get some room here.

L: You know what? I want to do it a bell.

P: A . . . a bell?

L: Yeah.

P: What do you mean, a bell. You want to do the house with a bell in it? Where? Show me [looking through the brochure together].

L: ———— .

P: You want to build it, huh?

L: Yeah.

P: Okay.

In the preceding sequence, I continued the conversation by reinforcing the use of the term *apart*. Then Leandro used a formulaic phrase ("You know what?") to initiate another request for how he wanted the house to look, but again I did not understand. Finally, I decided he may have meant *build* instead of *bell,* and we proceeded.

P: Are you getting all the pieces you need?

L: Yeah.

P: How about some windows? Can you get some windows?

L: The door is a square [looking at the brochure].

P: The door is a square?

L: Yeah. [pause while he goes through the pieces] Can't find.

P: There's no . . . oh, come on, there's got to be a door in here some-where. There are a lot of things in here. Here're some windows.

L: Windows . . . Here [having found a door].

P: There's a door! Good. Now.

L: No, here's a door ———— .

P: Uh! We have two doors. . . . Now we need lots of pieces, right?

Here Leandro introduced the terms *door* and *square,* used a negative construction correctly ("can't find"), and answered some of my ques-tions appropriately.

P: Let's see if we can get this door here.

L: How?

P: We have to go up to the top here . . . We need the . . . lintel (pushing pieces around).

L: And what is for that [showing me a piece]?

P: That's for the corners.

L: For the what?

P: Corner. To go around a corner. Oh, look at this nice big long one. I'm looking for something to go on top of my door.

L: Look at one like that, and one like that.

P: Yeah . . . And here's another one. That can be the other side.

In this sequence Leandro initiated a question about a particular piece (getting the sequence of words slightly wrong) and then asked for a clarification about a new vocabulary item (*corner*).

L: You know what?

P: Oh, here's a window.

L: Lot of windows . . .

P: You need a lot of windows?

L: The house has a lot of windows. [pause] I know what, why have windows?

P: Why?

L: 'Cuz to we can see outside.

P: That's true.

L: It's tru-u-u-e.

P: You couldn't see outside if you didn't have a window, right? [pause] Do you think it would be very dark inside, Leandro, without a window? It would be dark, wouldn't it?

L: Yeah . . .

In this complicated sequence, Leandro showed off his ability to construct sentences in English. First, he started with "lot of windows" and put together "The house has a lot of windows." Then, rather than merely making a statement about why houses have windows, he used his knowledge to construct a rhetorical question ("I know what, why have windows?") and the answer ("'Cuz to we can see outside"). Although neither of these phrases was correctly formed in English, it is possible to see how far Leandro had come in the process of developing ways to communicate these more complex ideas. Interestingly, Leandro's question and answer encouraged me to pose several more questions that seemed to be too sophisticated for Leandro to follow, perhaps because he did not understand the vocabulary.

L: I think that window, window . . .

P: Is that one of these windows? One of these corner windows? Let me put it on the corner, huh?

L: Corner . . .

P: Can you get that one to go the right way?

L: Can you put it?

P: There, you can do it. You just had to get those things lined up. (pause) Good. I think you got it. . . .

L: The corner window.

P: Yeah. . . .

L: Corner window. I didn't know it was a corner window.

This conversation returned to the vocabulary item *corner* about which Leandro had asked for a clarification earlier. Here I used the word, then Leandro repeated it alone and with the term *window*, ending with a statement about his previous lack of knowledge about this term.

L: And we have to do it like that [pointing to the picture].

P: Really big?

L: Yeah.

P: We'll have the world's biggest house, huh?

L: Like . . . [gesturing with his hands like a roof].

P: You mean with a roof?

L: Yeah . . .

P: Okay. That looks like it's going to be hard.

L: Yes. How we going to put it . . . ?

P: I don't know.

L: I think we're going to do it with windows.

P: Okay. We'll have a solar roof.

This sequence demonstrates the full range of Leandro's communicative skills, from nonverbal use when demonstrating the need for a roof to construction of a complex sentence such as, "I think we're going to do it with windows."

From these excerpts, it is possible to see how volatile the language abilities of young second-language learners are. When they have both the vocabulary and the grammatical form under control, they can express themselves in highly sophisticated ways, but when a piece is missing from the puzzle of their knowledge, they have to drop back to techniques that they used in previous stages of their development of the second language. This is what makes conversing with young second-language learners such an adventure, as well as what makes assessment of their language skills a very complicated process (see Chapter 9).

It is also possible to see from these excerpts, however, that by the spring, Leandro had developed all of the building blocks necessary to continue to develop his second-language ability, acquiring vocabulary items and grammatical forms from the interactions he was able to initiate with the English speakers in the study classroom setting. From his first day at school in September, Leandro had been working hard at figuring out how to understand and make himself understood in this new language environment, and by April he was certainly well on his way.

As mentioned previously, however, Leandro was more advanced in his second-language skills than the other children who entered the study classroom at the same time. Chapter 5 explores the reasons for individual differences in second-language learning in young children.

Chapter Five

Individual Differences in Second-Language Learning

The previous two chapters establish that the second-language–learning process for young children follows a particular developmental pathway. As in all developmental processes, however, there are definite individual differences in how children approach this developmental pathway, and there are differences in how quickly they proceed along it. This chapter discusses these individual differences and the factors that may be involved in creating these differences.

THE APPLICATION OF COGNITIVE AND SOCIAL STRATEGIES

At the beginning of her study of Spanish-speaking children from Mexico, Wong Fillmore (1979) expected that

> The second language development of the five [children] would be fairly uniform after 9 months of exposure to the new language. . . . But the results were quite different. By the end of 3 months of observations, it became quite clear that there would be enormous differences among the five children in what they would achieve during the study year. In fact, after just 3 months of exposure, one child, Nora, had already learned

more—or at least she was producing better-formed and more varied sentences—than two of the others, Juan and Jesus, would be able to manage by the end of the study period. And by the end of the study period, Nora herself was speaking English as well as her friends who came from bilingual homes, and very nearly as well as her English mono-lingual friends. (p. 207)

In looking for the reasons behind these differences, Wong Fillmore (1979) came to believe that "the individual differences found among the five learners . . . had to do with the way in which cognitive and social factors of language acquisition interact together" (p. 207). There-fore, Wong Fillmore used her data to derive a set of strategies that she believed the children had used in the second-language–learning situation. As she explained, "These strategies are phrased as maxims that the children might have formulated for themselves" (pp. 208–209). The level of proficiency that any individual child achieves in the sec-ond-language–learning setting might well be related to how well these strategies are employed by the child. The following are Wong Fill-more's (1979, pp. 209–218) social and cognitive strategies:

Social: Join a group and act as if you understand what's going on, even if you don't.

This strategy is critical as a first step in exposure to a new language. After entering a group situation in which others are speaking the new language, the second-language–learning child will begin to hear language embedded in that context and relevant to that situation. For example, by joining a group of children about to make soup with a teacher, by finding a spot at the water table next to an English-speaking child, or by helping a group of children build a tall tower of blocks, the second-language–learning child demonstrates that he or she is ready to be part of the social network in the classroom. A child who is reluctant to put this strategy into play will remain isolated from helpful social situations and will have less exposure to the new language.

Cognitive: *Assume that what people are saying is directly relevant to the situation at hand or to what they or you are experiencing. Metastrategy: GUESS!*

To make sense of the new language, the second-language–learning child will need to assume that actions and words are connected. When a teacher is holding an object and talking, the second-language–learning child will need to assume that one of the words being used refers to that object, particularly if one word is repeated or emphasized. If another child uses a gesture or action accompanied by a word or words, the second-language–learning child will need to take a chance and act accordingly, testing the hypothesis that the action and the words are connected. The second-language–learning child who is not prepared to take these risks will take longer to make the necessary connections between the immediate context and the language used.

Social: *Give the impression—with a few well-chosen words—that you can speak the language.*

Cognitive: *Get some expressions you understand and start talking.*

These strategies show why the development of telegraphic and formulaic phrases is so critical. Socially, it is important that second-language–learning children be able to begin to sound like members of the group in order for them to get further exposure to the language; cognitively, these phrases give second-language–learning children material to begin the process of deconstruction and reconstruction that will eventually lead to the productive use of the language. Furthermore, by beginning to use phrases in the new language, second-language–learning children will receive feedback on what does and does not work. A child who does not pick up on the possibilities of using telegraphic and formulaic phrases may remain socially isolated, will have less information about how the new language works, and will have fewer opportunities to use his or her cognitive processes to unravel the new language.

Cognitive: Look for recurring parts in the formulas you know.

Cognitive: Make the most of what you've got.

Cognitive: Work on big things; save the details for later.

All three of these strategies deal with the process of moving from using formulaic phrases to productive use of the new language. Getting beyond the use of formulaic phrases requires considerable cognitive work on the part of the second-language–learning child. It seems as if the child must understand that there are regularities and commonalities in the phrases that he or she hears, extract them for future use, be willing to try them out, and be relatively unconcerned about being wrong. The second-language–learning child who is willing to take chances and use all of the language resources available at any given time will continue to make progress both in comparing his or her own language output to what is heard and in eliciting language input from others. The child who is less ready to employ these cognitive strategies will require a longer period of time in developing productive control over the new language.

Social: Count on your friends for help.

In Wong Fillmore's (1979) study, this meant primarily that the children needed to count on the English-speaking friend who was paired with them for the purposes of the study, but in other contexts, it could refer to both adult and child friends. Of course, it is imperative that the friend be a speaker of the new language that the child is trying to learn. To develop information about the new language, the second-language–learning child must be in communicative contact with those who speak the language; having a friend who is able to maintain this communication is an important part of the process of breaking through the social isolation that accompanies the second-language–learning situation. In a classroom situation, that friend may be a teacher at first or another child who is particularly tuned in to the social needs of a second-language learner. (See Chapter 6 for suggestions about how to provide this of friend for second-language learners in early childhood classrooms.) The second-language–learning child who is able to recruit a friend or friends in the second-language–learning situation will be included in the social network and will be exposed to more input in the new language; the second-language–learning child who finds this a difficult social challenge will have a harder time eliciting useful input in the new language, thus slowing down the second-language–learning process.

To proceed with rapid second-language learning, children would optimally use these social and cognitive strategies to the fullest extent possible, depending on where they are along the pathway of second-language development. But, as we have seen from Wong Fillmore's (1976, 1979) study, as well as what I found in my study in the English-language classroom, young children's second-language development progresses at very different rates. Which underlying factors, then, are involved in determining how available these strategies are to young children in the second-language–learning situation?

UNDERLYING FACTORS

Based on the research on young children learning a second language, there are at least four factors that may determine how available the social and cognitive strategies discussed previously may be to an individual child and, therefore, may strongly influence the progress that a child makes in the second-language acquisition process. These four factors are motivation, exposure, age, and personality.

Motivation

A young child must want to learn a second language. This decision to actually take on the process of learning a new language is one that different children come to at different times and in different ways.

It is known that this is an actual decision for children, because there are some children who decide *not* to learn a second language. For example, in Saville-Troike's (1988) study, there was a 5-year-old Japanese girl who informed a Japanese interviewer that English was too hard, so she was not going to speak to people who spoke English. She actually followed through with this plan and did not learn any English during the course of the yearlong study.

In the same way, Juan, one of the children studied by Wong Fillmore (1979) "refused to have anything to do with English-speakers, and would only play silently beside the ones I attempted to pair him with for the purposes of the study" (p. 206). Unlike in the study mentioned previously (Yim, 1984; see Chapter 3) of a young Korean girl learning English in a book-reading situation, the same process of my reading a book with another second-language–learning child, in this case a 3-year-old Korean boy, was a total failure. Unlike Young-joo, the boy listened politely but made no effort to repeat the English words or phrases I was using.

In all three of these cases, therefore, the children simply refused to play the game of second-language acquisition, at least for a particular time period. And, as long as children are placed in communicative situations in which they can continue to speak their home language or in which they can get by without speaking the second language, they may choose not to undertake the difficult task of learning a second language.

Even in situations in which children eventually do decide to begin the second-language acquisition process, it is possible that the amount of time they spend in the nonverbal period may be related to how long it takes for them to make the decision to start learning the new language. As mentioned previously, the early period in his early childhood classroom was considered a rejection period for Takahiro, the Japanese child studied by Itoh and Hatch (1978). One explanation for this, they believed, was that he "was attempting to avoid dealing with the second language . . ., hoping it would not be necessary to cope with this new learning task" (p. 78).

Other children, although not cutting themselves off entirely from the second-language–learning situation, find ways of avoiding learning much of the second language being used around them. In situations in which there are sufficient numbers of children who speak the same first language, some children will continue to associate with their same-language friends, forming social groups on that basis. For example, Meyer (1989) studied a group of Korean girls in an English-speaking early childhood classroom who spent most of their time in class playing with each other. When they sought communication outside their group, they were highly selective, most often concentrating on communication with their teachers rather than with their English-speaking peers.

In bilingual classrooms in which some children speak the same home language, the children can function by using that language in play situations and with any adults in the classroom who speak their language. If there are also English-speaking adults in the classroom, the children may develop receptive understanding of English, but they may not feel sufficiently motivated to begin speaking the language themselves.

A final factor in how motivated young children may be to learn a new language might have to do with what their parents tell them about language. Children who are short-term visitors may understand that learning a new language is not a high priority for their family; they may develop enough receptive knowledge to get along in the classroom and perhaps a few high-utility phrases to get into play with other children, but they may not advance beyond that level. If families have come to the United States to stay, however, and/or if learning English is given high priority within the family, young children will be exposed to a different attitude and may therefore make more of an effort to learn English. (Chapter 8 discusses the kinds of decisions that families face when learning English is a high priority and the ways that teachers can help advise parents for whom this is a concern.)

Young children, then, certainly seem to understand that learning a second language is a cognitively challenging and time-consuming activity. Being exposed to a second language is obviously not enough; wanting to communicate with people who speak that language is crucial if acquisition is to occur. Children who are in a second-language–learning situation have to be sufficiently motivated to take on this cognitive challenge.

Exposure

Another factor related to how children approach the second-language–learning process is exposure, both prior exposure to the second language and the quantity of exposure in the second-language–learning environment.

Obviously, if a child arrives in the second-language–learning setting with prior exposure to the new language, this may affect how quickly he or she might start to use the second language in this new situation. In the English-language classroom I studied, a 4-year-old Japanese girl, Akemi, joined the class in January. Although she had not been in school, Akemi had been in the United States for approximately a year before coming to the classroom and had apparently spent considerable time with English-speaking children in her neighborhood. For this reason, Akemi never went through a nonverbal period in the classroom but began to show off her high-utility language skills right from the start. On the first day I observed her, Akemi went into the playhouse, picked up the toy telephone, and said, "I know. How are you? You go. Okay. Okay."

The amount of time spent in contact with the new language is also important in terms of the speed with which a child may acquire the language. At the English-speaking study classroom, parents had the option of enrolling their children in school for two, three, or five mornings a week. Only Leandro, the child who made the most progress among the second-language learners, attended the classroom 5 days a week. Furthermore, Leandro had two older brothers who were attending public school, and his parents reported that the boys often played together using their new language. Leandro, therefore, could be said to have been in a high-exposure condition during the year that he attended the English-language classroom.

Children are also exposed to different levels of a second language depending on how they spend their time in the second-language setting. If they remove themselves from English speakers and keep mostly to themselves or remain in a group of children who speak the same home language, they will be exposed to less second-language talk than if they solicit interaction from the English speakers in the classroom. In my study, for example, when comparing Ling Ling, Naoshi, and Leandro, I found that Ling Ling communicated the least with English speakers, and when she did use English, it was mostly with adults. In contrast, Naoshi talked more often than Ling Ling with English speakers but concentrated mostly on English-speaking children. Leandro, who spent the most time (of these three children) communicating in English, started with a strategy of talking with the English-speaking adults and then moved on to talking primarily with English-speaking children. At the end of the school year, Leandro had made the most progress in English. Naoshi and Ling Ling had also both made progress, but their achievement was not as great as Leandro's.

Age

Age may also play a distinct role in how a child approaches the second-language situation. As Chapter 1 discusses, young children are at an advantage in second-language–learning situations because the cognitive demand of what they must learn is quite low; they do not have to use language in as sophisticated a way as older children. However, younger children are also at a disadvantage because their cognitive capacity is not as great as that of older children. For this reason, younger children may take longer to move along the developmental pathway than older children.

First, as shown in the Chapter 3 description of the study involving the two Chinese brothers, younger children may persist in the use of their home language for a longer period of time than older children. This may be because it takes younger children longer to figure out that the language they are speaking is not being understood and that it is *another*, completely different language that is being spoken to them.

Second, younger children may spend a lengthier period in the nonverbal period as well. As mentioned in Chapter 3, there seems to be an inverse relationship between the age of the child and the length of time spent in the nonverbal period. For Panos, who came to the United States from Greece when he was 2 years old, this period lasted for almost $1\frac{1}{2}$ years. For Ervin-Tripp's (1974) children, who were 5 and $6\frac{1}{2}$ years old, the period lasted for only a matter of weeks. It can be assumed that it may take younger children longer than older children to formulate a strategy for breaking out of the nonverbal period.

Third, younger children may also take longer to acquire formulaic phrases, to develop strategies for breaking down phrases into useful pieces, and to create productive phrases in their new language. In Chapter 4, the differences between the phrases used by the children in my study (who were 3 and 4 years old) and those used by the children in Wong Fillmore's (1976, 1979) study (who were 5, 6, and 7 years old) are striking: The older children were able to acquire and use much lengthier phrases. All other things being equal, then, this seems to indicate that older children move into productive second-language use much more quickly than younger children.

Age, then, may be a critical factor in how quickly a child moves along the developmental pathway of second-language acquisition. Because of their more limited cognitive capacity, it may take younger children longer to mobilize their learning skills and apply them to the challenging cognitive task of learning a second language. This lengthier mobilization period may extend the time a child spends in any or all of the stages of second-language acquisition.

Personality

Personality may also play a part in the way an individual child approaches the second-language–learning situation. Researchers studying young children's second-language acquisition have observed that there seems to be a personality continuum stretching from shy and reserved at one end to outgoing and socially tuned in at the other end. Where an individual child's personality can be located along this continuum may have an impact on how quickly that child learns a second language.

Children who tend to be shy and reserved are more likely to approach the second-language situation with more caution. These are the children who take a long time to go public with their newly acquired language skills, spending their time practicing quietly to themselves before anyone can hear them. Byong-sun certainly fit this profile (see Chapter 3), mouthing other children's words before he began to say them out loud himself. In Saville-Troike's (1988) study, six of the nine children entered a nonverbal period during which five of them used private speech as a means of mobilizing information about the new language. (The sixth child who entered a nonverbal period was the Japanese child mentioned previously in this chapter, who decided not to learn any English.) Saville-Troike characterized the five children who used private speech as inner directed and more reflective in their general learning style. In Wong Fillmore's (1979) study, she characterized Juan, the child who did not want to communicate with English speakers, as the "most cautious of all" of the children she studied, a child who "rarely said anything in English unless he was quite sure of himself" (p. 224).

At the other end of this personality spectrum are the children who approach the second-language–learning situation in a more outgoing and socially oriented fashion. The most detailed example of the use of this style comes from Nora, the child in Wong Fillmore's (1979) study who learned the most English during the study year. Wong Fillmore characterized Nora as

> Quite uninhibited in her attempts at speaking the new language. After the first 2 months, she was able to get by almost exclusively with English, and from the first she was far more concerned with communication than with form. She used what she knew to say what she needed to say, and she usually made good enough sense. (p. 224)

Although she was the youngest of the children studied by Wong Fillmore (5 years, 7 months of age at the beginning of the study), Nora "experienced spectacular success as a language learner" (1979, p. 221). None of the other children in the study even approached her level of achievement. Wong Fillmore commented,

> Nora was particularly motivated by the desire to be part of the social group that spoke the new language, and thus she sought out the company of the children she wanted to be with. At the other extreme, Juan avoided contact with people who did not speak his language. Thus Nora was in

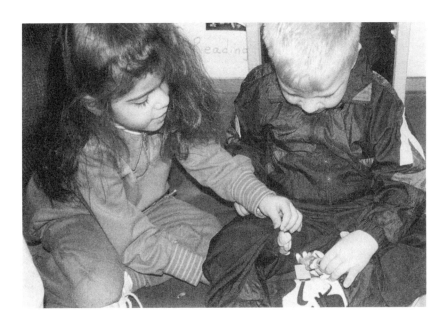

a position to learn the new language where Juan was not. That difference presumably had nothing to do with intellectual or cognitive capacity. It was solely a matter of social preference, and perhaps of social confidence as well. (p. 227)

It is easy to see why more outgoing, socially oriented children find the second-language setting a particular kind of challenge. If they want to communicate with the children who speak the new language, they have to make every effort to learn the new language as quickly as possible. These risk-taking children often plunge almost fearlessly into communication in the new language, making many mistakes but getting by nonetheless while receiving a lot of exposure. Instead of hanging back until they believe they are totally competent, they use whatever words they have and hope for the best, counting on those around them to help in the process of getting the message across.

Of course, most children do not fall at the outer extremes of this personality continuum. For most young children, the process of learning a second language means finding a balance between their social needs and their knowledge of the new language. Juggling the social and cognitive demands of the second-language setting is the hard work that these children do on a daily basis.

Obviously, these four factors—motivation, exposure, age, and personality—may combine in any number of different ways for different children, and they can also be highly interrelated. In my study, Leandro was the child who learned the most during the study year. In Leandro's case, it also happened to be true that he was the oldest of the second-language learners (4 years, 2 months of age in September), that he came to the classroom every morning, and that he was an outgoing child who made friends easily with both adults and children. This combination of factors, rather than one particular factor, certainly gave Leandro a definite advantage in the second-language–learning situation and can be seen to be the source of his success. We can only guess at how different his level of achievement might have been if one or more of these factors had varied.

CONCLUSION

In both Wong Fillmore's (1976, 1979) study and my study, the objective was to document the process of second-language acquisition among young children. In neither case did the researcher make any attempt at intervention in or manipulation of the second-language–learning process. The variations in the achievement levels of the children at the ends of the study periods were therefore seen to be the result of the interactions among the strategies and factors that this chapter discusses.

The fact that children gained more or less control over their new language within a certain time period was seen to be the end product of a series of natural processes. The implication of this research is, *That is just the way it is.*

From an educator's point of view, however, how quickly a child gains control over a second language may be of more than simply academic interest. Educators of children who will soon be moving into or are already involved in primary school classrooms are certainly under pressure from parents and other educators to help children progress as quickly as possible along the developmental pathway of second-language acquisition. The second part of this book therefore presents information about the role that teachers can play in supporting and facilitating the second-language–learning process in their classrooms, as well as their role in working with parents and assessing young second-language learners' progress.

Part Two

The Teacher's Role

Using Information, Communication, and Classroom Organization to Support Second-Language Learning

E arly childhood educators may encounter a variety of second-language–learning situations in their classrooms, from one child who speaks a language other than English to an entire classroom of children who speak the same or a variety of different languages. Of course, no matter what the second-language composition of a classroom may be at the beginning of the school year, there may be a very different configuration by the end of the school year. Furthermore, one year may not look anything like the next.

Even so, there are some basic ingredients common to all early childhood classroom situations in which there are second-language learners. These commonalities make it possible for early childhood educators to plan effective classrooms for second-language–learning children. This chapter presents information concerning the teacher's role in communicating with second-language–learning children and their families and in organizing the classroom to support second-language learning.

GATHERING INFORMATION ABOUT THE CULTURAL AND LINGUISTIC BACKGROUNDS OF SECOND-LANGUAGE–LEARNING CHILDREN

One of the first questions on an early childhood educator's mind at the beginning of the school year no doubt is, "Who are these children in my class?" Answering this question is complicated enough when there is a match between the cultural and linguistic backgrounds of the teacher and the children; when this is not the case, the task of getting information about the children may be even more complicated.

Following are some rules for early childhood educators to use as guidelines when embarking on the process of getting information about children in an early childhood education classroom.

Rule #1:   Do not make any assumptions about a child's cultural or linguistic background without getting further information.

This is clearly the starting point for any data-gathering activity and should apply equally to all of the children in a classroom. In the process of collecting information from the families, interesting and helpful characteristics may be discovered, such as other languages spoken or countries visited, that would otherwise never be known. In addition to identifying children whose families speak a language other than English at home, it is important to identify second-generation speakers of English (i.e., children whose parents are not native speakers of English, although English is the home language) and internationally adopted children (see Chapter 11), because both of these groups of children may have specific language-learning issues.

Rule #2:   Decide what information is important to know.

If the primary interest is in collecting cultural and linguistic information, then there are certain categories of information that will be important as children move into the early childhood education situation. These categories include 1) basic demographic information, 2) linguistic practices in and outside the home, and 3) relevant cultural practices.

Basic demographic information includes information about where the child was born; when the child arrived in the community; what the family configuration is (including extended family); what, if any, religious affiliation the child has; and what the other child care arrangements are for the child. Basic linguistic information includes the language(s) spoken at home, the family members who speak those languages, and the language(s) to which the child has been exposed, including when and where. Important cultural practices information includes child-rearing beliefs about discipline, toileting behavior, and separation problems; food preferences and feeding practices; and how children are expected to behave toward adults and in group situations. Further information might also be collected about culturally appropriate behaviors that diverge considerably from practices in early childhood education classrooms.

Rule #3: Plan how to get this information.

This type of information can be collected from formal questionnaires, trips to the library, or searches on the Internet and/or informal chats with parents or other cultural representatives. In many situations, there is an intake interview when a family applies for admission to an early childhood education program or during a home visit within the first few weeks of the school year. In either of these situations, basic demographic and linguistic information could be developed from questions asked at that time. If sitting down with the family to have questions answered is not an option, sending home a questionnaire with demographic and linguistic questions is a possibility, but one that does not always yield results. If a questionnaire is sent home without response, it may be necessary to have someone with the appropriate linguistic skills visit or call the family to get the answers.

Information on cultural practices may be more difficult to acquire. One good starting point for the early childhood educator is the library, where books on individual countries, religions, or linguistic groups might provide some insights and some relevant background information. Books or magazine articles also provide historical information that might be important in understanding why a particular family has recently arrived in the community. Internet searches may yield the same type of information and might be more up to date. Information developed along these lines should certainly be shared within the early childhood community and should be checked with cultural representatives.

Again, however, it is certainly helpful for an early childhood educator to have the option of asking parents about their cultural practices. As one Head Start teacher remarked,

On the home visit paperwork, we have a form that the office wants anyway. What country are you from? What foods do you eat? Do you celebrate any holidays? But those, they don't get down to the behaviors and the traditions, the taking off the shoes things. For me, it depends on the parent a lot; if they seem like they're the willing kind, I'll come out and ask them.

The early childhood educator may also consider asking the parents to include him or her in a community-wide celebration, which could provide important cultural information as well as let the parents know that the educator values their cultural traditions and is interested in knowing more.

Rule #4:   Think about using a variety of ways to get this information.

Getting information from second-language families can be a challenge. One of the most basic hurdles is, of course, finding an effective way to communicate. Here are some suggestions.

First, face-to-face communication in the second language may be the most difficult for the parents. Face-to-face communication requires quick language processing and formulation of a response in real time. This takes a relatively high level of proficiency in a language. It is important to remember that if face-to-face communication is used in a language that is a second language for the parents, the questions may be difficult for them to understand and they may have difficulty putting together their answers. Therefore, if face-to-face communication is used, the same question should be asked more than once using slightly different wording to confirm that consistent answers are being given.

Second, written communications in the parents' second language may give them a chance to read and respond in a way that is less pressured than face-to-face communication. Reading ability in a second language may be stronger than speaking ability. Furthermore, written communications can be shared with other members of the same first-language community who can read and write the second language. Parents with low levels of proficiency may seek out a translator to help complete a questionnaire. For this reason, it is important to remember that a completed questionnaire may not represent the actual language abilities of the parents but may represent their ability to recruit translation help when needed.

Third, communications that can be arranged in the parents' home language (either oral or written) will likely be the most comfortable for the parents. Many programs have parent liaisons who are bilingual in English and one of the languages spoken by parents in the program. In this case, both written and oral communications can be translated into the home language, and responses can then be translated for the benefit of staff members who do not speak that home language. If a program does not have access to parent liaisons, it will be necessary to develop relationships with community members who can act as translators. Public schools, churches, community agencies, community newspapers, and even local grocery stores are good places to ask about translation services.

These same community resources may also be a good place to seek out cultural information as well (see also Williams & De Gaetano, 1985). Frequently, individuals identify themselves as cultural representatives and make themselves available to discuss the cultural differences that they have noticed between their home culture and the culture in their new community. If one of the parents in a classroom assumes such a role, it can make the teacher's job much easier. As the same Head Start teacher quoted previously told me,

> Like Peilan . . . she's great at answering questions. She has been the life-saver in this room because . . . in the beginning of the year she didn't understand as much, but now she can translate back and forth between Mandarin and English—and that's just been wonderful.

The CD-ROM and Appendix A contain a sample questionnaire that can be adapted and/or translated for use in a variety of situations. Questions can be added or dropped, depending on the particular information that is needed. In deciding what information to ask for, teachers should think about its usefulness in the early childhood education context.

COMMUNICATING WITH SECOND-LANGUAGE–LEARNING CHILDREN

By collecting the kind of information that is requested in the sample questionnaire, teachers will have a better idea of the backgrounds of the children who are coming into or are already in their classrooms. But this information will be only a starting point when it comes to actually communicating with a child who knows little or no English. This section discusses ideas about how to communicate with second-language–learning children in ways that will help them understand and begin to use English.

Starting with What the Children Know

A common practice for the teachers I interviewed was for them to ask parents of children whose home language was not English to provide a few important words in their home language, so that the teachers could do some low-level communicating with the children in the first few weeks in the classroom. Words for *listen, bathroom,* and *eat* were very useful in this early period in the classrooms and helped the teachers and children feel connected. At the same time, by asking the parents to provide these phrases, teachers also deliver the message that they value the home language and are open to finding out more about how the home language sounds and is used.

A handy technique for collecting these words is to have parents tape-record them so that teachers can listen to them and practice them by playing them over and over. These tapes can also be played for the children in the classroom so that everyone can learn words in another language. Furthermore, these tapes could also contain comforting messages from home that could be played for children with separation difficulties.

Starting Slowly

One of the features of the English-language classroom that I observed was that the teachers did not make immediate efforts to communicate with the second-language learners beyond a welcoming smile and greeting. In fact, they gave the second-language learners a lot of time to become familiar with the classroom situation before approaching them with questions or directives in English. Several times in the first few weeks of school, Marion even referred to Byong-sun in the third person (e.g., "Let's give Byong-sun a chance," "Let's show Byong-sun how to pick this up"), including him by using his name without actually directing her speech to him. This approach established the fact that Byong-sun was being considered part of the group but that specific responses would not be required of him. By setting up such a low-demand situation, the teachers gave the second-language learners time to start the adjustment process in this new cultural and linguistic setting.

In fact, the language that the teachers used around the second-language learners in the first month of school was probably too complicated for them to understand anyway, because only 30% of the teachers' communications involved simplified language. This language use was probably similar to, if not the same as, that which they used to address all of the children, including the English speakers, in the classroom. After all, in the first few weeks of school, the teachers did not know very much about many of the children in the classroom. So, their choice was to use talk appropriate for young children generally when addressing any of the children. For the second-language learners, this early exposure probably made it possible for them to begin at least to tune in to the sounds of the new language, even though they probably did not understand what was actually being said.

After the first month, however, the teachers switched to less-complicated language in an attempt to help the children begin to understand English. This reminded me of how adults in American culture speak to infants as though infants can comprehend sophisticated speech until the infants are old enough to actually start acquiring receptive abilities, at which time adults begin to simplify their speech to get their messages across.

This is not to say, however, that teachers should not be responsive to communicative efforts made by the second-language learners. In fact, the rule in the study classroom seemed to be to always respond, even if the message from the child was not understandable. Just like the teacher mentioned previously who engaged in dilingual discourse with the Chinese brothers in Saville-Troike's (1987) study (see Chapter 3), the adults in the study classroom tried to guess the topic of the message and responded accordingly. For example, one day at the drawing table, Poram showed her completed project to Marion and said something to Marion that was unintelligible (i.e., her utterance sounded like a sentence, but it was not possible to understand what she had said). Marion replied anyway, "Oh, are you making that?"

Buttressing Communication

When the teachers in the study classroom started the process of communicating with the second-language learners in their classroom, they frequently "doubled the message" by using words along with some type of gesture, action, or directed gaze. For example, one morning two Japanese sisters, Kumiko and Kaori, arrived with a paper bag full of vegetables. They approached Rosa, who *pointed to the bag* and asked, "What's in there?" Kumiko opened the bag and showed Rosa what was inside. Rosa said, "How about feeding Ponytails [the guinea pig]?" and she walked to the guinea pig cage, *gesturing for the sisters to follow*. At the guinea pig cage, Kumiko began taking the vegetables out of the bag and handing them to Kaori to put in the cage. Rosa *named each vegetable as it was put in the cage*, "Another carrot, and lettuce."

On another occasion, after watching Leandro wander around the room for a while with a painting he had made, I said to him, "Do you want to put it in your cubby?" He started to go to the cubby area, then he stopped and *touched the paint* on the picture. It was still wet. He *showed me this*, so I said, "Shall I hang it up?" *indicating the line* strung up to dry paintings. He brought the picture to me, I hung it up, and he went to the block area. In this example, Leandro used nonverbal communication to indicate what the problem was with my first suggestion. My response about hanging the picture on the line was reinforced by indicating the location that I was talking about, because this was a special arrangement for hanging up pictures and I was not sure that Leandro would understand what I was saying.

One of the teachers I interviewed referred to this as using "body language" to help a second-language–learning child understand. I call this technique buttressing communication, because the additional information delivered by a gesture, an action, or a directed gaze adds another dimension that helps the child tune in to exactly what is being talked about, making it easier to get the message.

Repetition

Another technique that is used successfully when communicating with second-language–learning children involves using repetition. Saying the same thing more than once gives a child more than one opportunity to catch on to what is being said. If the repetition involves a single item, it may also provide an opportunity for the child to actually learn the word. For example, one morning at the drawing table, the following sequence occurred in rapid succession:

Marion to Jennifer: See how Sook-whan did her *hand?*

Rosa to Poram: Are you going to cut out your *hand?*

Marion to Jennifer: Look at that *hand,* Myong's right *hand.*

Marion to Miguel: Do you want to trace your *hand,* too?

Frequently, the teachers also emphasized the words as they said them and put them at or near the end of the sentence for better comprehension.

Talking About the Here and Now

One major feature of successful communication with second-language learners is that it is grounded in the here and now. Talking about what is right there gives the second-language learner a chance to narrow the field of what the conversation is about and focus on a more restricted number of options for response as well. As second-language learners begin to use their productive abilities, the context in which the conversation is held also helps the teacher understand what the child is talking about.

For example, one day, outside on the playground, I was sitting on a large rubber tire when Poram came to sit down next to me. Quickly, Poram discovered that the tire had writing all around it (Firestone and so forth). She and I started to name the letters and numbers. Poram had little difficulty with any of the letters, except the ones that were upside down, because of where we were sitting on the tire. Noticing that there was a problem, Poram gestured to me that the letters were in a strange position. I told her "upside down," and she repeated it. The next time she had the same problem, she said, "Upside down." She also stumbled over the number 8. After I told her what it was, Poram was able to identify it correctly later.

In this example, the fact that we were sharing the same physical space and could refer to the same information on the tire helped to make this a successful communicative experience for both of us, including my being able to provide some missing vocabulary items for Poram.

Expanding and Extending

Once children begin to demonstrate their developing capabilities with their new language, teachers can use communicative opportunities as ways of helping children expand and extend their language skills. In this technique, it is necessary to start with what a child already knows and work from there. For example, one morning when I sat down at a table where children were working with playdough, Sook-whan held up a round piece of playdough to me and said, "Cookie." I replied, "Is this a chocolate-chip cookie? May I eat it?" Sook-whan nodded, and I pretended to eat the cookie. I then told Sook-whan, "That's a good cookie." Later, Sook-whan held up a cube-shaped piece of playdough and said, "Chocolate." We followed the same procedure as before as I pretended to eat the piece of chocolate and commented on how good it was. This play routine used Sook-whan's original utterance as a starting point and then developed parallel verbal constructions to extend and expand her linguistic knowledge. This turned out to be successful both as communication and as play.

Upping the Ante

One of the difficult judgment calls that teachers have to make when communicating with second-language learners is when to be more insistent that the children get beyond the nonverbal techniques that they have developed and actually use language to get their point across. To push the process along, it is often necessary for a teacher to up the ante, insisting on verbal communication, for example, before complying with a request.

This was demonstrated one day when Miguel approached Marion with a suspender that had come loose. The following interaction occurred:

Marion: You're trying to tell me something.

Miguel: [No reply.]

Marion: Do you want me to do something?

Miguel: [No reply.]

Marion: Do you want me to do something with your suspender? Put it on my nose? [Starts to do so.]

Miguel: Red. [Showing her his pants.]

Marion: Yes, red . . . red what?

Miguel: Red pants.

Marion: Do you want me to attach this to your red pants?

Miguel: Yes.

Marion: Okay. I'll do that for you.

I found myself in just this same situation one day with Leandro. As I was leaving the art table, Leandro walked by, stopped in front of me, and pointed to his untied shoelace. I said, "What do you need?" He paused for a moment and said, "Please do my shoes." I said enthusiastically, "All right!" letting him know how pleased I was at his linguistic accomplishment.

Fine-Tuning

When communicating with second-language–learning children, teachers must always estimate what level of proficiency a child has achieved so that their language can be calibrated to that level. Of course, this task is very difficult, and many mistakes can be made along the way to successful communication. Fortunately, most communicative situations allow for a process of fine-tuning in which it is possible to reiterate a message in a form that might be more understandable. Not surprisingly, successful communication with second-language learners requires a lot of fine-tuning on the part of teachers.

For example, after lunch one day in early November, I found Leandro alone in the block area looking at a book. He had a pair of plastic glasses with him that he had been wearing off and on all day. I picked them up and said, "I like your glasses. Are they yours or do they belong here at school?" This complicated question did not get a reply. Then I said, "Do these come from school?" and Leandro shook his head and said, "House." Then I said, "Are they from Halloween?" And he said, "Yes." Slightly later, Leandro spotted a piece of candy in my pocket. He asked, "What's this?" I replied, "Candy," and he repeated, "Candy." I said, "Sally gave it to me." He said, "Halloween?" I answered, "Yes."

By realizing that my first question was perhaps too complicated for Leandro to answer and by rephrasing it to make it simpler, I made it possible for Leandro to understand what I was asking. I then took a chance that he would know the term *Halloween,* as there had been a lot of talk about Halloween in the classroom. He not only knew what I was talking about but demonstrated how much he knew by turning the conversation around later and using the term to ask me a question. By fine-tuning my initiation, I was able to prolong a conversation that turned out to be very successful.

Combining Techniques for Communicating with Second-Language Learners

Although these techniques for communicating with second-language learners have been presented individually, they rarely appear separately from each other. In any attempt to communicate with second-language learners, teachers combine techniques and keep trying until they find out what works in any given situation. The transcript of my discussion with Leandro at the end of Chapter 4 shows a variety of these techniques used simultaneously in my efforts to keep the conversation going.

Furthermore, although these techniques have been presented as relevant for communication with young second-language–learners, they are, in fact, very similar to techniques used to communicate with first-language learners of a slightly younger age group. Marion, for example, talked about how similar the second-language children were to prelinguistic toddlers:

> When I first started here I had a lot of children who really had no English at all, and then—since I'm comfortable with toddlers, toddler was one of my favorite periods with my own children and the use of preverbal communication—that was sort of the level on which I began things.

Intuitively, Marion discovered that she could use the same communicative techniques with her second-language learners that she had previously used with 18-month- to 2½-year-old first-language learners. Teachers who have worked with a younger age group will certainly recognize many of these techniques as being those that are needed to communicate successfully with toddlers. Imported into the second-language–learning early childhood classroom, they make it possible for teachers and second-language learners to communicate more quickly and with less frustration right from the beginning.

ORGANIZING THE CLASSROOM
FOR SECOND-LANGUAGE LEARNERS

How the classroom is set up can have a major impact on how comfortable and secure a second-language–learning child may feel there. As discussed in the previous chapters, there is a strong social component to a second-language–learning child's adaptation to the classroom. Classroom organization can be used to ensure that adaptation occurs more smoothly and more quickly.

Physical Setup: Providing Safe Havens

In observing second-language–learning children in early childhood education classrooms, I have often noticed that they choose to settle down to play in physical settings where manipulatives like LEGOs, puzzles, playdough, or small blocks are available. As the portrait of Byong-sun in Chapter 2 shows, his first choice that morning was to go to the table where the LEGOs were available and to play there for quite some time, either alone or in proximity to another child, whom he ignored. The obvious advantage of these locations is that they provide an activity that a child can pursue without asking for help from anyone else or having to negotiate play with other children. As long as a space and some materials are available, a child can proceed to play without interference, eventually making a decision about whether to interact with other people.

In setting up a classroom for second-language learners, teachers can make sure that they are providing places in the classroom where second-language learners can feel comfortable, competent, and occupied. These areas, which I think of as safe havens, can provide the children with a base of operations from which they can move into the rest of the classroom activities when they are ready.

Classroom Routines:
Helping Children Become Members of the Group

The social aspect of the study classroom that proved most helpful for the second-language learners was the presence of a consistent set of routines for the children. These routines meant that, with a little observation, the second-language–learning children could pick up cues regarding what to do and when, using the English-speaking children as models, even before they could understand the language being used around them. The daily schedule of arrival, free play, cleanup, snack time, outside play, and circle time gave the second-language learners a set of activity structures to acquire (e.g., put jackets in a cubby, go to rug, find a place at a table for snack, help put toys away), which immediately allowed them to act like members of the group.

For example, one morning early in the school year, when Marion began to organize a soup-making operation at one of the tables, Sook-whan was standing nearby watching. Marion asked her, "Would you like to help, too, Sook-whan?" Sook-whan nodded her head. Marion then announced, "Okay, there will be five helpers." Sook-whan sat down at the table as Marion named the five helpers, including Sook-whan.

In this example, Sook-whan is addressed by the teacher in a questioning tone that includes her name. This routine is similar in general format to routines that occur again and again in the classroom: The teacher begins to display particular types of materials for a project and invites children to engage in the project. From previous experiences, Sook-whan can guess that Marion has asked whether she wishes to join the group. Then, when she hears her name and sees the other children start to sit down at the table, Sook-whan does the same, indicating that she understands that she has been included. Even without knowing anything more than her own name, Sook-whan could look like she knew what was being asked of her because the situation was routine in the classroom.

Other researchers have observed similar situations with young second-language learners. In their case study of a 5-year-old Taiwanese boy acquiring English in a child care center, Huang and Hatch (1978) found that "Paul's prompt non-verbal responses to verbal commands were frequently misleading. For example, on his second day at school, when the teacher . . . said, "Paul, would you like to sit there?" he smiled and sat down immediately" (p. 121). The researchers' speculation was that

> If he responded to any verbal cue at all it would be to "Paul." More likely he saw the other children seating themselves and [the teacher] pointing to the chair as she spoke to him. His response was the expected one and could not be taken as evidence of sentence comprehension. (p. 121)

Because children are so good at using established routines to guess what an appropriate action might be in a given situation, it is only when a child guesses incorrectly that this strategy is fully revealed. One day in the study classroom, Naoshi and Rebecca were sitting side-by-side working independently with story pieces. I sat down next to Rebecca, who was having a difficult time setting up the pieces on the plastic stands. Naoshi, however, had figured out how to set up the pieces and was putting some together. Rebecca said to me, "I want to do what Naoshi did." I answered, "Go ahead." She said, "I don't know how." I said, "Ask Naoshi to help you." Rebecca turned to Naoshi and said, "Can you help me to do that?" He handed her one of the plastic pieces. She asked again, "How do you do it?" He gave her the plastic bag that still had one extra piece in the bottom.

In this example, Naoshi's best guess is that Rebecca has asked him to provide her with pieces that she cannot reach, a typical request in this situation; not actually understanding what she has said, he still responds with an appropriate, if misguided, action in an attempt to be helpful.

In interviews, both Marion and Rosa pointed to these routines as being an important aspect of the classroom, particularly for the second-language learners. (In the following interview, P is the author and M is Marion.)

P: What kind of patterns do you think you have established with the kids? . . . What helps the kids, particularly the second-language kids?

M: I think, one thing, the structure and rhythm of the day is fairly well set. We do have a definite routine . . . at the beginning particularly we try to be fairly consistent about the routine. . . .

P: Does it surprise you . . . how quickly the kids seem to pick up on the routines and fit right in and, on the whole, not be confused and . . . ?

M: Right, it really does.

P: It surprised me!

Rosa mentioned that in the beginning it was a lot of work to establish the routines in the classroom—she could not just stand back and "let it happen"—but, in the long run, it was worth the effort.

Just how powerful routines can be in helping children become members of a group occasionally becomes apparent when a routine changes without the child's being aware of the change. Snow (1983) observed just such an incident in Amsterdam, The Netherlands, where a 5-year-old English girl, Nicola, attended a kindergarten classroom. Nicola seemed to be a fully functioning member of the class:

> She participated in art projects, listened attentively during story reading, executed all the steps to the dance during music class. Her only failure came one day when the teacher announced, while passing out snack, "Today we're going to wait until everyone is back at his seat before we open our milk." Nicola failed to observe this deviation from the standard routine, since she understood not a single word of Dutch, and she was soundly scolded for having disobeyed. Nicola had done such a good job of acting as if she spoke Dutch that betrayal of her ignorance was treated as obstinacy rather than poor language learning. (pp. 148–149)

Fortunately, most teachers of young children in second-language–learning situations are more sensitive than the teacher in this situation to the possibility of a child's not understanding verbal instructions. But Nicola's reliance on classroom routines as a basis for her activities, particularly in the absence of any understanding of the language being used, is quite typical of young second-language–learning children.

In setting up a classroom for second-language learners, teachers can capitalize on the helpfulness of routines. Early in the school year it may be desirable to have a strict schedule to get children oriented to a set of routine situations. Minimizing confusion and maximizing structure will help the second-language learners tune in to the classroom and feel more secure sooner. Allowing children to participate in activities in easily understood ways will help them join the social group and be exposed to more language.

Small-Group Activities: Ensuring Inclusion

In the study classroom, the teachers were always careful to include a mix of first- and second-language children in organized small-group activities. Whenever there was an activity underway, such as making pizza muffins or soup, teachers would invite groups of children to join the activity, particularly mentioning the names of the second-language–learning children so that they would know they were being included. This inclusionary policy had many benefits:

1. The invitation from the teacher made it possible for the child to join the group without having to negotiate entry.

2. Once included around the table, the child would be in social proximity to the other children, making interactions easier.

3. The child would hear a lot of language relating to the activity that was being pursued.

In setting up a classroom for second-language learners, teachers can use small-group activities as an ideal time to begin to get second-language learners involved. Small-group activities, under a teacher's direction, can help second-language learners begin the transition from more isolated to more coordinated play activities.

Social Support: Getting Help from the English-Speaking Children

In the English-language study classroom, the support that was provided to the second-language–learning children came almost entirely from the adults; the English-speaking children chose to play with English-speaking playmates in the classroom until the second-language–learning children began to communicate in English. This pattern developed, no doubt, because the English-speaking children probably believed that the second-language children's unresponsiveness to their social advances was meant as rejection rather than an inability to understand.

This meant that the second-language–learning children had to wait for months to acquire English-speaking friends and to get involved in activities such as sociodramatic play that are heavily dependent on language. Is it possible to get second-language–learning children into contact with English speakers more quickly? If so, would this enhance the acquisition of the second language for these children?

These questions were the basis for an intervention study by Hirschler (1991, 1994) in an early childhood classroom serving 3-, 4-, and 5-year-old Khmer-, Spanish-, and English-speaking children at the Demonstration School of the University of Massachusetts, Lowell. This school is based on a multilingual and multicultural model (Tabors, 1988). In this model, children's preliteracy development in their first language is supported during language periods taught by native-speaking teachers. At other times of the day, however, the children join group activities that are conducted primarily in English. Hirschler believed that the English-speaking children in this classroom could act as valuable language resources for the second-language–learning children if the English speakers could be persuaded to interact effectively with the second-language–learning children.

Recognizing that children are capable of modifying their speech to communicate with less proficient speakers (Shatz & Gelman, 1977), Hirschler (1991) designed an intervention in which she trained five English-speaking children in a variety of strategies for approaching and sustaining interaction with the second-language learners in the classroom. These strategies were ones that Hirschler developed from a review of the literature on input shown to be most beneficial for second-language learners. They are summarized in Table 3.

To introduce these techniques, Hirschler (1991) and an assistant used role playing to model the desired behaviors before the entire group of children and then individually with the five children chosen for the study. All of the strategies were understood by the children, and all but recasts were successfully elicited during the training sessions. To remind the children of these strategies, each was equipped with a reminder bracelet and posters were placed in the classroom as well.

Interactional data collected pre- and postintervention indicated that rates of initiation to second-language learners increased from 2.5 to 3 times for four of the five children. Rates of turn-taking and utterances per turn also increased, as did language modifications. The overall effect of the training, then, was to increase contact between the English-speaking target children and the second-language learners earlier than would have been the case otherwise.

After the intervention, one particular English-speaking child took on a protective and teaching role with several of the Khmer speakers, consequently greatly increasing her interaction with them. In the example on the following page (Hirschler, 1991), Tiffany was showing Therry some shells on the science table.

Table 3. Strategies for interaction used in training English-speaking children to communicate with second-language learners

- *Initiation:* Children were taught to approach other children, establish eye contact, and ask the children to play with them or with a particular toy.
- *General linguistic aspects:* Children were taught to speak slowly with good enunciation.
- *Reinitiation:* Children were taught to repeat the initiation if it met with nonresponse.
- *Request clarification:* Children were taught to request clarification of a response by the second-language learner if the response was not understood.
- *Recast/expansion:* Children were taught to repeat an utterance with slightly different wording when the second-language learner indicated a lack of comprehension through nonresponse, noncontingent response, or other nonverbal signs.

From Hirschler, J. (1994, Winter). Preschool children's help to second language learners. *Journal of Educational Issues of Language Minority Students, 14,* 227–240; The Bilingual Education Teacher Preparation Program, Boise State University; adapted by permission.

Tiffany: O.K. have to smell this. O.K.? That don't smell, does it? Ha! That don't smell. That don't smell.

Therry: [Giggles]

Tiffany: Hear the ocean? Hear the ocean? Hear it? Oh, this one is loud! You can hear this one. Can you hear it? Wait, come here. Come here. Want to hear it? Look, hear this. Hear the ocean? (p. 100)

In this example, Tiffany was functioning much like a teacher working with a second-language learner, using repetition and talk about the here and now to deliver her message.

By helping the English-speaking children understand that the second-language learners needed help and by providing information about how they might help, Hirschler made it possible for the second-language learners to hear more contextualized language than would have been possible if their only conversational partners had been the teachers in the classroom.

In these circumstances, the second-language–learning children did not have to wait until they could begin to produce English to be included in social groupings with their English-speaking peers. Hirschler (1991) speculated that "this benign form of social engineering could act as a catalyst to language development" (p. 125) for the second-language learners. She suggested that it would be useful to integrate "into the multi-cultural classroom, through discussion and group activities, the idea that some children are learning to speak English and there are ways that we can help them" (pp. 125–126).

In setting up a classroom for second-language learners, teachers can point out to English-speaking children that there are children in the classroom who speak a different language, that it will take time for the second-language learners to begin to speak a new language, and that there are some ways that the English-speaking children can help in this process. Teachers might even ask for volunteer helpers or buddies who could be partnered with second-language learners early in the school year to help reduce the isolation of the second-language learners and increase their contacts with English-speaking children. Rather than making the second-language learners feel different (they are already feeling different), this approach can help them feel more connected while giving English-speaking children valuable information about how to help other children.

CONCLUSION

The suggestions in this chapter related to classroom organization can be seen as ways of accomplishing a particular objective in a second-language–learning setting termed *lowering the affective filter* (Krashen, 1980). Because the social situation can be so difficult for young second-language–learning children, it is possible for emotional factors to override the language-learning process. By making second-language–learning children more comfortable in the social situation, teachers increase the likelihood that their communicative efforts—and those of the English-speaking children in the classroom—will begin to make sense to the second-language learners. By setting up a classroom environment that helps second-language learners feel secure and competent, teachers make the child's second-language–learning task that much easier.

Chapter Seven

Using the Curriculum to Facilitate Second-Language and -Literacy Learning

In the English-language classroom that I studied, there were no overt efforts made to tailor the curriculum to the second-language–learning children. Instead, as discussed in Chapter 1, the teachers proceeded with a general developmental curriculum that included an activity period, during which children could be involved in free play or in teacher-directed activities; a storytime, when the children listened to books read aloud by the teachers; snack and lunchtimes, when children gathered at the individual tables in the room; an outside time, when children climbed on structures, rode tricycles, and played games; and a circle time, when all of the children gathered together with the teach-

Some of the material in this chapter is adapted from Tabors, P. (2002). Language and literacy for *all* children. *Head Start Bulletin, 74,* 10–14. This article is available on the included CD-ROM.

105

ers to sing songs and discuss events of interest. What was evident was that this structure, although fulfilling the developmental needs of the English-speaking children in the classroom, also made it possible for the teachers to incorporate many techniques that helped the second-language learners. This chapter discusses the ways in which the early childhood classroom curriculum can help second-language learners develop language skills and begin to develop literacy skills as well.

LANGUAGE AND LITERACY IN THE EARLY CHILDHOOD CLASSROOM

Many early childhood education classrooms are organized around principles characteristic of high-quality early education programs outlined in a position statement by the National Association for the Education of Young Children (NAEYC) (1996). Furthermore, the NAEYC and the International Reading Association (IRA) have jointly issued a position statement detailing practices that have been shown to facilitate the development of reading and writing skills in young children (NAEYC, 1998). What are these principles and practices, and how do they relate to second-language–learning children's experiences in early childhood classrooms?

In summarizing the guidelines for early childhood professional practice related to "teaching to enhance development and learning," the NAEYC position statement (1996) stated:

> Adults are responsible for ensuring children's healthy development and learning. From birth, relationships with adults are critical determinants of children's healthy social and emotional development. At the same time, children are active constructors of their own understanding, who benefit from initiating and regulating their own learning activities and interacting with peers. Therefore, early childhood teachers strive to achieve an optimal balance between children's self-initiated learning and adult guidance and support. (p. 11)

How would these principles work for second-language learners? As mentioned in Chapter 1, first-language learning occurs in the context of social interactions within the family. For young second-language learners, a similar context, in which understanding adults can fine-tune their language to the children's needs and other children can provide further input, recapitulates the successful environment for first-language acquisition. In both cases, it is the child's interaction with the environment that makes it possible for learning to take place. An early childhood classroom environment that does not allow the child the opportunity to interact freely and often with speakers of the second language will mitigate second-language learning; conversely, a classroom in which children are encouraged to engage in meaningful interactions with helpful others will facilitate second-language learning. This is just the type of classroom that is advocated by the NAEYC.

The joint position statement from NAEYC and the IRA (NAEYC, 1998) concerning reading and writing concluded,

> [T]he picture that emerges from research in [the] first years of children's reading and writing is one that emphasizes wide exposure to print and to developing concepts about it and its form and function. Classrooms filled with print, language and literacy play, and writing allow children to experience the joy and power associated with reading and writing while mastering basic concepts about print that research has shown are strong predictors of achievement. (p. 5)

The joint statement also included the following comments:

> Children who are learning English as a second language are more likely to become readers and writers of English when they are already familiar with the vocabulary and concepts in their primary language. In this respect, oral and written language experiences should be regarded as an additive process, ensuring that children are able to maintain their home language while also learning to speak and read English (Wong Fillmore, 1991). Including non-English materials and resources to the extent possible can help to support children's first language while children acquire oral proficiency in English. (p. 4)

What this means is that a high-quality early childhood classroom serving second-language–learning children needs to include strategies for home language use in the classroom, as well as planful ways for second-language learners to begin the process of language and literacy development in their new language. The remainder of this chapter focuses on some strategies that have been found to be effective in promoting first- and second-language and -literacy learning in the early childhood education classroom.

ORAL LANGUAGE DEVELOPMENT FOR SECOND-LANGUAGE LEARNERS

There are many opportunities throughout the day in a developmental classroom when curriculum planning can facilitate oral language development for second-language learners.

Activity Time

Activity time in a developmental classroom is frequently the time when children are most actively involved in exploring and learning about their environment. In many classrooms, it is during this time that children are engaged in hands-on activities that introduce them to materials, concepts, and vocabulary that help them expand their understanding of the world. In many classrooms, it is also during this time that children are given the opportunity to develop their social skills in interaction with other children around play themes that they develop. In each of these types of activity structures—either teacher-directed or child-initiated—there are opportunities for language to be used in helpful ways with second-language learners.

Teacher-Directed Activities   An extremely useful technique utilized by teachers when working with young second-language learners is to provide what I call *running commentary* or what others have called "event casting" or "talking while doing." This takes the form of the teacher explaining his or her actions and the actions of others as an activity unfolds. The advantage of this use of language is that it is directly connected to the objects that are present and the actions that are being performed. This technique can provide children with vocabulary items as well as syntactic structures in English.

For example, one morning Byong-sun was participating in a pizza-making operation with Marion and some of the other children at one of the tables. Marion gave Byong-sun some sauce to put on his pizza muffin. Next, she provided the grated cheese and said, "We have to put the cheese on. Would you like to put the cheese on? Andrew put cheese on his. Jessica put cheese on hers. Now you are putting cheese on yours." In this example of running commentary, Marion is combining buttressed communication—talking about the cheese as she is handling it—with repetition. The repetition of the word *cheese* helps it stand out as a particular item among the other sounds that Byong-sun is hearing Marion use. Furthermore, she is providing a minilesson in pronouns for Byong-sun by varying only the subject (i.e., Andrew, Jessica, you) and the matching possessive pronoun (i.e., his, hers, yours) in each rendition of the sentence while keeping all of the other elements in the sentence the same.

Child-Initiated Activities   Although the English-speaking children in this classroom were slow to initiate conversations with the second-language learners, they did eventually begin to be helpful communicators when the second-language learners were able to demonstrate some ability in understanding English and using some formulaic phrases. When this happened, the children often spent activity time in free play activities that gave the second-language learners a chance to hear much *context-embedded language*—language related to the immediate situation—particularly in the course of sociodramatic play.

For example, one morning in December, Leandro was successfully involved in a long play sequence that he initiated by taking up residence on a small platform area built into the loft and declaring, "Here my bed." First Andrew responded by saying good night, then Jessica gave him a good-night kiss, saying, "Good night, sweetheart" before leaving the area. Then Myong arrived on the scene, and Rebecca, who had been playing with a telephone nearby, told her, "Leandro's sick." Myong replied, "I got some medicine." At this point, Joanna came by. Seeing Leandro in bed, she said, "Good night." He answered, "No, sick!" "Oh, you're sick. Who's the doctor?" Joanna asked. Myong responded, "I'm the doctor," and she went to the dress-up area to find the proper attire for her role, coming back with a long white coat and a white apron. Joanna helped her get the coat on and tied the apron around her waist. As this was going on, Rebecca reassured Leandro by telling him, "The doctor will come soon." Joanna then suggested that Myong might need some paper so she could write down her prescription for Leandro. Myong went off to find paper and a marker. Leandro got out of bed to follow her, but Rebecca told him, "Stay in bed. You're sick. Stay in bed." Leandro climbed back into bed.

Then Myong came back and helped Leandro get arranged in bed. Rebecca said, "He needs a shot." Myong started to give Leandro "an examination" while Rebecca went into the house area to get a shot. When Rebecca came back Myong said to her, "Take the medicine, okay?" and Rebecca said to Myong, "Here's the shot." Then Rebecca said, "He needs a shot right in his tummy," and both girls hovered over Leandro administering the shot. While this was going on, Rebecca commented to Leandro, "You're sick," and Myong commented, "I'm a good doctor."

After giving Leandro the shot, Myong asked Rebecca about what had caused his condition. Myong asked, "How did he get sick?" Rebecca replied, "Someone made him sick and he had to go to the doctor." Myong continued to work on Leandro, declaring, "He has the rash." Rebecca, however, announced that Leandro was well, and Myong and Rebecca began a new play sequence about going to the swimming pool, leaving Leandro to languish in his bed alone.

In this play sequence, words like *doctor, shot, medicine,* and *sick* are repeatedly used in the context of the play, giving Leandro a great deal of exposure to these words. An indication of the effectiveness of this type of play for vocabulary acquisition came after Rebecca and Myong had left Leandro alone. At this point, Leandro got out of the bed and went over to the telephone Rebecca had been using. He picked up the telephone and said, "Hello, doctor! Doctor!" Then he put the telephone down and picked up the coat that Myong had been wearing. He announced, "Me's doctor" as I helped him put on the coat. Although he no longer had an audience (other than me) for this play, it was clear that Leandro was beginning to develop the necessary vocabulary so that he could adopt another role in future play sequences.

Book-Reading Time

One of the most challenging times for teachers with both first- and second-language children in their classrooms may be book reading. Trying to keep all of the children engaged in listening to a book being read aloud can be difficult when only some of the members of the group may actually understand what is being read. For this reason, particular attention must be paid to developing a book-reading time that works for all of the participants. Here are some suggestions for teachers:

1. *Keep it short.* Second-language–learning children cannot be expected to sit for long periods of time listening to material that they are not able to comprehend. To keep the book-reading time from becoming an endurance contest, teachers should choose books that can be presented in a reasonable amount of time. If the book is long and/or the group attention span is short, teachers should consider purposely stopping part way through and, after eliciting what the children think might happen next, putting the book away to be finished at a later time. This technique helps children develop anticipation for book reading, keeps them interested, and helps them focus on the story line of the book. When the reading recommences, it will also be an opportunity to recap what happened in the story up until that time, giving children a reason to "stay tuned."

2. *Consider small-group book reading.* When teachers sit down with a book and a small group of children, they can tailor how the book is presented and decide how to respond more carefully to the questions from the group. On some occasions, teachers can choose to have a small group that includes both English-speaking and second-language–learning children in the group. At other times, only English speakers or only second-language learners might be included, so that the presentation can be fine-tuned for that particular audience.

3. *Choose books carefully.* Presenting a book to a group of children requires preparation. Different children's books lend themselves to different types of presentations, and teachers should be aware of the possibilities of each book before it is read to the group. Any book used in the classroom should be carefully reviewed for content, vocabulary, length, and special features, including cultural sensitivity.

There are many types of books for young children. Everything from alphabet and naming books to sophisticated renderings of fairy tales are available. The selection of a book should be made with the interests and understanding of the children in mind, as well as the integration of the material with other activities going on in the classroom. Information detailing types of books for young children can be obtained from sources such as *Children and Books* (Sutherland & Arbuthnot, 1991). Local librarians are, of course, also excellent resources for choosing books for particular audiences.

Predictable books are of particular interest for use with second-language learners because they feature highly repetitive and simplified text that makes it easy for second-language learners to become engaged with them. Books like the "Spot" series (Hill, 1980) can provide scaffolded text, making it easy for children to respond to them when they are read aloud.

4. *Talk the story, rather than read it.* If the illustrations and story in a particular book are appealing, but the children being read to are not likely to understand the text, teachers can modify the story by telling a version of it in a way that the children will understand. Of course, with often-read books, some children may know the text by heart and want the "real" version. This would be a good moment to explain that sometimes it is necessary to do things a little differently so everyone in the class can understand the story.

5. *Read books more than once.* Multiple readings of books help children get more information from them each time they listen to the story. Vocabulary that was not understood the first few times may become more accessible with repeated readings. Each time through the book, different aspects should be highlighted so that the presentation will keep the children's interest high.

6. *Encourage children to "read" to other children.* Once children become familiar with a book, they can then become readers of that book to other children, particularly second-language learners. Again, it is not necessary that they have the text exactly right. What is important is that they can convey their interest, excitement, and understanding of the story to another child. A second-language learner may feel more comfortable asking for clarification or definition from another child than in a larger group with the teacher.

Snack and Lunchtimes

Mealtimes in early childhood education classrooms are usually times when teachers are involved in many management activities. Just getting the food onto the table and not on the floor takes a lot of work and patience. Snack and lunchtimes, however, can also be thought of as important times for adults and children to have conversations that can help second-language learners.

One day in a Head Start classroom (Smith, 1996), a teacher was sitting with children during lunch. The following interaction occurred:

Teacher: Do you know what vegetables these are?

  Child: No.

Teacher: What's the green vegetable?

  Child: B-b-broccoli.

Teacher: Broccoli. What's the orange vegetable?

  Child: Carrots.

Teacher: And what's the white vegetable?

  Child: Fish.

Teacher: No.

  Child: Flower.

Teacher: Cauliflower.

  Child: I said that, but I didn't say cauliflower.

Teacher: That's a long name. . . . It's a long name to remember.

  Child: I know what that's called—cauliflower.

By taking the time to help this child develop and confirm vocabulary related to the food being eaten, the teacher was able to turn an ordinary event into an opportunity to learn. Although this interaction occurred between a teacher and an English-speaking child, it is the type of exchange that could also be useful for a second-language–learning child as a participant or as a listener.

I observed how conversations among a group of children might also work to help second-language learners. One day, Naoshi, Supat, and Andrew were eating lunch at the same table. As Naoshi poured out his drink for lunch, he showed it to me and announced, "Cocoa." Then he turned to Andrew to show him his drink, announcing "Cocoa" again. Then he pointed to Andrew's drink and said, "Cocoa." Andrew replied, "No, this is milk." Then Naoshi pointed to Supat and said, "Cocoa." Andrew said, "No, his is probably apple juice." Then Andrew showed Naoshi his Thermos and said, "This is in here milk." Naoshi said, "This is [pause] cocoa!" Then Naoshi said, "Milk cocoa." Andrew repeated, "Milk cocoa?" As lunch continued, Andrew took items out of the paper bag he had brought from home. The bag had ink stamps on it for decoration. Twice Naoshi asked, "What's this?" pointing to an object on the bag. Andrew told him "spider" and "giraffe." Naoshi had a pile of orange sections in front of him on the table. He began to count them out loud, "One, two, three," and then, pointing to his mouth, he said "Four." Andrew looked over and saw only three sections, so he said, "Three orange pieces." But Supat, who had not said anything up until this point, understood what Naoshi was doing. He told Andrew, "That was four and he ate one." Later Naoshi further refined his orange-section–counting technique (after eating another section) by counting "One, two" on the table, "three" pointing to his mouth, and "four" pointing to his stomach.

In this sequence, Andrew and Supat are something of a captive audience for Naoshi, who takes full advantage of their presence to collect data on English vocabulary and grammar as well as to demonstrate his knowledge and conversational skills.

In many early childhood classrooms, children's names are taped to chairs, and children find their chairs to sit in for snack and lunch. By placing chairs in particular configurations, it is possible for teachers to promote interactions of these sorts at mealtimes by placing sociable English-speaking children with second-language learners, making it easier for second-language learners to get into conversation with English-speaking peers.

Outside Time

Most early childhood educators think of outdoor activities as chances for developing gross motor skills and cooperative game playing. Most of the outdoor activities I have observed do not require a great deal of language use, which may well be the reason that this time is such an important time for second-language learners. In other words, outside time might well be a time when second-language learners can demonstrate physical competence without being put at a linguistic disadvantage.

Furthermore, outdoor games that have highly routinized rules can give children a participation structure that is obvious and easy to get into. Many large-group games have repetitive linguistic features (e.g., "Duck, Duck, Goose"), which are easy for second-language learners to key into and start using themselves. An effective method for using outdoor games as a time for second-language acquisition would be to partner second-language learners with English-speaking children and have them work cooperatively throughout a game.

Establishing social and play relationships with other children during outside activities may make it easier for children to develop social and play relationships with these same children inside the classroom as well. Teachers who are alert to the possibilities of partnering children socially could use outside time as an ideal opportunity for getting English-speaking children and second-language–learning children together.

Circle Time

In many early childhood classrooms, circle time is a time when all of the children and adults come together, often sitting down in a big circle on a rug or enclosed area. Various activities occur at circle time. Some of the most common are taking roll and noting who is or is not in class, talking about the day of the week and the weather, talking about the schedule for the day and/or upcoming events, asking the children to make choices for activity time, singing songs, and perhaps doing exercises together. If the classroom curriculum is organized around themes, these themes are often introduced at circle time.

Circle time in a classroom with second-language learners can be organized in a way that will make the time particularly useful for them. First, as in other areas of classroom organization, it is important for teachers to keep to a certain routine during circle time. By calling the children's names, then talking about the calendar, and then discussing the weather report, teachers can help second-language learners predict the sequence of events and their required response.

Second, teachers should include songs and movements with highly predictable components and should introduce the words of the songs first without music so that the second-language–learning children have an opportunity to catch on more quickly. In addition, giving children many opportunities to return to their favorite songs also reinforces their learning. Frequently, second-language learners "find their voice" or "go public" for the first time in their new language as they are singing songs during circle time.

Third, the introduction of theme material during circle time should be kept short, simple, and as visual as possible. By being explicit about the vocabulary involved, teachers can also provide second-language learners with the necessary words to participate in the activities around the theme material.

Fourth, children should be allowed to respond to teachers' questions in unison or on a voluntary basis at circle time. By calling on a second-language learner to respond in front of the entire class, teachers may well render even the most confident child speechless. For example, at circle time one rainy morning in November in the English-language classroom, Marion called on Naoshi to ask him what might get wet on a rainy day. Naoshi made some motions with his hands (a typical circle time response), so Marion asked the question again, and Joanna tried to help by making raining motions and touching Naoshi's hair, asking, "Did your hair get wet?" This time Naoshi shook his head (another typical circle time motion). Marion interpreted this as a negative response to Joanna's question and scaffolded the situation by suggesting *umbrellas* as an answer as she held up an imaginary umbrella. This brought the sequence to a successful conclusion, but what was clear was that Naoshi was not yet ready to respond in this high-demand situation. Letting him offer an answer along with the other children or letting him indicate that he had an answer before calling on him would have made it a much more comfortable situation for Naoshi.

THE LANGUAGE ACQUISITION PRESCHOOL

As mentioned previously, most developmental early childhood education classrooms have a variety of goals for the children enrolled in them, including social, emotional, physical, and cognitive development. This chapter's discussion thus far has emphasized that a general developmental curriculum offers many opportunities for teachers and other children to help in the second-language–learning process. These suggestions highlight how second-language learning can be accomplished in the context of a developmental classroom, without requiring a restructuring of the classroom curriculum to incorporate them.

It is possible to imagine, however, a classroom in which language acquisition is the main goal guiding curriculum planning and classroom activities. In fact, just such a classroom has been developed at the Language Acquisition Preschool (LAP) at The University of Kansas (see http://www2.ku.edu/~splh/Clinics/LAP.html). This school, now affiliated with the local school system, serves typically developing children, children with specific language impairments, and children for whom English is their second language (Bunce, 1995; Rice, 1991; Rice & Wilcox, 1990, 1995). The LAP classroom shares many of the features of other developmental early childhood settings, providing activities that are aimed at the development of social skills and school readiness. What differentiates the LAP classroom from others is an emphasis on language development throughout the curriculum, the presence of a variety of children with limited language skills but age-appropriate social and intellectual skills, the consistent emphasis on verbal activities, and the encouragement of verbal interactions among the children.

Beginning with the premise that language is learned in socially interactive settings and that children construct their linguistic systems from the language they hear from adults and more capable peers, the creators of LAP have developed the following intervention strategies to facilitate language development.

1. *Provide opportunities for language use and interaction.* First, LAP teachers provide rich and interesting activities. The curriculum is based on an integrated approach in which a specific weekly theme is used to structure many of the activities for the week. For instance, during a week for which the theme is vacations, props for dramatic play, art

activities, storytime, group time, and music selections all relate to the theme, with options including everything from taking an airplane trip to singing the "Mickey Mouse" song (see Bunce & Watkins, 1995). These activities are meant to engage and interest the children and get them involved in interactions related to the activities.

Second, LAP teachers concentrate on allowing quiet times when they are not talking to provide an opportunity for children to initiate conversation about what they find interesting. As Bunce and Watkins (1995) wrote,

> A language-facilitating preschool classroom requires teachers and aides who are comfortable being quiet; if adults in the classroom constantly fill up the language "space," there is little incentive or opportunity for children to participate in verbal interchange. Quiet moments in a class-room are not negative. On the contrary, they provide time for reflection and they encourage child initiations. (p. 45)

Third, the teachers in the LAP classroom arrange the environment so that not all materials are readily accessible, to encourage children's efforts at interaction. "In brief, the idea is to provide opportunities for children to learn and practice requesting materials or assistance when they need it" (Bunce & Watkins, 1995, p. 45).

2. *Provide focused stimulation on particular language features.* The teachers in LAP develop plans that include targeted sounds, words, or forms to be used with particular children. These forms are then modeled in comments or statements made during conversations with the children, and the children are encouraged but not required to repeat the models. These forms are usually ones that the children have not yet produced themselves. Furthermore, teachers recast forms that children do use to maintain their meaning, but change their form to another, grammatically altered form. Finally, teachers recast their own utterances, repeating an idea in a different way, to provide several structures for children to compare.

3. *Develop routines to help children connect events and language.* Several of the routines used by the teachers at LAP are the same as ones that have been mentioned previously. These include establishing familiar daily routines such as arrival time, circle time, and snack time so that children can anticipate what is coming next and prepare themselves to participate (see Classroom Routines: Helping Children Become Members of the Group in Chapter 6) and using event casting (running commentary) to describe their actions or the actions of the children during these events (see Teacher-Directed Activities in this chapter).

One activity in the LAP classroom, however—sociodramatic play—is handled quite differently. In the classroom I studied and in many classrooms I have visited, sociodramatic play is most often initiated by the children and facilitated by the teachers (i.e., teachers provide materials and often contribute ideas to ongoing play as Joanna did in the sick-in-bed sequence discussed previously, but, on the whole, sociodramatic play is developed by the children themselves). As I noted, however, this means that second-language–learning children are often not included in sociodramatic play until they have been in the classroom for a considerable period. In fact, in the English-language classroom there were *no* observed instances of verbal interactions by the second-language–learning children in the house area during socio-dramatic play until December. As Garvey (1977) pointed out, sociodramatic play imposes particularly high demands on children's linguistic abilities.

In the LAP classroom, the teachers have taken this aspect of the curriculum and made it the centerpiece of their planning, calling it scripted dramatic play. As Bunce and Watkins (1995) explained, "Scripted play is a valuable intervention procedure because it provides opportunities for verbal communication within a meaningful context" (p. 48). Rather than merely providing materials, the teachers at LAP initiate the scripted dramatic play by introducing the roles and the props available for the play, as well as giving background information in a discussion or demonstration prior to the play activity. Each day, the teachers introduce a new activity that exposes the children to a variety of information, vocabulary items, and language routines related to each script (see Bunce, 1995, for further information about these techniques and activity guides from LAP). In this fashion, the children in the LAP classroom are exposed to and participate in a particularly rich and supportive language environment.

4. *Stimulate social interaction between children.* In a technique that is the mirror reflection of Hirschler's (1991) training of English-language children to interact with the second-language learners at the Demon-stration School (see Chapter 6), LAP teachers help children interact with each other by redirecting their requests for help by suggesting that they seek help from another child. When a child asks a teacher to intervene with another child, the teacher provides the child with a model of how to initiate the interaction; for example, by saying, "Ask Shauntaye, 'May I use this truck?' " If a teacher sees that a child is interested in joining an activity but has not made any verbal request to be included, she might suggest, "Ask Larry, 'May I have some play-

dough?' " In this way children are provided with a model phrase and the necessary vocabulary, and, because the teacher remains nearby to mediate the communication, usually experience a successful start to further social interaction.

As mentioned previously, many of these strategies are, of course, already in common use in other early childhood classrooms. At LAP, however, these techniques have been brought to the forefront of the curriculum effort, whereby they provide the framework for daily planning and for interaction between teachers and children. By highlighting the use of these techniques for language facilitation, the teachers at LAP have been able to help children with language impairments make significant progress within the context of the classroom while providing an optimum environment for typically developing English-speakers as well as second-language–learning children.

LITERACY DEVELOPMENT FOR SECOND-LANGUAGE LEARNERS

There are five types of activities that early childhood educators are likely to use to help prepare young children for the challenges of reading and writing:

1. Activities that target letter recognition (alphabetic principle)

2. Activities that emphasize the sounds that make up words (phonological awareness)

3. Activities that show how books look and how they work (book and print concepts)

4. Activities that emphasize words and their meaning (vocabulary)

5. Activities that encourage telling stories, explaining how the world works, or building a fantasy world (discourse skills) (Tabors, 2002)

Let's think about how each of these types of activities might work with second-language learners.

Children develop alphabetic knowledge when teachers use activities that target letter recognition. These activities can be anything from singing the alphabet song, to identifying the first letters in children's names, to having children work with magnetic letters to begin using invented spelling. Simultaneously, teachers can help children develop phonological awareness by pointing out the sounds that words are made up of and how those sounds relate to letters of the alphabet. Concentrating on sounds in words that are highly familiar and important to children—like their names or names for objects in the room—will yield the best results. Using rhyming text in songs and poetry will also help children key into how when one sound in a word changes, it changes the meaning of the word.

Learning about the English alphabet is clearly useful for second-language–learning children, and it is something that they can begin quite early in their exposure to English. Furthermore, any activities that help English-speaking children develop phonological awareness in English will also be helpful for second-language–learning children. In fact, I found that the second-language learners in the study classroom concentrated on watching people speaking English to see how the sounds of English were formed with mouth, teeth, and tongue. Consequently, teachers who help children in the classroom "tune in" to the sounds of English will be helping both English speakers and second-language learners.

Book and print concepts are developed when teachers talk to children about various aspects of how books work. Book readings can include information about where the front and back of a book are, what kinds of information can be found on the cover (the title, the name of the author, the name of the illustrator), where the print is on the page, how the print is read, what a sentence looks like, and what different kinds of punctuation mean at the end of sentences. Including these types of information as part of the book reading process helps children who do not have a lot of book reading experience begin to understand the ins and outs of books.

What about book and print concepts for second-language learners? Here I think teachers need to think carefully about what these children can understand in the book-reading situation and plan accordingly. As mentioned in Chapter 6, one technique for effective book readings with second-language learners involves developing more small-group book readings with particular groups of children so that the information provided during the session can be tailored to the group. As the children gain more understanding of English, they can be involved in more extensive discussions of book and print concepts.

Words, words, words, words. The more words children know, the more words they will have available to connect to the letters and sounds that they will meet in print when they begin to read. Teachers help children develop their vocabulary by intentionally presenting new words for children to learn as part of *every* activity in the classroom, by using and explaining new words in conversations with children, and by reading new words to children and helping them understand their meanings. Children should be learning 6 to 10 new words *a day* in the early childhood period. If they are spending time in early childhood classrooms, then the talk they hear and are involved in there needs to include lots and lots of new words.

Developing a vocabulary in English is, of course, one of the first jobs for second-language–learning children. In my research, I found that the study children would often pick up objects from around the classroom and bring them to someone to have them say the word for the object in English. Teachers who are aware that second-language learners need to learn lots of words in English will make sure that they are thoughtful about helping them understand what words mean. So, a classroom where the teacher is aware of the vocabulary needs of the children and is always explaining, defining, or showing children what a word means will be a supportive classroom for both English-speaking and English-learning children.

Finally, the talk that children hear and are involved in should help them develop more advanced discourse skills as well. What does this mean? We think of discourse skills as being able to use language in structured ways to go beyond the basics of conversation—for example, to tell a story about a past event, or to explain how something works, or to build a fantasy world with words. Teachers encourage the development of these types of linguistic structures when they ask open-ended questions such as, "What did you do over the weekend?" or "Why do you think the stone sinks in the water?" or " What did your baby do when you put her in the carriage?" But asking the question should not be the end of the interaction, just the beginning, because teachers need to support children's efforts to use language to answer these sorts of questions, extending the conversations so that children develop the ability to sustain the interaction for a number of turns.

Given that English-speaking children are still developing these skills during the early childhood period, it should not be surprising that these higher-level skills in English are the most difficult for second-language learners. I found in my research that the area of the classroom where the English-speaking children used their discourse skills to the greatest extent was the sociodramatic play area, and it was not until the spring of the year that *any* of the second-language learners participated in play in this area. Apparently, they knew that they didn't know enough English to be effective participants in that type of play earlier in the school year. However, teachers who are aware of second-language learners' proficiencies and their need to develop discourse abilities can make sure that they have conversations with them, as well as with English speakers, that begin the process of building more sophisticated structures in English.

But are these language and literacy activities the only ones that can be meaningful in a classroom with children from diverse language backgrounds? What about the home languages and literacies of the second-language–learning children? Can they be incorporated into the classroom as well in ways that would be socially useful and cognitively challenging for all the children? The answer is "Absolutely." Not only *could* activities related to the home languages and literacies of the second-language–learning children be included, but they *should* be included. Why? For two very different but complementary reasons:

1. *This addition to the curriculum will be socially useful.* For the second-language–learning children, the inclusion of their home languages and literacies in the classroom curriculum provides them with the opportunity to be the experts and builds pride in the languages and cultures of their families. For the English-speaking children, the inclusion of other languages and literacies in the classroom curriculum provides them with insight into the capabilities of their classmates and their classmates' families and clues them into why these children may not be using a lot of English in the classroom right away.

2. *This addition to the curriculum will be cognitively challenging.* Both groups of children benefit from comparing languages and literacies in ways that help them develop metalinguistic awareness, which is the ability to think about how language works.

So, what would teachers need to do to follow this recommendation? Although many languages use an alphabet that is the same or similar to the one used in English (e.g., Spanish, French), many other languages are alphabetic but with different writing systems (Arabic) or are not alphabetic at all (Japanese). Finding out about the different writing systems represented among the languages of the children in the classroom can be a complicated job, but engaging parents or knowledgeable others in conversations along these lines—and then making that information available to the children—can be a very worthwhile activity. Labeling objects in the classroom using different colors for each label in a different language can help children see what different languages look like when written down and can help them begin the process of understanding that different languages look and sound different but that they are all used to talk about the world.

Of course, as soon as different languages are brought into the classroom, children will notice that the languages have different sounds. Often children can mimic the sounds of a language that they have heard even before they have begun to acquire any actual facility in a language.

I call this learning the tune before learning the words of the song. For children to understand that these sounds represent meaningful messages to the people who use them, it is important to have speakers of different languages (parents or others) come to the classroom to read stories, sing songs, or present an activity in those languages. If there is a match between the language of the visitor and some of the children in the classroom, this will give those children a chance to be the experts and help their classmates to grasp what is happening.

Introducing books written in different languages will raise all children's awareness of the different forms that books can take. Finding books that are written in different scripts (e.g., Bengali, Chinese) or that are read from the back to the front (e.g., Hebrew) and having speakers of these languages demonstrate how these books are read emphasizes for children the variety of languages and literacies in the world. If printed books are not available and if there is enthusiasm for a parent involvement activity, it would be wonderful to have books written and illustrated by parents in their home language that would become part of the classroom library.

Children will be much more aware of the importance of words if they learn new names for the objects and concepts that they already have names for in one language. For the English-speaking children, this process will teach them that all languages use words as the building blocks for communication. For the second-language learners, this will make them the experts in providing names in their home language while they are acquiring new names in English. I would suggest that there be an even-up trade in the word department: Every time a second-language learner wants to know a name for an object or concept in English, the trade-off would be to find out what that word would be in his or her home language. In this way, everyone in the classroom becomes a language learner.

In terms of discourse, I think it would be a good idea to concentrate on storytelling in different languages. This discourse form is nearly universal, although the way that storytelling is structured may be a bit different from culture to culture. For storytelling to be engaging in a language that some of the children don't understand, it will probably be important to have pictures or visuals of some kind to accompany the story or to have a plot line that the children already know. Again, the children who already speak the language in which the story is being told will be the experts and can act as the interpreters (but not the translators) of the story for their classmates. If they can take active roles in the storytelling, that will be even more exciting and affirming for them.

FACILITATING SECOND-LANGUAGE LEARNING IN EARLY CHILDHOOD CLASSROOMS

The model of the classroom that works best for second-language–learning children that emerges from this chapter and Chapter 6 is one in which the adults in the classroom provide opportunities for children to engage in useful and purposeful first- and second-language and -literacy interactions with sensitive interlocutors, both adults and peers. To achieve this goal, teachers should consider providing the following types of opportunities in their classrooms:

1. A routine and consistent organizational structure in which activities happen at regular intervals and in predictable ways

2. A curriculum that brings the home languages of the second-language learners into the classroom

3. A language- and literacy-rich environment in which teachers use techniques that help second-language learners understand, and then begin to use, their new language and literacy skills

4. Discussions with, or perhaps training of, English-speaking children in the classroom to help provide socially appropriate partners for second-language–learning children

5. A variety of organizational and curricular modifications (e.g., small-group inclusion, safe havens, voluntary sharing at circle time, engaging book-reading sessions, cooperative games, appropriate first- and second-language and -literacy activities) that will help second-language–learning children feel more comfortable, included, and competent

By providing an environment that includes these opportunities and by encouraging children to take advantage of these opportunities, early childhood educators can help individual second-language–learning children make progress at the rate and in the way that best fits their social capabilities and cognitive strengths.

Chapter Eight

Working with Parents of Second-Language Learners

Involving parents in the education of their young children is a clear objective of early childhood education. Understanding that parents are the first educators of their children, early childhood educators must strive to build a partnership with parents so that home and classroom activities complement and reinforce each other. When parents speak a different language and come from a different culture, building this partnership may take more time and effort because of communication difficulties and cultural differences. This extra effort is well worth it, however, as parents begin to contribute to teachers' and children's understandings of cultural differences and teachers begin to contribute to parents' understandings of the new cultural contexts in which their children are being placed. The discussion in this chapter focuses on ways to include parents of second-language–learning children in the classroom and on the information educators may be called on to discuss with parents. The suggestions in this chapter are meant to help teachers and parents build the type of partnership that will be the most beneficial for children.

INCLUDING PARENTS IN THE CLASSROOM

Most early childhood programs bring parents into the classroom periodically to lend a hand or to demonstrate a specific talent or skill.

These roles should be extended to parents of second-language–learning children as well. In other words, rather than restricting parents of second-language learners to the role of cultural interpreters, educators should offer parents opportunities to become involved in all aspects of the program.

How can this be done? Some suggestions, along with the benefits that might arise from them, follow.

Lending a Hand

Many parents find this the least difficult role to assume in a classroom. Parents of second-language–learning children can be invited to visit the classroom just to spend time there and see what goes on and then can be encouraged to help out in a variety of ways, from pouring juice to cleaning up the paint area. This type of participation is low demand from both a linguistic and a responsibility point of view. During the course of a visit of this kind, parents can get a firsthand look at what goes on in the classroom and can begin to feel more comfortable with the activities that occur there.

Demonstrating a Talent or Skill

Many early childhood programs consider parents to be valuable resources to be tapped in a variety of ways to enrich the classroom curriculum. To find out what types of talents are available among the parents, teachers might want to consider a questionnaire that would ask all parents about the types of activities they might like to share with the children. This questionnaire could have a few suggestions of successful types of activities that have occurred previously in the classroom, but the activities being solicited should not be restricted. Activities to suggest might include those that the parents enjoyed doing as children themselves and those that they have enjoyed doing with their own child. In this way, a parent will not be limited to demonstrating a stereotypical and perhaps inappropriate cultural artifact but will be able to present an activity with real personal meaning.

This type of activity is, of course, much more demanding in terms of language and organizational responsibility. To be successful, teachers and parents will have to spend time together planning these activities. For many parents, it might be easier to work with a small group of children at first. As a parent's confidence and comfort levels increase, it may be possible to plan activities for the whole group.

Working with Parents Around Cultural Issues

Many teachers believe that it is appropriate to ask parents of second-language–learning children to come to their classroom to teach some songs in their native language, demonstrate national dress, or develop an ethnic cooking project. If presentations of this sort are made in the context of the overall classroom curriculum, they can certainly be effective in introducing young children to a variety of cultural experiences. For example, in one Head Start classroom that I visited, there were many children from China. At the beginning of the school year, three of the children who came to the class had never used forks and spoons. To make them feel more comfortable, the teachers provided chopsticks, and one mother came to the class and helped all of the children learn how to use chopsticks. After the lesson, chopsticks became a permanent feature of the house area so that all of the children could continue to develop their expertise.

If cultural activities are presented in this type of accepting fashion, they can help all of the children feel more comfortable. If cultural activities are presented as strange and exotic, however, they may, in fact, heighten children's feelings of difference rather than those of commonality. Again, planning and communication before any event will be necessary so that it will be received successfully by all of the children in the classroom.

Maintaining Home-Language Development in the Classroom

Parents of second-language–learning children can also help bring the home languages of the children into the classroom. Rather than restricting parents to the role of translator, teachers should encourage the parents of second-language–learning children to use their home language in meaningful ways when they are in the classroom. This strategy could take the form of the parent presenting an activity using the home language or reading a book to the children in the home language. In this way, the child whose home language is being used in the activity will have the experience of being part of the activity without having to struggle with the language being used, and the children for whom the language being used is not their home language will have the experience of trying to be part of an activity without understanding the language. Involving parents in language and literacy activities as recommended in Chapter 7 will make it possible for all of the children in the classroom to be aware of other languages, how they sound, what they mean, and their importance in the lives of their classmates.

Benefits

Some benefits of bringing the parent of a second-language learner into the classroom are obvious—the parent learns about what goes on in the classroom, and the teacher receives some help. There may be other benefits as well. When a parent of a second-language learner spends time in the classroom, the other children will be able to observe the parent and child talking together, perhaps realizing for the first time that a particular child speaks a different language. If the parent is encouraged to conduct an activity in the home language, the other children will benefit from the experience of being second-language learners themselves.

Furthermore, the presence of the parent of a second-language–learning child may increase the child's social confidence and comfort in the classroom. In the classroom I observed there was a young girl, Elena, who spoke Russian at home and was very quiet in the classroom. But when her mother came to class one morning, Elena was a different child. She chattered happily with her mother in Russian and participated wholeheartedly in all of the singing and movement activities at circle time. These types of revelations may make it easier for a child to feel more comfortable and find social acceptance in the classroom.

TALKING WITH PARENTS

Most early childhood education programs include opportunities for teachers and parents to talk with each other about a child's development and future. These opportunities may range from a quick, informal chat as a child is being dropped off or picked up to a sit-down conference at a prearranged time. The following sections describe examples of questions that parents may ask and the kind of information that educators can use in a conference no matter where or under what circumstances it is held.

How Is Our Child Doing in Class?

The most basic concern that all parents will have, of course, is that their child is settling into the classroom and participating in the activities being offered there. Teachers will need to be prepared to explain to parents that the process of adjusting to the classroom situation, particularly if there are no other speakers of the child's home language in the classroom, may be slow, requiring patience on the part of the parents and their child. In conferencing with parents of second-language–learning children, therefore, it will be particularly important for the teacher to have in mind developmental milestones that can be emphasized in areas other than language.

Different parents will place different levels of emphasis on the acquisition of English as a primary reason for the child's enrollment in the classroom. On the basis of questionnaires or conversations with parents, teachers should develop an understanding of the parents' attitudes on this topic and anticipate the types of questions that parents will ask. Understanding the developmental pathway for second-language acquisition discussed in this book will help both parents and teachers gauge an individual child's progress.

One question that parents may have is whether their child is developing friendships with other children in the classroom. As discussed in Chapter 2, social isolation is a common situation for young second-language–learning children in an early childhood education setting. The double bind that causes this situation—not being able to socialize because they do not know the new language and not being able to develop proficiency in the new language because they cannot socialize—is probably a necessary stage for young children in acquiring a new language in a group setting, so parents will need to be told that this is the case. Parents will also want to know what steps are being taken to reduce their child's isolation and to speed up the process of social acceptance. Having a well-developed plan for including second-language–learning children in classroom activities and being able to articulate that plan to parents will help the teacher allay parental concern in this important area.

Furthermore, teachers can also make a strong recommendation that parents should try to ensure that their children have the opportunity to be in social situations with other children with whom they *do* share a language so that they can continue to develop their social skills in situations in which they are not at a linguistic disadvantage. Parents might be making different decisions on the assumption that they are speeding up the process of language acquisition by keeping their children in all-English situations (see the following section). However, for both maintenance of their home language and development of age-appropriate social skills, it can be critical that young children continue to actively engage in social situations with speakers of their home language.

What Language Should We Be Speaking at Home?

This question is extremely important for many families. Teachers of second-language–learning children will need to understand the dynamics of language acquisition and the circumstances of individual families to help parents arrive at a satisfactory answer to this question.

For families that do not intend to remain in the United States, this question does not arise. These parents realize that although their young child may learn some English in an early childhood program in the United States, a return to their native country will require maintenance of and continued development in the child's first language. Usually, under these circumstances, families continue to speak their native language at home, sometimes taking on the task of developing the child's preliteracy and literacy skills as well. In these families, there may be a need to think about developing some strategies for how they might maintain their child's English proficiency after returning home, but there is never a question that their home language will be supported and maintained by the family. Knowing families' long-term plans, therefore, can help teachers evaluate whether the question of home-language use will even arise for an individual family.

Families who intend to remain in the United States, however, face a dilemma. For them, the message that comes through loud and clear is, "To be successful in school, your child should learn English as quickly as possible." Many parents believe that the simplest route to fulfilling the promise of this message is to abandon the home language and concentrate on English as the language of choice, even if they have little proficiency in English themselves. But, at the same time, they realize that they will be giving up a great deal in terms of cultural and personal identity along the way. Panos's father mentioned to me in an interview,

> If we end up staying in the States, we would like him to keep . . . a good deal of his Greek. . . . We would be happy if we could talk to him in Greek . . . even when he grows up. We feel we communicate better that way. . . . We feel that we will be closer. (Tabors, 1982, pp. 10–11)

As Wong Fillmore (1991a) wrote,

> What is lost when children and families can't communicate easily with one another? What is lost is no less than the means by which parents socialize their children: When parents are unable to talk to their children, they cannot easily convey to them their values, beliefs, understandings, or wisdom about how to cope with their experiences. . . . When parents lose the means for socializing and influencing their children, rifts develop and families lose the intimacy that comes from shared beliefs and understandings. (p. 343)

Abandoning a first language may have extensive personal, familial, religious, and cultural implications. Is it worth the sacrifice? Is this sacrifice necessary? To answer these questions, it is important to go back and examine the first part of the dilemma mentioned previously, the contention that to be successful in school a child should learn English as quickly as possible. In fact, there are good reasons to believe that this is a false premise. What research has shown is that the bilingual children who do best in school are those who have had a strong grounding in their home language, perhaps including development of literacy in that language, before being exposed to a second language (Collier, 1987). Why would this be true?

Much of the cognitive work that children do during the early childhood period involves developing concepts about how the world works and learning the vocabulary that helps them express these understandings. Children engage in data gathering about the world by asking questions of adults who are willing to take the time to answer their questions. In this way, children develop an extensive knowledge base about the world that gives them a cognitive framework to apply to the information they will be taught later in school. What is important about these interactions is not which language is used but the concepts and vocabulary that are developed.

As mentioned in Chapter 1, the early childhood period is also a time when children are developing discourse skills in their first language. During this period, children begin to use language to put ideas together across a number of utterances. This might be thought of as speaking in paragraphs. Helpful adults again play a role in this development, frequently by asking questions rather than answering them (see Chapter 1). Again, what is important about these interactions is not which language is used but the extended discourse skills that are developed during the interactions.

What happens if a family decides to abandon the home language and begins to use only English in the home? First, it is unlikely, except in unusual cases, for both parents to be equally proficient in English and/or that either of them is as proficient in English as in their home language. Therefore, their interactions with their child will be less rich in vocabulary and less facile in extended discourse in English than they would be in the home language. In other words, not only are parents who are second-language learners themselves rarely good language models for their children, they may also be less well equipped to help children develop the concepts, vocabulary, and extended discourse skills that are needed in school.

As Richard Rodriguez (1983) wrote about the time after his parents were convinced by the nuns from his school that they should speak English instead of Spanish at home,

> [There] was a new quiet at home. The family's quiet was partly due to the fact that, as we children learned more and more English, we shared fewer and fewer words with our parents. Sentences needed to be spoken slowly when a child addressed his mother or father. (Often the parent wouldn't understand.) The child would need to repeat himself. (Still the parent misunderstood.) The young voice, frustrated, would end by saying, "Never mind"—the subject was closed. Dinners would be noisy with the clinking of knives and forks against dishes. My mother would smile softly between her remarks; my father at the other end of the table would chew and chew at his food, while he stared over the heads of his children. (p. 23)

Convincing parents that there is a benefit to continuing to speak the home language may not be easy for a teacher, because most of the input that parents receive from the popular press, the education system, and even perhaps their own cultural group will point in the direction of switching to English at home as soon as possible. What can teachers tell parents?

One teacher in a workshop mentioned that she tells parents that their role is to teach their children about the world, whereas her role is to teach them the English to talk about what they understand about the world. In this way, she splits the responsibilities for concept formation (to be done at home) and second-language acquisition (to be done at school).

Another teacher, when asked what she tells parents about language, replied,

> I've had parents in the past who have said "I want him to go to school and speak English and we're going to start speaking English," and I have to explain to them, you know, don't let them lose their native language, that's *so* important to their self-esteem and, I mean, it's just so important to the family. You know you don't want them to lose that, it could become really valuable. What if he gets older and he needs this job, most people can't speak two languages. This is really important. He might get a job someday over someone else, like me, I can only speak one language, and I tell them only having one language is really hard. . . . If I could speak Spanish or Mandarin or Creole, I wish I had a second language like that.

If Our Child Does Not Want to Speak Our Home Language, What Should We Do?

As mentioned in Chapter 5, young children often take some time to decide that they are willing to devote the cognitive effort necessary to learn a second language. But by the same token, once they have undertaken that task, they are likely to try to lighten the cognitive load by switching off their first language. This tendency, coupled with a general societal message that English is the preferred language, may lead young children to go from monolingualism in their home language, to active bilingualism (when they are developing both languages), to passive bilingualism (when they stop producing their home language, although they still understand it), and then back to monolingualism but now in English. Ironically, parents may decide to commit themselves to maintaining their home language, only to have children as young as 4 or 5 years old announce that they will no longer speak the home language and wish to converse only in English.

Wong Fillmore (1991a) wrote about a young Chinese girl named Mei-Mei who arrived in the United States from Beijing when she was 3 years old. She and her mother had come to join her father who was already in the United States as a student. Mei-Mei and her mother both began the process of acquiring English as a second language. For Mei-Mei, this meant attending an English-language early childhood program and embarking on the developmental process that has been outlined in this book; for Mei-Mei's mother, this meant faithfully attending English as a Second Language (ESL) classes. Predictably enough, after 3 years, Mei-Mei had "achieved a native like competence and fluency in the new language" (p. 31), whereas her mother was still struggling with pronunciation and grammar.

At first, Mei-Mei's parents were enthusiastic about using English at home so that Mei-Mei's mother could practice her new language and Mei-Mei would be ready for school. This plan did not work, however, because Mei-Mei's mother never learned enough English to be able to use it with her. For this reason, the language of the home remained Chinese. However, during the period of a year, Mei-Mei began answering in English when addressed in Chinese, and then began not even understanding what was being said to her in Chinese. When her father asked her to speak Chinese, she would say, "Papa, I can't say it in Chinese. Can I say it in English? English is easier."

This course of events, when young children start answering in English when addressed in the home language, then move on to claiming not to even understand the home language, and finally answering only when they are addressed in English, is not uncommon. The problem with this situation is that the child's language development in the home language is truncated, and, just as happens when parents abandon the home language for English, the family loses the sense of intimacy and cultural connection that the home language would otherwise provide. When this happens, parents' concerns turn from, "Will my child ever learn English?" to "How can I keep my child from abandoning our home language?"

Successful home-language maintenance requires parents to be aware that their young children may try to embark on a campaign to stop speaking the home language and, therefore, to have a countercampaign in mind. As mentioned in Chapter 1, Taeschner (1983) was determined to raise her two daughters as German-Italian bilinguals. Her original strategy was to speak German with her daughters, whereas her husband would speak to them in Italian. Taeschner's daughters, however, soon discovered that she also spoke Italian, so they began to speak Italian to her, although they still understood her when she spoke German to them. At this point, her daughters had entered a period of passive bilingualism during which they understood both languages but would speak only one. To combat this loss of active bilingualism, Taeschner instituted the following strategy:

> [I] began pretending not to understand most of what they said in Italian. When they spoke to [me] in German, [I] answered immediately and fulfilled their desires. But when they spoke to [me] in Italian, I answered *Wie bitte*? ("What, please?") or *Was hast du gesagt*? ("What did you say?"). . . . After awhile, in order to avoid having to say the same thing twice, they began to speak to [me] directly in German. (pp. 200–201)

Even after this strategy proved successful with the girls, Taeschner continued to seek out a variety of ways to keep her daughters interested in German, including trips to Germany, periods of time in German schools, and the hiring of a German-speaking household helper. Furthermore, she made sure that the children learned to read in both Italian and German, so that their understanding of German could be extended through literacy as well as through personal contact with German speakers. By the time they were 9 years old, both girls were balanced bilinguals who were eager to show off their ability to speak another language with new friends or even casual acquaintances.

There are a variety of recommendations, therefore, that teachers might make to parents. For example, with young children, if the rule has been established that communication must be in the home language at home, then parents might want to institute the practice of not understanding requests made in English. Furthermore, discussions about why it is important to maintain the home language can also prove invaluable with slightly older children. Beyond conversation, reading books written in the home language and watching appropriate television programs or videos or DVDs produced in the home language are other family-oriented activities that can be used to strengthen home-language development.

Just speaking a language at home, although a good start, may not be enough to allow for the full development of the language. For this reason, many families make sure that their children have multiple and frequent opportunities to speak the home language outside the home in settings in which there is high communicative demand, such as in playgroups, with extended family, or at religious or community gatherings. In these types of circumstances, children learn not only to communicate in different situations with people outside the family but also the culturally and linguistically appropriate ways to do so. If trips to visit family still living in the areas where the home language is spoken can be arranged, these will also provide high communicative demand situations for young children.

Some families believe it is important for children to acquire literacy in their home language and find that the only way to do this is through an after-school or weekend-school program. In fact, there is a long tradition in many immigrant groups of children attending such schools as a supplement to home-language use. Teachers can endorse parents' use of these schools as a way to continue the development of the home language.

Raising a child bilingually in the United States does not just happen—it requires vigilance and persistence on the part of parents and cooperation and continued practice on the part of the child (see also "How Can Teachers and Parents Help Young Children Become [and Stay] Bilingual?" on the included CD-ROM). Given that there are personal, cultural, cognitive, and even economic reasons to maintain bilingualism, many parents think it is worth the effort.

How Should We Go About Choosing a School Program for Our Child?

To answer this question, teachers must have considerable information available to them, including 1) an assessment of the individual child's skills (see Chapter 9), 2) the family's educational goals, and 3) the school programs available to the child. Teachers should be able to gather the appropriate information about the first two issues within the context of the early childhood education setting and in conferences with parents. The third issue, however, will require an information-gathering strategy that goes beyond the confines of the early childhood education program.

To be able to advise parents of second-language–learning children about what programs are available to them, early childhood educators will have to do more than the usual research. Knowing what types of follow-on programs are available for young children has always been part of an effective early childhood program, but unraveling the intricacies of programs for second-language learners may offer a further challenge. Knowing what types of programs exist, knowing what questions to ask and what to look for when visiting programs, and knowing how to convey that information to parents will make it easier for teachers to help parents make informed decisions.

Educational programs that serve second-language–learning children, whether public or private, can usually be classified as one of the following: 1) first-language programs, 2) transitional bilingual programs, 3) two-way bilingual programs, 4) general education programs with ESL support, or 5) general education programs with no ESL support. Each of these types of programs, including their defining characteristics, is discussed here.

First-Language Programs   A truly first-language program is a program that is dedicated to the exclusive use of the home language of the children in the program for every interaction in the educational context. As mentioned in Chapter 1, there are researchers and educators who are strong advocates of this approach to education, particularly for young children (Wong Fillmore, 1991b). Historically, immigrant groups were able to establish such school programs, but practice now stresses the development of programs aimed at English-language acquisition with various amounts—from none to a lot—of support for first-language development. For these reasons, it is the unusual community that offers first-language programs except as after-school or weekend options.

Transitional Bilingual Programs   Transitional bilingual education is actually an umbrella term that covers a variety of instructional and programmatic options. In most school systems, transitional bilingual education involves having children who speak the same first language attend class together so that at least part of their instruction each day can take place in their first language. The impetus in most of these programs, however, is to make sure the children leave the bilingual classes as quickly as possible and continue their schooling in general education classes. When evaluating transitional bilingual education programs, it is important that teachers keep the following questions in mind:

- *What are the qualifications of the teachers?* Many bilingual programs cannot keep up with the demand for certified teachers and therefore grant waivers to fill classroom teaching slots. Just being able to speak a particular language is obviously not a sufficient qualification for being an effective teacher. In some school districts, parents are put in the position of having to choose between a bilingual program in which their children will be taught in their first language by inexperienced teachers or general education programs in which their children's first language will not be supported but the teachers are more proficient.

- *How is language used throughout the day?* Just as simultaneous bilingual development is accomplished most effectively when young children have one model for each language, children in a bilingual educational context learn best when the languages are not mixed and when translation is not available. Bilingual classrooms should have a clear plan for the use of the two languages in appropriate instructional and conversational situations.

- *Is the first language maintained? How?* In fact, for young children, this question should really be, "Is the first language being actively *developed?*" A commitment to the development of the first language in the early grades can be found in the reading and language arts instructional program, where the use of the first language would be critical.

- *How are assessments made concerning children moving into the general education program?* Every school system will have a set of criteria for assessing when a child is ready to leave the transitional bilingual program. Concerns about these assessments and about the timing of bilingual children entering general education programs have been common (Collier, 1989; Cummins, 1984).

- *How are English-speaking children included in the classroom?* One of the greatest concerns with bilingual education programs is that they segregate second-language–learning children from the English-speaking students. This is troubling for two reasons: 1) a second language is acquired in communicatively demanding situations, and therefore contact with English-speaking peers is vital to the process, and 2) social segregation results in "us versus them" attitudes, and therefore contact with English-speaking peers is critical so that such attitudes, which are so difficult to overcome, will not develop.

Many school systems try to include second-language–learning children with English-speaking peers in nonacademic classes such as art and gym but discover that these efforts are often too little and too late (see Smith & Heckman, 1995). Other systems have adopted more effective plans, for example, by pairing bilingual and general education classrooms with children of the same or different age levels. When students from both classrooms are together, teachers organize lessons using context-embedded English, sometimes structuring the lessons so that the second-language learners are the "experts," even if their English is not as advanced as that of the children who are first-language English speakers. Mixing the classrooms as often as once a day for lessons in science or social studies and including plenty of hands-on opportunities and work in small groups helps the bilingual children make gains in English and helps the English-speaking children understand that the second-language–learning children have abilities other than language.

Two-Way Bilingual Programs   A particular type of bilingual program, called two-way bilingual or dual-language, has become increasingly popular (Christian & Whitcher, 1995). These programs match equal numbers of English-speaking children and children from another first-language group and are meant to foster second-language acquisition for each group. In a Spanish-English two-way program such as the Amigos Program in Cambridge, Massachusetts, for example, the Spanish-speaking children learn English and the English-speaking children learn Spanish, and each group has its first language maintained as well.

Even though this type of program has many appealing features, including the social inclusion of the children, the maintenance of the first language, and the development of the second language in a communicatively demanding situation, there are some pitfalls to its adoption as *the* form of bilingual program. First, there must be as many English-speaking parents who want their children to learn the second language as there are second-language–speaking parents who want a two-way program. In practice, what this has meant is that a two-way program will more likely survive if the second language is Spanish than if the second language is Khmer or Punjabi. Second, even if the second language is one that parents have decided is useful for their children to learn, the societal message to their children is the same as the one delivered to second-language–learning children and their parents: English is the important language in the United States. This means that two-way programs are more likely to be successful in promoting English acquisition among second-language–learning children than in promoting second-language acquisition among English-speaking children.

General Education Programs with ESL Support   In school systems in which there are not enough second-language–learning children from a particular language group to require a bilingual program, children often attend general education classrooms with support from an

ESL program. In these programs, children who come from a variety of first-language backgrounds are taught English together.

Not surprisingly, ESL programs can be more or less effective, depending on how they are structured. The least effective programs are characterized by inappropriate drill and skill approaches to second-language learning, with little or no attention to coordination with activities that are occurring in the child's general education classroom. The most effective programs are characterized by developmentally appropriate second-language use included with and/or in support of the curriculum in the child's general education classroom.

No matter how well developed an ESL program is, however, there is not an option within these programs to support first-language acquisition. Parents who wish to maintain their child's home language, therefore, will have to seek other means of doing so.

General Education Programs with No ESL Support

In certain school systems with no previous experience with second-language–learning children, there may be no provision for support for these children. In this case, it will be up to the general education teacher to develop an individualized program for the child. An inappropriate approach to this situation is to consign second-language–learning children to the farthest reaches of the classroom until they are "ready to participate." An appropriate individualized program would include many of the techniques of social inclusion and language use discussed in this book for early childhood classrooms, adapted to the primary school setting.

As in the case of general education programs with ESL support, there would be no support for maintenance of the first language in this situation. Again, parents wishing to maintain and develop their children's first language would need to find other ways of doing so.

Choosing a School Program: Summary

From these descriptions, it should be clear that labels mean very little in terms of what experience a second-language–learning child may have in any given school system's program. Teachers who wish to be informed about the different programs available to the children leaving their classrooms will need to visit programs, ask questions, and observe in classrooms to find out how any program actually works.

Despite this variety of program types and degrees of effectiveness within those types, there are still some basic criteria that should be applied to any follow-on program for second-language–learning children. These criteria are that the program should provide the following:

1. A strong, developmentally appropriate curriculum, including parent involvement

2. Contact with English speakers in a communicatively demanding setting with social and linguistic support

3. Multicultural understanding and/or support for first language development

If programs with these characteristics do not exist in the community served by the early childhood education program, it might well be time for early childhood educators to get involved in negotiations with school systems regarding these issues.

Chapter Nine

Assessing the Development of Second-Language Learners

A ssessing young children's development in meaningful ways is a topic of concern and controversy in the early childhood education community. Tests that involve placing a child in a new situation and/or with new people, tests administered only once, and tests that are constructed to display what children do *not* know rather than what they do know have all been criticized as being both invalid and unreliable indicators of young children's capabilities. As Meisels (1994) stated,

> Measurement in preschool is marked by recurrent practical problems of formulation and administration . . . Many measurement techniques used with older children are inappropriate for use with children below school [age] . . . For example, the following methods are extremely unlikely to yield valid information about normative trends in development: paper and pencil questionnaires, lengthy interviews, abstract questions, fatiguing assessment protocols, extremely novel situations or demands, objectively-scored, multiple choice tests, isolated sources of data. None of these methods are consistent with principles of "developmentally appropriate assessment." (pp. 210–211)

If these practices are not appropriate for young children in general, their inappropriateness for children from different linguistic and/or cultural backgrounds can certainly be taken as a given (see Genishi & Brainard, 1995). What, then, can teachers do to assess the development of young second-language learners in their classrooms?

GUIDELINES FOR DEVELOPMENTALLY APPROPRIATE ASSESSMENT

A variety of assessment techniques, known collectively as formative assessments, are considered developmentally appropriate for young children. These techniques, which have been growing in popularity among early childhood educators, involve the systematic collection of information on a child in the classroom during typical classroom activities by the teacher who works most closely with the child (see Bailey, 2008, p. 14, and McKay, 2006, p. 116, for discussions of the validity of formative assessments). These are also the types of assessment that are most appropriate for young second-language–learning children.

The National Association for the Education of Young Children (NAEYC) published a position statement that outlines the indicators of effectiveness for assessment in early childhood education programs (NAEYC, 2003). These indicators are as follows:

- Ethical principles guide assessment practices

- Assessment instruments are used for their intended purposes

- Assessments are appropriate for ages and other characteristics of children being assessed

- Assessment instruments are in compliance with professional criteria for quality

- What is assessed is developmentally and educationally significant

- Assessment evidence is used to understand and improve learning

- Assessment evidence is gathered from realistic settings and situations that reflect children's actual performance

- Assessments use multiple sources of evidence gathered over time

- Screening is always linked to follow-up

- Use of individually administered, norm-referenced tests is limited

- Staff and parents are knowledgeable about assessment. (NAEYC, 2003, p. 3)

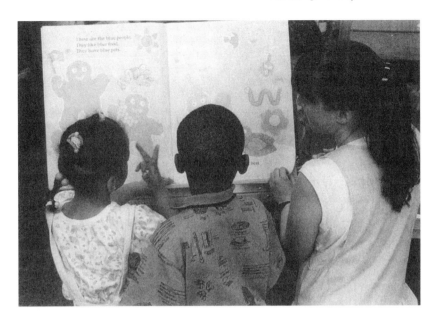

NAEYC summarized its position in the following statement:

> To assess young children's strengths, progress, and needs, use assessment methods that are developmentally appropriate, culturally and linguistically responsive, tied to children's daily activities, supported by professional development, inclusive of families, and connected to specific beneficial purposes: (1) making sound decisions about teaching and learning, (2) identifying significant concerns that may require focused interventions for individual children, and (3) helping programs improve their educational and developmental interventions. (2003, pp. 2–3)

Of course, these indicators constitute an ideal set of requirements for assessing young children and can be difficult enough to achieve under ordinary circumstances. For early childhood programs that serve children who are learning English as a second language, these indicators are even more challenging. Acknowledging these challenges, a committee of practitioners and researchers concerned about the screening and assessment of young English-language learners developed a supplement to the NAEYC position statement (NAEYC, 2005a; the supplement text also appears on the included CD-ROM). Some of the key indicators for assessment in this document include the following:

3a. Programs rely on systematic observational assessments . . . as the primary source of guidance to inform instruction and to improve outcomes for young English-language learners.

3b. Assessments for young English-language learners are based on multiple methods and measures.

3c. Assessments for young English-language learners are ongoing; special attention is given to repeated assessments of language development over time. (p. 4)

Using these indicators as a framework, teachers working with young second-language learners will be off to a good start. What is needed beyond these indicators, however, are some specific strategies for using them effectively with second-language learners. Providing help with these strategies is the goal of the following section.

ASSESSING THE CAPABILITIES OF YOUNG SECOND-LANGUAGE LEARNERS

Teachers working with young second-language learners need to think about how they will go about assessing those children's capabilities. This process can be divided into three steps: 1) deciding what should be assessed, 2) obtaining assessment information, and 3) using assessment information. This section discusses these three steps in the assessment process for young second-language learners.

Deciding What Should Be Assessed

The first question a teacher must ask when considering the task of assessing a young child is, "What do I want to know about this child?" For a second-language–learning child, the areas of interest might be divided into three categories: 1) the child's capabilities in terms of cognitive, social-emotional, and physical development; 2) the child's capabilities in his or her first language; and 3) the child's capabilities in his or her second language.

The classic division of capabilities for young children into cognitive, social-emotional, and physical development (Goodwin & Goodwin, 1982) is certainly a starting point for the assessment of all young children, including second-language learners. For second-language learners, however, difficulties arise quite quickly because the first two of these areas (cognitive and social-emotional development) as well as perhaps the third (physical development) are extensively involved in and affected by the process of second-language acquisition. In other words, a child's ability to acquire and display information in the cognitive realm may be hampered for a time because of an inability to understand or use the language of the classroom. Furthermore, a child's social-emotional development may be impeded because of a transitory lack of ability in the language used by the other children. Even a child's level of physical development may be difficult to ascertain because of an unwillingness to become involved in games or play. Therefore, teachers must approach assessment in each of these areas with an understanding of the types of constraints that a second-language–learning child is facing. A child's performance in each of these areas must be interpreted with regard to where the child is in the developmental sequence of second-language learning.

Knowing how a child is doing in terms of first-language development can also be crucial in putting together a complete picture of the child's capabilities. For teachers in bilingual settings, this information can be procured in the same way that second-language information is collected. For teachers who do not have access to bilingual resources, however, this important information may remain a missing piece of the puzzle unless specific steps are taken to obtain it.

In addition, teachers will, of course, want to know how a child is progressing in the developmental sequence of second-language acquisition. Even teachers who have an idea of what the milestones are in this developmental process will not have enough information without having strategies for finding out what a child understands and is able to do with the new language.

Finally, if possible, it will be important to be able to assess a bilingual child in both the first and second languages over time to be aware of how the two languages are contributing to the child's conceptual and linguistic development.

Obtaining Assessment Information

Knowing what should be assessed is only the first step. Knowing how to go about doing an assessment is the next step.

Assessing Cognitive, Social-Emotional, and Physical Development   The first and strongest caution in terms of assessing a second-language–learning child's overall cognitive, social-emotional, and physical development is for the teacher to give the child sufficient time to adjust to the classroom and to begin to get beyond the linguistic and social constraints of the second-language–learning situation (see Chapter 2) before embarking on any type of assessment except the most informal ones. In other words, the teacher's careful observation of the child's activities is entirely appropriate, but conclusions based on early observations and placement decisions based on these conclusions can be very misleading and perhaps even detrimental to the child's later development.

Furthermore, in assessing a second-language learner's overall cognitive, social-emotional, and physical development, teachers will need to be particularly aware of the abilities that a child can demonstrate *without* the use of language. For example, when a second-language–learning child sits alone at a table and sorts a collection of blocks into different colors, he has demonstrated an understanding of those colors as separate and distinct from each other, even if he is unable to name the individual colors in English. When a second-language–learning child helps another child by filling her juice glass, she has shown an understanding of appropriate social behavior, even though she might not have known what to do if she had been asked. When a second-language–learning child finally does the Hokey-Pokey at circle time after many days of only watching the other children, he has demonstrated a physical capability that was present all along but that he was only then willing to show off.

With second-language learners, it is always necessary to remember that when a child does not respond as expected to any assessment mediated by language, teachers will not know if it is because the child has not developed that capability, has not developed enough language to know what is being asked, or does not have enough language proficiency to respond. For these reasons, teachers will need to develop a series of language-free assessments for cognitive, social-emotional, and physical understandings, and/or will need to be keen observers of children's activities as they occur to document what children can and are doing without being asked.

Assessing First-Language Development   Assessing a child's first-language development is crucial to evaluating a child's overall development. If the child's teacher is a proficient speaker of the child's first language, then it may be easy for that teacher to appropriately assess the child's first language in the course of activities in the classroom. If there are few opportunities, however, to speak the child's first language in the classroom or if the child does not feel comfortable displaying first-language capabilities in the classroom situation, then additional steps will need to be taken. Furthermore, if the teacher is not a proficient speaker of the child's first language, it will be necessary to seek other ways of gaining information about the child's language development.

The best place to observe a child's first-language abilities is in the home context. There are many advantages to doing a first-language assessment in the home. The home is where the child is most likely to speak the first language, the child is most likely to feel comfortable speaking the first language, and the people with whom the child speaks this language most often can be found. An informal language assessment can proceed at home in much the way that it would proceed in the classroom. The difference would be, however, that the child can be observed in interaction with parents, grandparents, and/or siblings rather than with the adults and children in the classroom.

Several different methods could be used to obtain information about first-language use during a home visit. First, a bilingual teacher could take notes about the interactions observed in the home, concentrating on whom the child talks to and the level of appropriateness of these interactions. Second, these interactions could be audiotaped with the permission of the parents. In this situation, a teacher who is not bilingual could get help in evaluating the audiotapes later by consulting someone who is proficient in the first language. Third, if either of the first two options is not available, the teacher might consider interviewing the parents about their child's first language use, probing for how appropriate they believe their child's language use is in relation to what they expected. Fourth, if none of these options are available because of a lack of a common language between the teacher and the parents, the teacher can simply observe the child in communication with family members to see how fluent that communication is, even if the teacher does not understand the language being used.

One teacher I interviewed mentioned using a combination of these techniques. This teacher (M), who is English speaking, told me (P) about how she evaluated a Mandarin-speaking child in her classroom:

M: Actually at the beginning of the year I had some concerns about Kaikai, but then I went to his house and I heard all the talking he was doing in Mandarin. And I was like "He doesn't have a problem. He just hasn't picked up on the English yet."

P: So, one of the things that you have found the home visits useful for is that if you are trying to assess a child's progress in English and not much is going on, you might be worried about whether this is a general problem or whether he's moving into English and this is taking a little bit longer. So going home and seeing how they interact with their parents helps you decide . . . this isn't a big deal.

M: And I also ask the parents. If I think this is a real problem and I don't have a clue, then I ask the parents. And if they say no [it is not a problem], then I don't push the issue.

Assessing Second-Language Development   The next area of assessment that is relevant for young second-language learners is assessment related to their acquisition of the second language. One pioneering effort in developing a system of assessment for young bilingual children is the California Early Language Development Assessment Process (McLaughlin, Blanchard, & Osanai, 1995)[1], which used the developmental process outlined in this book as a starting point and developed both guidelines for assessment of young bilingual children and a detailed process for collecting assessment information.

The following guidelines were developed for the California Early Language Development Assessment Process:

1. *Assessment must be developmentally and culturally appropriate.* "In addition to taking into account the social and cognitive aspects of development (Bredekamp, 1987), appropriate assessment for language minority children must take into consideration the unique cultural aspects that affect how children learn and relate to other people" (McLaughlin et al., 1995, p. 7).

2. *The child's bilingual linguistic background must be taken into consideration in any authentic assessment of oral language proficiency.* "Bilingualism is a complex concept and includes individuals with a broad range of speaking, reading, writing, and comprehending abilities

---

[1]This publication is now available online from the National Clearinghouse for English Language Acquisition and Language Instruction Educational Programs (http://www.ncela.gwu.edu/pubs/pigs/pig22.htm).

in each language. Furthermore, these abilities are constantly in flux" (p. 7).

3. *The goal must be to assess the child's language or languages without standardizing performance, allowing children to demonstrate what they can do in their unique way.* "Assessment must be accompanied by a strong professional development component that focuses on the use of narrative reporting, observation of language development, and sampling the child's language abilities" (pp. 7–8).

4. *A fully contextualized account of the child's language skills requires the involvement of parents and family members, the students themselves, teachers, and staff in providing a detailed picture of the context of language learning and the resources that are available to the child.* "Assessment of the child needs to take into account the entire context in which the child is learning and developing" (p. 8).

Using these guidelines, McLaughlin et al. (1995) recommended what they call instructionally embedded assessment. This type of assessment is congruent with the guidelines mentioned concerning appropriate assessment in early childhood education because it is "intrinsically linked to program goals and affects instructional practice"; in other words, "the teacher is constantly observing what her children can and cannot do at different times and in different contexts and adjusting her instruction accordingly" (p. 9).

To carry out this assessment procedure, teachers follow a six-step process:

1. Make a plan about what, when, and how to assess a child, keeping in mind the need to observe all children, even the ones who are very quiet, to see what they understand.

2. Collect information from a variety of sources, including observations, prompted responses, classroom products, and conversations with family members.

3. Develop a portfolio for the child, which could include observational notes, results of prompted responses, such as audiotapes or dictations, and notes of formal or informal conversations with family members, being careful to collect information about both of the child's languages.

4. Write narrative summaries periodically to combine the material in the portfolio into a form that can be used in conferencing with staff and parents.

5. Meet with family and staff to present information from the portfolios and narrative summaries and to plan instructional strategies.

6. Use the information to inform curriculum development related to a particular child's level and needs.

By combining these assessment steps with knowledge about the developmental pathway that young children take in a second-language acquisition situation and understanding the individual differences that have been discussed, teachers can chart how a child is progressing in acquiring a second language. Keeping in mind that second-language learners' abilities are extremely volatile (see Chapter 4), teachers will need to constantly evaluate not only what the child is doing but also the circumstances surrounding the child at that time.

One way to keep track of the observations developed during this assessment procedure would be to use a checklist such as Observing Children Learning English (OCLE), presented in Appendix B and on the CD-ROM. This checklist is based on the developmental process outlined in this book and provides a way to track the progress of young children learning English as a second language over time. Items on the checklist may be completed when observed in naturally occurring communication, or they may be elicited by the teacher.

The checklist begins with basic vocabulary and provides an opportunity to note when the child understands a vocabulary item, when the child repeats a vocabulary item, and finally when the child uses that item when it has not been used recently near the child. Next, the checklist documents the child's repetition and then use of formulaic or social interaction words or phrases. Finally, the checklist includes examples of productive language that may be used by the child. By charting the dates of the observations and filling in any helpful comments, it is possible to keep track of the progress that any individual child is making toward the productive use of English.

Assessing First- and Second-Language Acquisition Together

What about finding out about children's abilities in *both* of their languages simultaneously? Why might it be a good idea to have a way to keep track of the development of both languages at the same time? The supplement to the NAEYC position statement on curriculum, assessment, and program evaluation (2005a) stated,

> There are several reasons to recommend a dual-language assessment approach. There is no one path to learning a new language (Wong Fillmore 1985); there are multiple environmental influences and individual differences that interact to shape second-language acquisition. To get an accurate picture of progress in the language domain, it is therefore useful to monitor progress in both English and the child's home language. Also, young children perform better when the language of assessment matches the language of instruction (McAfee, Leong, & Bodrova 2004; Gonzalez,

Bauerle, & Felix-Holt 1996). Young children are "instructed" both at home and in the education setting, but the content and skills developed may be different, and they may be differently revealed in assessments in either the home language or English—but not equally well revealed in both languages. For these and other reasons, whenever feasible, assessment should involve both languages to most accurately reveal children's knowledge and skills. (p. 10)

In other words, to get the fullest picture of a bilingual child's language development, it is necessary to take into account both languages, Furthermore, this type of approach also makes it possible to see whether a child is continuing to make gains in the home language while making progress in English. How can this be done?

To track a child's dual language development it is important to use parallel sources of information so that direct comparisons can be made between the child's development in each language and, if possible, the environmental changes that may affect that development. Research in this area was done by Barbara Pearson and her colleagues (Pearson & Fernández, 1994; Pearson, Fernández, Lewendag, & Oller, 1997) in a dual-language vocabulary study of 24 children raised bilingually in Miami. In this study, the researchers accounted for the words that the young children knew in each language by using parallel, modified forms of the MacArthur Communicative Development Inventories in English (Toddler and Infant forms) (Fenson et al., 1991) and in Spanish (Jackson-Maldonado & Bates, 1988) and asking the bilingual parents participating in the study to report on their children's capabilities. At the same time, the researchers also tracked the amount of exposure the children had in their two languages from 8 to 30 months. Although all 24 families intended to use equal amounts of each language with their children, the exposure of almost all of the children was unbalanced (i.e., more in one language than in the other) and/or varied (i.e., changed over time). The exposure patterns were related to the numbers of words learned in each language at different times during the study, with a lag of about 2 months between a change in the amount of exposure and a change in vocabulary composition.

In Figure 2, the effect of the change in one child's language environment is graphically displayed. In this case, the child experienced Spanish input an estimated 70% of the time (white background) until 20 months of age, at which time English input (dark background) increased from 30% to 60% and remained high for the remainder of the study. At the time of the change, the child's vocabulary in Spanish (SV) was well advanced over that in English (EV). However, when the language environment changed, the child's Spanish word learning plateaued and the child's English vocabulary surged. The

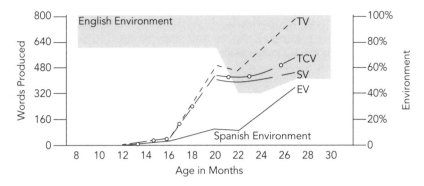

Figure 2. One bilingual child's language development in English, Spanish, and both languages together, from ages 8 months to 30 months. (*Key:* TV = Total vocabulary; TCV = Total conceptual vocabulary; SV = Spanish vocabulary; EV = English vocabulary.) (From Pearson, B., & Fernández, S. [1994]. Patterns of interaction in the lexical growth in two languages of bilingual infants and toddlers. *Language Learning, 44*[4], 632; reprinted by permission.)

other two lines on the graph—Total Vocabulary (TV) and Total Conceptual Vocabulary (TCV)—explain further what was happening. Clearly, the child was adding new words in English, so the Total Vocabulary (SV plus EV) increased accordingly. But instead of adding words in English that represented new concepts (i.e., words the child did not have in Spanish), this child was adding English words for already known words in Spanish, adding only a little to Total Conceptual Vocabulary.

By using parallel instruments to collect information about dual-language vocabulary development, four different types of information are available: a child's vocabulary level in one language, the child's vocabulary level in another language, the child's total conceptual vocabulary (all of the words the child knows in the stronger language plus those known in only the other language), and total vocabulary. If only one of the child's languages was assessed, it is obvious that a great deal of information would be lost and assumptions about the child's knowledge and skills would be very restricted.

Another research program with slightly older children points to the same necessity of collecting dual-language information. In the Early Childhood Study of Language and Literacy Development of Spanish-Speaking Children (Tabors, Páez, & López, 2003; Páez, Tabors, & López, 2007), more than 300 4-year-old children from Spanish-speaking homes were assessed on a series of language and literacy tasks in both English and Spanish. In Figure 3, the vocabulary results in both languages are displayed for the entire sample. In this figure, the results of the English vocabulary test (Picture Vocabulary; Woodcock, 1991) are plotted along the vertical axis, and the results of the

Figure 3. Individual bilingual 4-year-old children's vocabulary scores in Spanish and English. (From Tabors, P., Páez, M., & López, L. [2003]. Dual language abilities of bilingual four-year olds: Initial findings from the Early Childhood Study of Language and Literacy Development of Spanish-speaking Children. *NABE Journal of Research and Practice, 1*[1], 82; adapted by permission.)

Spanish vocabulary test (Picture Vocabulary; Woodcock & Muñoz-Sandoval, 1995) are plotted along the horizontal axis. The dark dotted line indicates the mean score (100) on each test that would be expected if these children were monolingual speakers of English or Spanish. The lighter dotted line indicates the mean for this sample of bilingual children (68 in English and 65 in Spanish).

Each dot represents the intersection of the two scores for an individual child. For example, Child 1 scored 87 in English and 27 in Spanish, indicating, perhaps, a child who is losing Spanish as she acquires English. Although her English vocabulary score is almost a full standard deviation (15) below the monolingual mean in English, she is well above the mean for this sample of bilingual children.

Child 2 scored 105 in English and 80 in Spanish, indicating that his English vocabulary acquisition has surpassed the monolingual mean but that his Spanish acquisition has slowed. If these children's English results were the only ones available to school personnel, these first two children would certainly be considered to be doing quite well in English acquisition. However, if their Spanish results were also available, it would be helpful for decisions related to placement, for example, in bilingual classes.

Child 3 scored 37 in English and 110 in Spanish, while Child 4 scored 35 in English and 45 in Spanish. If their results in English were the only ones available to school personnel, both of these children's English results might well raise red flags and concern related to language delay. However, Child 3 has scored over the mean for monolingual speakers of Spanish and is therefore unlikely to be a candidate for referral. Only the fourth child is likely to need further assessment.

How can information of this type be collected for young children in early childhood classrooms? One possibility is to use the Bilingual Early Language Assessment (BELA; Heise-Baigorria & Tabors, 2004), which was developed by researchers and practitioners[2] to be used for dual-language administration with young children over time. The BELA is available free of charge from the Cambridge Public Schools web site (http://www.cpsd.us/bela) in parallel versions in English and in Mandarin Chinese, Spanish, Haitian Creole, and Portuguese. The instrument is available to be translated into other languages and therefore may be used for even low incidence languages.

The following are distinctive features of the BELA:

- It is designed to be administered by home visitors or other professionals, either with a caregiver present or in any other socially familiar situation so that the child will feel more comfortable during the assessment.

---

[2]The Bilingual Early Language Assessment (BELA) is a revised version of the *Preschool Language Interview for the Child (PLIC)* which was developed in 1995 by a group of teachers and administrators from the Cambridge (Massachusetts) Public Schools. Participants included Margarita Cordoba, Bilingual Teacher, Spanish; Josianne Barnes, Bilingual Teacher, Haitian Creole; Carmen Medeiros, Bilingual Teacher, Portuguese; Helene Smit, English as a Second Language Teacher; Cornelia Heise-Baigorria, Project Leader of the Bilingual Home-Based Program; Linda Cravens, Bureau of Pupil Services; Patton Tabors, Consultant, Harvard Graduate School of Education; and Mary Cazabon, Acting Director, Bilingual Education. Further development work was supported by an Early Learning Opportunities Act (ELOA) Grant to the Cambridge 0–8 Council and the Cambridge Public Schools in 2002–2004.

- It is designed so that concrete materials are used during the tasks (see Cocking & McHale, 1981) and the child is operating with familiar objects or with illustrations.

- It is designed to assess the child's knowledge of basic concepts such as body parts, colors, and numbers, as well as the child's linguistic ability.

- It is designed to be administered both in the child's home language and in English so that it will be possible to ascertain whether a child is having difficulty with a concept (e.g., which shape is a square) or with the vocabulary item (e.g., the word *square* in English).

- It is designed to be used more than once so that a child's developing competencies can be assessed and home visitors and other professionals can use the assessment information to inform their work with the child.

The BELA is administered first in the language that a parent feels is the stronger language. A subsequent administration of the BELA is conducted in the other language. After scoring the results of the two assessments, a comparison can be made across the two score sheets to ascertain the child's level of demonstrated competence in terms of concept development and ability in the two languages. If the child has gotten an item correct in both languages, there is no reason for that item to be administered in the future. If the child gets an item incorrect or does not respond for both administrations, then that item can be targeted for conceptual development in both languages. If the child gets an item correct in one language but incorrect or does not respond in the other language, then that item can be targeted for vocabulary development in the other language.

Furthermore, because the BELA is designed to be administered over time, progress in both languages can also be charted using the dual-language record. Figures 4 to 7 show hypothetical results for four administrations of the BELA for four children with different patterns of results. In Figure 4, the child shows a pattern of increasing competencies in both languages simultaneously. Figure 5 displays the results for a child who is making very little progress in either language. In Figure 6, we can see a pattern in which the child begins with strong development in the home language and then begins rapid acceleration in English while continuing some gains in the home language. Finally, in Figure 7, the child begins with much stronger results in the home language, followed by increases in English competencies, and then continued increases in English and a decrease in the home language score.

BELA Dual Language Record

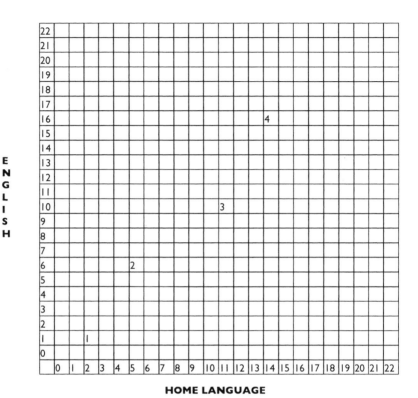

Figure 4. This pattern of results over a school year indicates a child who is gaining proficiency in both languages simultaneously. (From Heise-Baigorria, C. & Tabors, P. [2004]. *Bilingual Early Language Assessment [BELA]*. Cambridge, MA: Cambridge 0–8 Council/Cambridge Public Schools. Retrieved July 2, 2007, from http://www.cpsd.us/bela; adapted by permission; copyright © Cambridge 0–8 Council/Cambridge Public Schools through Early Learning Opportunities Act [ELOA] Grant 2002–2004.)

By using the results of the item analysis from each dual administration and charting a child's dual language results over time, a good deal of useful information can be obtained that otherwise would not be available.

Using Assessment Information

The information that can be collected and summarized for each child with the recommended assessment methods can be used in at least four ways: 1) to inform curriculum, 2) to inform parents, 3) to inform

BELA Dual Language Record

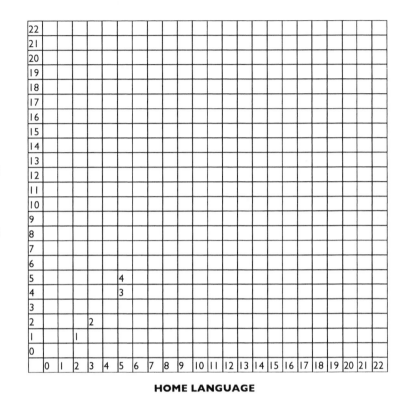

Figure 5.   This pattern of results over a school year indicates a child who is making very little progress in either language. (From Heise-Baigorria, C. & Tabors, P. [2004]. *Bilingual Early Language Assessment [BELA]*. Cambridge, MA: Cambridge 0–8 Council/Cambridge Public Schools. Retrieved July 2, 2007, from http://www.cpsd.us/bela; adapted by permission; copyright © Cambridge 0–8 Council/Cambridge Public Schools through Early Learning Opportunities Act [ELOA] Grant 2002–2004.)

other educators who will be working with the child, and 4) to inform decisions about referring the child for further evaluation.

Informing Curriculum   There are many ways that individual assessment of children can inform the curriculum in the classroom. Knowing where a child is in his or her developmental pathway of second-language acquisition means that a teacher can fine-tune any of the techniques suggested in Chapters 6 and 7 to fit a particular child's needs. McLaughlin et al. (1995) presented the following narratives developed during the assessment process as examples of how assessment can help teachers make curriculum decisions.

BELA Dual Language Record

HOME LANGUAGE

Figure 6. This pattern of results over a school year indicates a child who starts by making gains in the home language and then begins rapid acceleration in English while continuing some gains in the home language. (From Heise-Baigorria, C. & Tabors, P. [2004]. *Bilingual Early Language Assessment [BELA]*. Cambridge, MA: Cambridge 0–8 Council/Cambridge Public Schools. Retrieved July 2, 2007, from http://www.cpsd.us/bela; adapted by permission; copyright © Cambridge 0–8 Council/Cambridge Public Schools through Early Learning Opportunities Act [ELOA] Grant 2002–2004.)

Kim Loo

Narrative summary. After eight months of exposure to English, three-year old Kim is usually silent when she interacts with other children and adults. She is eager to participate in group activities but uses nonverbal means almost entirely. . . . Her comprehension of English is improving. She follows directions well and understands short statements and commands in English. According to her parents, Kim speaks and understands her home language, Taiwanese, as would be expected of a child her age.

Instructional strategy. The teacher decided to use the daily routines of the program to strengthen Kim's English. Because of the repetitive and concrete nature of many everyday routines, they are ideal for helping

BELA Dual Language Record

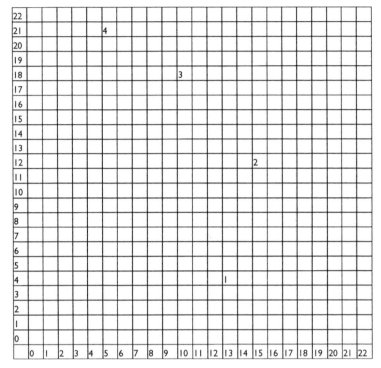

Figure 7.   This pattern of results over time indicates a child who begins with strong results in the home language but then continues to increase in English and decrease in the home language. (From Heise-Baigorria, C. & Tabors, P. [2004]. *Bilingual Early Language Assessment [BELA]*. Cambridge, MA: Cambridge 0–8 Council/Cambridge Public Schools. Retrieved July 2, 2007, from http://www.cpsd.us/bela; adapted by permission; copyright © Cambridge 0–8 Council/Cambridge Public Schools through Early Learning Opportunities Act [ELOA] Grant 2002–2004.)

children acquire vocabulary and word patterns. The staff labeled activities for Kim by talking to her and giving her the words for the activities: "It's snack time. We are having our snacks now. Ready for your snack, Kim?" The teacher also tries to involve Kim in choral activities with other children, such as reciting poems and rhymes. To develop her Taiwanese, the teacher has a Taiwanese-speaking aide read to Kim and other children whose home language is Taiwanese.

Tony Martinez

Narrative summary. Tony is quite advanced in his English for a four-year old child. He still has some problems finding the right word and his pronunciation is still developing, but he speaks English fluently and loves to participate in activities with English-speaking children. He uses Spanish at home and his parents say that his Spanish is also developing well.

Instructional strategy. The staff decides to encourage Tony to be involved in dramatic play to increase his English vocabulary. Tony rarely chooses dramatic play. The teacher knows Tony's father is a carpenter and Tony loves woodworking activities. The staff sets up a dramatic play area with tools and carpentry props. To assist in Tony's Spanish language development, the teacher also gives Tony's older sister, who is quite fluent in Spanish, some Spanish books to read with him at home. (p. 18)

By using these types of assessment methods and by charting an individual child's progress, preferably in both languages, teachers can avoid the one-size-fits-all fallacy of curriculum planning and can modify aspects of the curriculum intentionally to help specific children make developmental gains.

Informing Parents   As discussed in Chapter 8, parents will have many questions about how their child is doing in the classroom. By using observational and narrative techniques, teachers will have actual examples of activities and accomplishments to discuss with parents, helping them to really *see* what is going on in the classroom with their child. Furthermore, teachers will also be able to give parents specific ideas about how the curriculum will be shaped in relation to their child and may even suggest ways that they could work with their child at home.

Informing Other Educators   The transition from preschool to elementary school is a particularly important time for young second-language learners. The program placement that is made will have a major impact on the rest of a child's school experience. Early childhood teachers who have developed extensive information about a child's development will be in a position to convey that information to the next group of educators who will be working with the child. Recommendations concerning a particular child will carry much more weight if they are the result of systematic, periodic, and organized assessment than if they are general and vague reports developed only once near the end of the child's preschool experience. Developing methods for making sure that this important information about each child is made available to other educators should be an important part of the assessment process.

Informing Decisions About Referral   When a young second-language–learning child is having problems adjusting to the early childhood classroom, teachers will need detailed information to help them make decisions about whether a child might be a candidate for referral to receive other services. Sorting out which behaviors are typical for a young second-language learner and which would be considered a cause for concern should be part of the ongoing assessment process. Of particular concern would be assessments that showed that a child was having difficulty in both a first and second language (see Figure 3, Child 4), indicating the possibility of a general language delay. As the following case study illustrates, careful observation, conferencing with parents, seeking the help of other professionals, and making a plan for modification of the classroom environment can all be part of this process.

TARO: A CASE STUDY

The case of Taro, a Japanese boy who joined the English-language classroom in September at the age of 2 years, 9 months, shows how these assessment elements—observation, conferencing, consultation, and modification—came into play concerning one child's development. Because Taro was only one of the second-language learners in the classroom, because I was not in the classroom every day, and because I was not his teacher, the following observations are not as complete a record of Taro's activities as they might be. Even these observations, however, written each day after visiting the classroom, show how an observational record can help to reveal one child's consistent patterns of behavior and how this information helped teachers make decisions about how they might work effectively with Taro. (Observational notes are in bold; observer's comments are in italics.)

SEPTEMBER 19

Taro came in with his mother. He was very tentative and whimpered when he was greeted by Marion. His mother stayed for a good part of the morning, and he stayed in her vicinity but was not tied to her. Just before circle time, Marion asked if his mother was going to leave then. Marion promised that she would hold Taro if he were upset and that his mother could call and check on him. Taro's mother explained all of this to him in Japanese and then handed him over to Marion and left. Taro did cry loudly for several minutes; then when he was not sobbing, Marion brought him to circle, still keeping him on her lap. During outside time, he separated from her and remained relatively independent for the rest of the morning. After returning to the classroom, he began to play an escape game and doors were closed to contain him. It was very difficult to get him into the routines of eating, cleaning up, brushing teeth, etc. His father came earlier than any other parent for pickup and left quickly.

SEPTEMBER 28

. . . Taro's mother came over to say good-bye to him. He immediately left the water table (where he had been playing alongside Naoshi) and climbed into Marion's lap, even before his mother had left the room . . .

Taro seems to have all sorts of problems. Marion is trying to separate which problems might be due to language and which might be developmental.

OCTOBER 3

Taro clings to the teachers or runs away. He demands their full attention and screams and cries if he does not get it. Marion and Joanne have a conference scheduled with his parents. Marion is concerned that a conference may be difficult for the parents, but she really wants them to know what is going on.

OCTOBER 12

. . . Taro arrived with his father. Marion greeted them with "Good morning." Taro's dad said something to him in Japanese which included "morning" and Taro said, "Morning" to Marion, still clinging to his father's leg.

Taro is, indeed, doing better. But he still has a long way to go to become a model member of the class. He still "jitterbugs" around, cannot or will not sit down for circle, and has wild bursts of needing to be held but is unable to derive any comfort from it. Interestingly, there is no question in my mind that Taro's primary problems are not related to language needs, but are social/cognitive problems. A good countercase to thinking that all adjustment must depend on language facility.

At circle time, both Taro and Ling Ling left the circle and wandered around the room. Eventually Marion brought Ling Ling in to sit on her lap. Taro remained on the fringes.

This behavior of Ling Ling and Taro is very unsocial, the most direct repudiation possible of the process of becoming a member of the group.

OCTOBER 17

At circle time my main focus of observation was Taro because, for the first time that I have seen, Taro was a member of the circle for the whole time today. To begin with, when circle time was announced, Naoshi went to get Taro and brought him into the circle and held his hand, placing himself between Taro and Supat. When the first record was played, however, Taro left the area next to Naoshi and came to stand near the record player as all the other children (including Ling Ling) participated in doing the

movements for the record. When everyone sat down after the record, Taro left the corner and went to Marion (who had recently joined the circle). After climbing into her lap briefly, however, he got off and lay down on the floor near her, outside the circle, holding a toy car.

Naoshi's interest in helping Taro join the circle is interesting. I wonder how he perceives the situation. Does he see it as a big brother–little brother relationship? Naoshi has been a confident member of the classroom almost from the beginning. Will his influence help Taro to become included in the social milieu?

For the rest of the circle Taro migrated back and forth between Marion and Joanne . . . The only time he displayed his shrieking behavior was when Marion left the circle for snack.

Throughout the proceedings Taro never participated in any of the activities, but the fact that he was near the circle was a change from his previous behavior.

OCTOBER 19

Just as cleanup time was getting under way, I went into the block area and found Naoshi and Taro waltzing around and around with Naoshi holding Taro's hand. Taro was giggling and laughing as Naoshi pulled him around. When Naoshi stopped, Taro went out of the area for a minute, then he returned quickly, coming in shrieking in anticipation. Naoshi obliged him by spinning him around again.

Naoshi is definitely working on helping Taro. Marion and I later speculated whether or not Naoshi had been asked by either set of parents to try to help out or if he was undertaking this task on his own.

OCTOBER 24

During what should have been outside time, the class went to watch a movie in another room because of the rain. It was obvious that Taro was not going to make it through the movie, so I brought him back to the classroom. I got out the plastic pegs and shapes—an activity that he had shown an interest in previously—and for what was probably close to 20 minutes, he worked with piling shapes, dumping them over, and piling them again. At one point, he was working on circles and was able to pick them out from among the other shapes. I did a lot of naming of colors and shapes, but the only one that got repeated was "yellow one." Otherwise Taro did quite a bit of vocalizing that I couldn't understand.

This session with Taro represented the longest time I have seen him involved in any one activity. He was not as jittery as usual while he was working on this project, and he did not get distracted by anything else—perhaps because there were no other children in the classroom. I noticed that his hand–eye coordination is not good—he often missed the hole in the plastic pieces. He does not seem to have much digital dexterity either. A child with many problems it would seem. But each time I see him, he seems to be doing better in the classroom.

At circle time I spent a lot of time getting Taro into the songs. He was at least passively willing and stood in circle, first holding Naoshi's hand on one side and mine on the other, then letting me help him do the motions for the first set of songs. After that he broke away, however, and went to lie on the bench.

Taro is more involved in circle time than he has been before.

OCTOBER 31

Taro is sitting next to me at the circle table using the plastic shapes and the five pegs. I count as he and I take turns putting the shapes on. When he is finished, he turns them over, then starts again. At one point he picked up the pegs and started away from the table. I said, ''Taro, show it to Marion'' gesturing toward where Marion was painting children's faces (for Halloween) nearby. He did, and she remarked enthusiastically at what a good job he had done.

NOVEMBER 2

A long sequence developed in, around, and above the house area. It started with Byong-sun inside the house by himself looking out the window at the end near the bench where Taro happened to be. When Taro spotted Byong-sun in the window he started to giggle. Then they both giggled and laughed at each other.

When Taro stuck his head in the window, Byong-sun saw him and came back to the window, sticking his hand through again and giggling. Once inside the house, Leandro came to the end of the house with the window and stuck his head out. Taro, who was still on the bench, laughed at Leandro and then stuck his head in the window.

Taro and Byong-sun have had a few giggly interactions before, but this is by far the most extensive interaction between them.

At circle time, I again tried to keep Taro in the circle. He stayed for quite awhile—much of the time lying under my legs. Eventually he got up and left.

Taro seems to be making a lot of progress. Marion and I conferred several times during the day, and we both expressed the opinion that things were going much better. Taro is beginning to make contact with the other children, he is not running away, and he is at least passively a member of circle.

NOVEMBER 7

Today an observer from the local preschool intervention program was in class to observe Taro . . . At one point during the morning, Taro came to the playdough table and sat down next to Ling Ling. I got him some play-dough and showed him how the plastic coffee lid could be used to make a circle on the playdough. I also used one of the playdough toys to make a smaller circle. (All of this was being watched by the observer from the early intervention unit.) After this Taro mostly sat flapping the coffee can top with his fingers close to his face, not attending to the playdough.

In some ways, Taro's behavior was a step forward. He sat down at the table on his own and attended for awhile to what I was doing with him. But the flapping of the coffee can lid, as Marion told me later, was interpreted by the early intervention observer as "self-stimulation." Her feeling was that he was a candidate for referral and that he was operating more like a 2-year-old than the 3-year-old he is about to become.

As they were leaving the bench area, Andrew, Supat, and Jessica all stopped at the circle table where they found Taro. The three of them surrounded him and began going "Ah! Ah!" at him from all sides, calling his name, and putting their faces close to his. This developed into a chase game with the three of them chasing Taro into the cubby area and back into the room.

This behavior by Jessica, Andrew, and Supat is very interesting. I think the initial sequence—calling his name, saying "Ah!," and putting their faces near his—is some kind of mimic of how adults talk to babies. The chase game that followed was very exuberant, and Taro was a very willing participant.

NOVEMBER 16

As I moved over to the circle table, I found Taro on the bench with Byong-sun standing in front of him. Byong-sun was touching Taro's face very gently and smiling at him. While this was going on, Andrew came over and put his face near Taro's and said, "boo, boo," quietly. Then Andrew kissed Taro on the cheek and went away.

Here Byong-sun and Andrew are both treating Taro like a baby. Taro seems to enjoy this kind of attention, but the sequences never last very long.

Having spotted Taro alone in the cubby area, I decided to see if he would work with me on the pegs and plastic shapes for awhile. I went in to the

cubby area and brought him into the classroom to the circle table. I got out the pegs and plastic shapes and he sat right down and started picking out shapes. He picked up a circle. I said, "What's that? That's a circle. Circle?" And he repeated, "Circle?" Then as he continued to pick out shapes, he would ask me "Circle?" each time and I would confirm except once when he asked "Circle?" and I said, "No, diamond." He repeated, "Diamond." At another point I said, "Here's a blue one" and he repeated, "Blue one."

*This activity seems to be one of the few activities that Taro can sustain interest in. Is it because it is one of the few that he has been explicitly taught how to do? Perhaps he needs this kind of careful scaffolding to get into **any** activity. Are there children who have to be taught how to play?*

As Taro continued to work with the plastic shapes, Ling Ling came over and sat on the other side of Taro. Because he had recently dumped all the pieces off the pegs, there were some plastic shapes on the table in front of Ling Ling. Taro reached toward the box that still contained most of the shapes, but he did not take any more out. Ling Ling, seeing this, reached across Taro and brought the whole box over to her side. Joanne passed by and Ling Ling said to her, "(unintelligible) Taro." To which Joanne replied, "You're playing with Taro!" After this Taro left the table.

Taro did not object to Ling Ling's incursion on his project, but neither was he able to develop a coordinated effort with the pegs and shapes.

Having left the circle table, Taro went over to the water table, which was filled with straw and farm animals. Andrew saw him there and also came over, saying, "Taro" in a high tone. Andrew started to play with the animals, but Taro did not stay.

When Taro left the water table, he went back over to the circle table, where Ling Ling had finished piling the pegs with shapes and then had left. Taro picked up the peg array and dumped it over, spilling some of the shapes on the floor. Seeing what he had done, Taro bent down to pick up several shapes and returned them to the table top. Then he sat down and started to work on the pegs again.

I was very impressed with this sequence on Taro's part. First, because he went back to the activity without any urging from an adult. Second, because he pursued the dropped pieces and retrieved them successfully. And third, because he could organize himself to get back to work on the shapes, again without any adult supervision.

At cleanup time, Taro helped me put away the peg array and plastic pieces. He did very well getting the pieces in the box, but then he had trouble

with the box top, placing it squarely 90 degrees off where he needed it. I turned it around for him, and he placed the box and the array where they belonged on the shelf.

After this observation, I began to concentrate on taking notes on other second-language–learning children each time I visited the classroom, so I did not collect further detailed descriptions of Taro's activities. However, several events occurred that were important for Taro. First, in consultation with the preschool early intervention observer, a decision was made to recommend home visits with Taro and his parents around language and play issues. Second, a decision was made to keep Taro in the classroom for the remainder of the year, given the fact that he had made an adjustment and that any other placement would clearly have disrupted him again. After this decision, Marion brought a variety of play items into the classroom for Taro that were more appropriate to a toddler than those already in the classroom. Furthermore, the teachers developed a variety of plans for individualizing aspects of the classroom to promote Taro's development.

CONCLUSION

Clearly, one of the reasons that assessing young second-language learners is so difficult is that the use of language is such an integral part of the assessment process. Informal assessment, in particular, is based on being able to converse with children as they are involved in an activity. Children who cannot understand the questions being asked in the assessment situation or who do not have sufficient language proficiency to explain what they know are at a disadvantage unless the teacher is aware of these constraints and is prepared to pursue alternative methods of gaining the information. The strategies and techniques discussed in this chapter should provide a useful starting point for devising a systematic way of intentionally tracking young children's first- and second-language development that can be used to inform teaching and learning, reporting to parents, and communication with other professionals.

Chapter Ten

Developing Effective Early Childhood Programs for Second-Language Learners

Much of the information in this book is focused on how young children go about learning a second language in a social situation such as an early childhood classroom and how early childhood educators can support that developmental process. But most children who are acquiring a second language are acquiring a second culture as well. To plan effective early childhood programs for children who are linguistically and culturally diverse, the role of culture in development needs to be taken into consideration as well.

WHAT ABOUT CULTURE?

The basic question, then, is, What is the role of culture in development? Bowman and Stott (1994) wrote,

Developmental accomplishments thought to transcend cultural differences include such tasks as establishing mutually satisfying social relationships, organizing and integrating perceptions, learning language, developing category systems, thinking, imagining, and creating. Since children's growth and development are reasonably orderly, developmental achievements are learned in a similar fashion by all children and occur in predictable sequences. (p. 120)

In other words, all typically developing children, no matter what cultural group they belong to, are expected to engage in behavior meant to master the types of tasks listed by Bowman and Stott (1994). All of these tasks are certainly ones that early childhood educators would recognize as important in the early childhood period, and making appropriate developmental progress related to these achievements can be considered the work of early childhood.

This is, however, only part of the developmental picture. Bowman and Stott (1994) continued,

> Developmental milestones, however, take on their *meaning* only in the context of social life. The meaning of behavior is determined by the values and expectations of members of a culture as passed from one generation to the next. Children, therefore, learn to balance their needs and wishes with the constraints and freedoms of the social world in which they live, to express their developmental predispositions in ways that are consistent with their family's and culture's practices. (p. 120)

In other words, even the behaviors that young children share with all other children are expressed and interpreted within a cultural setting. For example, expectations and practices related to such issues as toilet training, discipline, separation, and socialization all take on cultural meaning and cultural interpretations. Families hold certain attitudes and beliefs about these issues, depending on their cultural heritage and their own personal experiences.

How does this play out in relation to how children learn? Bowman and Stott (1994) contended,

> Cultural factors play an important role in determining how and what children learn (Rogoff, Gauvain, & Ellis, 1984). They interface with age/stage potential, personal characteristics, and experience—giving them direction and substance. . . . Cultural differences can lead teachers to misunderstand children, to misassess their developmental competence, and to plan incorrectly for their educational achievement. (p. 121)

For these reasons, then, it is clear that early childhood educators need to be responsive to cultural differences as well as linguistic differences in planning curricular and assessment activities. Knowing what cultural differences make a difference for young children and finding out how they are expressed at home and in the early childhood setting are necessary components for effective early childhood education programs for children who are linguistically and culturally diverse. Bowman and Stott (1994) concluded,

> Educating all children will require the will and commitment to understand and respond to cultural difference. To the extent that teachers know and understand how children's past experiences have been organized and explained, they are better able to fashion new ones for them. (p. 131)

This concern for the importance of culture in development has sparked considerable discussion about just how appropriate the developmentally appropriate practice standards are that have defined effective practice in early childhood classrooms since the mid-1980s (Mallory & New, 1994). Clearly, if these standards are meant to express a single cultural representation—what might be called a European American representation—then they cannot be appropriate for all children, because many children come to early childhood classrooms from very different cultural backgrounds. For this reason, effective early childhood practice is now defined as being culturally as well as developmentally appropriate (Bredekamp & Rosegrant, 1992, 1995). What this means for early childhood education for children who are linguistically and culturally diverse is the topic of the next section.

RESPONDING TO LINGUISTIC AND CULTURAL DIVERSITY: RECOMMENDATIONS FOR EFFECTIVE EARLY CHILDHOOD EDUCATION

In recognition of the growing number of children from linguistically and culturally diverse families who are attending early childhood programs, the National Association for the Education of Young Children (NAEYC) (1996) issued a position statement titled "Responding to Linguistic and Cultural Diversity—Recommendations for Effective Early Childhood Education." This position paper made a strong statement concerning the potential problems related to the loss of a first language, and, in recognition of the variety of cultural representations with which children arrive in the classroom, recommended that early childhood educators develop flexible strategies for working with families from linguistic and culturally diverse backgrounds.

The position statement was divided into four sets of recommendations: recommendations for working with children, for working with families, for professional preparation, and for programs and practice. In the next section, each of the recommendations for developing an effective early childhood program for children who are linguistically and culturally diverse is discussed, particularly in reference to the material from this book.[1]

Recommendations for Working with Children

- *Recognize that all children are cognitively, linguistically, and emotionally connected to the language and culture of their home.* This recommendation reinforces and extends the important premise that parents are the first educators of their children. As discussed in Chapter 1, children's earliest learning experiences occur in the context of the home language and culture. An effective early childhood program recognizes and honors the importance of the cognitive, linguistic, and emotional understanding that a child brings to the early childhood setting from home. By collecting cultural information (see Chapter 6), by interviewing parents (see Chapter 6), and by making home visits (see Chapter 8), early childhood educators will be able to develop their own understanding about the meaning

---

[1]These recommendations, the bulleted entries in bold italics, are from the National Association for the Education of Young Children. (1996, January). NAEYC position statement: Responding to linguistic and cultural diversity—Recommendations for effective early childhood education. *Young Children*, pp. 7–12; copyright © National Association for The Education of Young Children.

of the home language and culture in the lives of the children they serve. As children who are linguistically and culturally diverse move from home to the early childhood setting, they should never be made to feel that they must choose between the ways of their family and friends and the ways of their school. Instead, they must be assisted in adding to their cultural and linguistic repertoire in this new setting without feeling that they must give up their cultural and linguistic heritage.

- *Acknowledge that children can demonstrate their knowledge and capabilities in many ways.* As discussed in Chapter 9, when children are at a linguistic disadvantage, it is not possible for them to demonstrate their knowledge through verbal communication for quite some time. Early childhood educators, therefore, need to develop other ways of helping children show what they know, including the use of extensive observations and nonverbal tasks.

  Furthermore, children from different cultural backgrounds may also have different ways of expressing themselves. Teachers need to be alert to the possibility that a child's behavior, although different from other children's, is an expression of that child's understanding at that time, and they need to use that as the relevant starting point for that child (see Espinosa, 2005, p. 848).

- *Understand that without comprehensible input, second-language learning can be difficult.* Comprehensible input refers to the types of modifications of language that educators can use when communicating with second-language learners, such as those discussed in Chapters 6 and 7. Techniques such as buttressed communication, repetition, running commentary, and context-embedded talk all make it more likely that a second-language–learning child will be able to understand what is being communicated and will begin to get an idea of how the new language works.

  For these techniques to work, however, early childhood educators need to ensure that second-language learners feel safe and included in the classroom. As discussed in Chapter 2, there is a double bind for children who are in a social situation in which they cannot speak the language: To begin to understand and speak the language, they need to be in social contact with those who already speak the language, but to get into social contact, they need to be able to speak the language. As discussed in Chapter 6, there are a variety of ways in which teachers can help second-language–learning children feel more comfortable and competent, including providing safe havens where second-language learners can play independently and developing small-group activities that include second-language learners. Involving the English-speaking children in helping the second-language learners can also be a key component of an effective program. Leaving second-language–learning children alone to figure it out by themselves is not an appropriate strategy.

Recommendations for Working with Families

- *Actively involve parents and families in the early learning program and setting.* It may be difficult to communicate with families who come from different cultural and linguistic backgrounds, particularly if there are no liaison personnel who speak the home language of the families. However, it should be possible for early childhood educators to get information about families, using techniques such as the questionnaires suggested in Chapters 6 and 8, so that each family's interests can be included in the classroom. Bringing the home language and culture into the classroom will make a child's transition to the new setting more comfortable, will let parents of second-language learners know that the program values their knowledge and interests, and will benefit the English-speaking parents and children in developing multicultural understandings.

- *Encourage and assist all parents in becoming knowledgeable about the cognitive value for children of knowing more than one language, and provide them with strategies to support, maintain, and preserve home-language learning.* As outlined in Chapter 8, parents of second-language–learning children often have questions about whether they should be maintaining and developing their home language with their children. Early childhood educators can support parents by letting them know how important their role is in their child's development and how important their home language is in accomplishing this.

    However, simply believing that maintaining the home language is a good idea may not be sufficient, because children are likely to try to reduce the cognitive load by dropping the home language. This is the point at which early childhood educators can play a crucial role, helping parents develop strategies for continuing the use of the home language within the family context, for seeking social situations outside the family where the language is spoken, and for traveling to areas where the home language is the primary language. To help parents with these issues, early childhood educators need to be extremely knowledgeable about the messages that parents receive from the media, the traditional educational establishment, and their children. Informing parents in advance about these issues will assist them in developing the strategies needed to maintain their home language before language loss begins.

- *Recognize that parents and families rely on caregivers and educators to honor and support their children in the cultural values and norms of the home.* Most of the discussion in this book has focused on the process that children who are linguistically and culturally diverse go through to become bilingual and bicultural in a second-language and second-culture setting. This recommendation, however, points out that early childhood educators also need to begin to accommodate their practice in ways that demonstrate that they are developing bilingual and bicultural sensitivities. To communicate effectively with parents who are linguistically and culturally diverse, early childhood educators need to let parents know that they understand and value family norms. Acquiring the necessary knowledge along these lines takes time and persistence (see Chapters 6 and 8 for suggestions) but certainly pays off in increased understanding and communication. Furthermore, once early childhood educators have developed cultural understandings, it will be possible to bring those understandings into the curriculum of the classroom and include them in the assessment process.

Recommendations for Professional Preparation

- *Provide early childhood educators with professional preparation and development in the areas of culture, language, and diversity.* Making sense of what children who are linguistically and culturally diverse experience in the classroom requires a theoretical and practical framework that goes beyond the basics of child development. Understanding, facilitating, and assessing second-language and literacy acquisition requires specific knowledge on the part of early childhood educators, knowledge that traditional coursework may not provide. Furthermore, early childhood educators need to take time to study and reflect on the cultural differences that may make a difference in young children's behavior and to think about how those differences can influence what goes on in classrooms (see also "What Early Educators Need to Know" on the included CD-ROM).

- *Recruit and support early childhood educators who are trained in languages other than English.* Bringing bilingual and bicultural professionals into the classroom with appropriate support can result in a myriad of positive effects. First, by recruiting and supporting early childhood educators who are bilingual and bicultural, a program demonstrates its commitment to broadening its scope and becoming more responsive to the needs of the children it serves. Second, if there are well-developed opportunities for constructive discussions among staff members, conversations can occur that will help all staff members develop an understanding of what it means to come from a different language and/or cultural background. Third, communication with children and parents who share the first language with a bilingual early childhood educator will be facilitated, and home and school contacts may be increased and may be more beneficial for both the parents and the program. Fourth, the presence of a bilingual and bicultural early childhood educator sends a powerful message to all children and all parents that more than one language and more than one culture is honored and valued by the program.

Recommendations for Programs and Practice

- *Recognize that children can and will acquire the use of English even when their home language is used and respected.* This recommendation actually combines two important points: Young children 1) can and will learn a second language in a supportive social setting, and 2) do not have to give up their first language to learn a second language.

    The first part of this recommendation is supported by the information concerning the developmental pathway of home-language use, nonverbal communication, formulaic language use, and productive language use, which research has shown is common for young children in a social setting in which a second language is used (see Chapters 3 and 4). Of course, like all developmental processes, there are differences in how individual children go about this process (see Chapter 5). These differences, based on underlying factors such as motivation, exposure, age, and personality, may affect the cognitive and social strategies that young children bring to the task of second-language acquisition, but it is clear that typically developing young children can successfully acquire a second language in a setting such as an early childhood classroom.

    The second part of this recommendation is more problematic, however, and refers to a common belief that to successfully learn a second language, the first language must be abandoned. Where does this belief come from, and how can it be countered?

This belief is rooted in a model of language learning that I call the single-container theory. In this conceptualization there is limited cognitive capacity available for learning language. This cognitive space can be thought of as analogous to an empty glass. As a child begins to learn a home language, the glass begins to fill up with the first-language liquid. Fortunately, in this view, the glass is just the right size to hold all of the first-language liquid; once the glass is full, the child has successfully achieved first-language acquisition.

In this model, however, difficulties arise if, part of the way through this process, a second-language liquid is poured into the same glass, with the same capacity, at the same time. In this case, the single-container theory predicts that there will be a mixture of the two languages as the two liquids flow together, resulting in semilingualism (incomplete learning of either language), or that there will not be enough room for the second liquid, resulting in an overflow and therefore lack of complete second-language acquisition. In either of these cases, the recommended remedy is to empty the glass of the first-language liquid so that there will be no competing language to confuse the child or to keep the child from learning the second language.

The competing model of language learning is what I call the multiple-container theory. In this theory, the child's first-language acquisition is again represented by a single glass that is filled with the first-language liquid, just as in the single-container model above. In this model, however, when the child is exposed to a second language, a new glass is added. This new glass comes with some liquid already in it—the child's knowledge of how language works—but it needs to be filled with second-language liquid for it to be useful to the child. In this model, the two glasses can continue to be filled simultaneously and can contain different amounts of liquid, depending on exposure to and use of the language. Furthermore, the amount of liquid in either glass can fluctuate, depending on the amount of language learning that occurs in either language at a given time. If the child is exposed to a third, fourth, or fifth language, this model provides that a new glass will be started for each, with no need to remove any of the previous glasses. If one of the languages is not used, however, the liquid in that glass will eventually dry up and ability in that language will be lost.

These two models represent two types of bilingualism called *subtractive* and *additive*. Educators may give parents entirely opposite advice, depending on which of these models of second-language learning they support. Educators who believe that a first language interferes with the learning of a second language, the single-container theory, often recommend to parents that they abandon the home language and make every effort to remove their children from contact with the first language. This policy results in subtractive bilingualism, the replacement of the first language with the second. As discussed in Chapter 8, research has shown that this model is not accurate and that the results of such policies have been detrimental to both children and families.

Educators who believe that well-developed first-language acquisition enhances the learning of a second language, the multiple-container theory, recommend that the home language be maintained and offer parents important advice related to strategies that they need to use to support development in the first language. This policy results in additive bilingualism, in which the second language is added to the first language. As discussed in Chapter 8, research has demonstrated that there are a variety of cognitive, emotional, and cultural benefits to first-language maintenance as children learn a second language.

This recommendation, then, refers to the second of these models, the one that supports additive bilingualism. For this recommendation to become accepted, educators who understand the importance of additive bilingualism need to be prepared to help explain the multiple-container model to other educators and to parents.

- *Support and preserve home language usage.* Given the negative consequences of subtractive bilingualism, the need to help parents continue the use of the first language at home with their children becomes obvious. This recommendation requires that effective programs for children who are linguistically and culturally diverse take an active stance in informing, strategizing, and supporting parents' efforts to keep the home language alive for their children (see Chapter 8).

- *Develop and provide alternative and creative strategies for young children's learning.* Having children who are linguistically and culturally diverse in the classroom means that early childhood educators must always take into consideration how each learning activity needs to be set up for optimum learning to occur. By providing a multitude of ways and modes that children can use to arrive at new understandings of a topic, early childhood educators will make it possible for all children to participate more fully in the construction of their own knowledge.

TEACHER PREPARATION AND STAFF DEVELOPMENT

Although only two of the previous recommendations have been placed under the category of professional preparation, it is obvious that both preservice and in-service programs for early childhood educators need to reexamine the premises on which they operate and reorient the way that they prepare early childhood educators if the NAEYC recommendations are to be put into effect. Some suggestions for the types of changes that will be necessary include the following:

1. Early childhood educators need to develop new understandings about the role of language and culture in development and the pathways that children take in becoming bilingual, bicultural, and biliterate.

2. Early childhood educators need to realize that developmentally appropriate practice must be interpreted to include development as expressed in other cultural groups.

3. Early childhood educators need to be prepared to examine their own cultural and linguistic heritage so they can begin to gain an understanding of the cultural lens that they bring to the classroom and to examine their attitudes about other linguistic and cultural groups.

4. Early childhood educators need to reflect on the ways that these understandings can and will affect their practice.

5. Early childhood educators need to be well versed in the research related to second-language and literacy acquisition so that they can help parents develop strategies for home-language preservation.

6. Early childhood educators need to learn how to observe and assess children during ongoing activities in the classroom (see Chapter 9), looking for alternative and nontraditional ways that children express their understandings.

Will all of these changes be easily or quickly accomplished? Of course not. Are they necessary? Absolutely. Given the statistics cited in Chapter 1 concerning the numbers of children from linguistically and culturally diverse backgrounds who are entering early childhood settings, it is clear that business as usual is no longer possible. Responding appropriately to children from families that are culturally and linguistically diverse requires new information, new attitudes, and new practices on the part of early childhood educators. The information provided in this book will help early childhood educators begin the process of developing these new understandings.

Part Three

Internationally Adopted Children

Chapter Eleven

What to Expect, How to Help

Six-year-old Maya lives in a suburb in Massachusetts. She is originally from China and has been adopted by an English-speaking family that includes her mother and father, and her brother, Patrick, who is 15 years old. Maya was 11 months old when her new family traveled to China to her. She had lived in an orphanage in China from shortly after her birth. When Maya's family met her, they were pleased to find her highly socially interactive and busily babbling, including *bababa* and *mamama* sounds. She also loved to have them read books to her. During the first few months of her being in the United States, however, they found that her babbling decreased, and she was not acquiring many sounds or words in English. By 13 months, she was using "dat'un" (that one) whenever she was pointing at or handing an object to someone, and "mama" to refer to her mother, to herself, and to pictures of women in books. At 13½ months, she was holding objects up to her ear and saying, "Hi." She also expressed hunger by smacking her lips. By 14½ months, she had three words: "ap(ple), " "hi," and "mama." More and more frequently, she was using a scream to get attention or to point out something of interest. Her parents decided it was time to have Maya evaluated by the early

The author wishes to acknowledge the help provided by Jeanne M. De Temple in the development of the material in this chapter, including providing references to research, revelations of personal experiences, and life-sustaining green muffins.

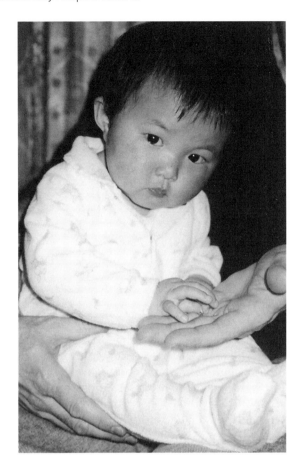

intervention unit in their community, where internationally adopted children automatically qualify for assessment.

Maya is not considered a bilingual child, as she has not been in a situation in which the Chinese she was exposed to as an infant could continue to be supported. However, she is an English-language learner. She is one of a growing group of internationally adopted children who are being introduced into early childhood programs in the United States. The number of international adoptions from all age groups has grown from 7,093 in 1990 to 20,679 in 2006; a total of 247,225 children were brought to the United States during that period. In 2006, the most common countries of origin of internationally adopted children were China (6,493), Guatemala (4,135), and Russia (3,706). Overall, internationally adopted children in the United States come from 21 foreign countries, none of which is English-speaking (U.S. Department of State,

Bureau of Consular Affairs, 2007). It is therefore increasingly important that early childhood educators have relevant information about this population of English-language learners. Because of their different circumstances, there are some definite differences that should be highlighted about these children as well.

IMPORTANT BACKGROUND INFORMATION

When an internationally adopted child comes to an early childhood classroom, there will be important information to collect from parents that will go beyond what is acquired using a basic questionnaire. It might be particularly important, then, to arrange to have an interview with the parents. A discussion of the areas that an interview might involve, and the reasons why these areas are of interest, follows.

The Child's Circumstances Before Adoption

The two main types of care situations that are common for internationally adopted children are orphanage care, which accounts for more than 80% of children, and foster care. Children from China, Russia, and certain eastern European countries are most likely to have been in care in orphanage situations, whereas children from South Korea, Guatemala, and some parts of Romania will most likely have been in foster care (Meese, 2005). In many countries where orphanages have been the norm, however, efforts are being made to increase the availability of foster care as awareness increases of the importance of stimulation and contact for young children (J.M. De Temple, personal communication, March 20, 2007).

Of course, knowing which of these two types of care a child was exposed to does not guarantee information about what that experience was like for the child. However, a commonly accepted generalization is that a child in foster care has been in a family-type setting in which everyday language was used to communicate with and around the child, whereas in an orphanage, each caregiver was responsible for many children and the child received less language input. When Sharon Glennen, Assistant Professor of Communication Sciences and Disorders at Towson University, spent 8 days visiting an orphanage in Russia while waiting to adopt her daughter, she found that her daughter was in a group of 10 toddlers who had 2 caregivers. Her observations were as follows:

- Children were segregated into groupings based on age and ability. They were rarely allowed to play or interact with older children who might have served as language models.

- Older toddlers ate independently at small tables with no adult interaction during meals.

- Younger children who needed help . . . were fed by caregivers. However, the caregivers rarely talked to the children and spent most of the time talking to the other caregivers.

- When children were carried, they were often held facing out, away from the caregiver. This limited interactions between caregiver and child.

- The children spent all of their time in the orphanage sleeping/play area, or outside in a small section of the playground. . . . They were never taken outside of the orphanage compound.

- When children were talked to, it was typically in the form of simple commands such as "come here," "sit down," "don't do that." Across the 8 days of visits, there were only 3–4 instances of interactions where caregivers described objects, actions, or provided other types of "teaching language" experiences. (Glennen, 2006)

As a result,

Two of the oldest children in the orphanage group produced a single expressive word; the other children were not talking. Of concern was the low frequency of any communicative vocalizations, including babbling. . . . Except for occasional cries, the children were eerily silent during their interactions. . . . When the assistant director of the orphanage was asked if any of the children in the group were speaking, her response was, "None of the children are talking; it is to be expected."' (Glennen, 2002, p. 337)

Other than this lack of language stimulation, other features of institutional care have been identified as being detrimental to the development of young children. These features include poor health care, inadequate nutrition, exposure to environmental toxins and infectious diseases, limited opportunities for cognitive stimulation, rotating shifts of caregivers who have little or no training, and regimented requirements for daily living (Johnson & Dole, 1999). Furthermore, many children are given up for adoption because of their birth history (e.g., low birth weight, prematurity, exposure to alcohol in utero, physical or medical handicaps) and the difficulties that their parents would have in caring for them (Johnson & Dole, 1999). Even Chinese infants, however, who are often abandoned simply because they are girls, have been found to have been affected in the same way by institutional care. Miller and Hendrie (2000) "concluded that children adopted from China demonstrate patterns of developmental and growth delays, as well as medical difficulties, similar to children from Romania, Russia, and other eastern European countries" (Meese, 2005, p. 62). In a survey of adoptive parents of children from Romania, "Groze and Ileana (1996) reported that delays in height, weight, fine and gross motor skills, and social and language skills related to the length of time spent in the institution" (Meese, 2005, p. 159).

To mitigate these effects of institutionalization, some countries have launched intensive efforts to improve the quality of programs serving orphans. In China, for example, organizations such as the Half the Sky Foundation (http://www.halfthesky.org) work closely with authorities to improve the physical surroundings in orphanages, as well as providing training for nannies, early childhood educators, and foster families. Consequently, the effects of institutionalization may be ameliorated for some children who have access to these programs.

Given this information, it is important for early childhood educators to inquire about the type and quality of care that an internationally adopted child received prior to adoption and the length of time that the child received that care. Adoptive parents will also have some information about the child's reported health history and will most likely have developed more information along those lines since the child's arrival. Special attention should be paid to the possibility of multiple ear infections and their effect on hearing. It should also be kept in mind that behavioral difficulties that are caused by institutionalization, such as attachment problems exhibited as indiscriminate friendliness, inattention, and overactivity, and quasi-autistic features (Meese, 2005) may also occur.

The Child's Circumstances Since Adoption

Most internationally adopted children will spend considerable time within the family context before being exposed to group settings such as an early childhood classroom. During that time these children will have an opportunity to adjust to an entirely new set of personal circumstances and begin the process of learning to communicate in an entirely new language. Unlike bilingual children who are placed in settings in which English is used but return daily to a home in which their first language is spoken, internationally adopted children are most often adopted by parents who do not have proficiency in the child's first language. Therefore, these children are completely cut off from the language that they have heard since birth. Consequently, it is necessary for them to acquire a first language a second time.

What researchers have found is that internationally adopted children, for the most part, begin to lose proficiency in their first language rapidly. At the same time, however, they begin to acquire skills in English extremely rapidly, some as rapidly as 2 weeks after adoption (J. Snedeker, personal communication, November 17, 2006). In fact, "the task and input of internationally adopted children appear to closely parallel those of infant learners. Like infants, adopted children get prolonged exposure to their new language in the context of meaningful social interactions" (Snedeker, Geren, & Shafto, 2007, p. 81) with family members and other important individuals all day long. Consequently, a prolonged silent period is not typical of these children.

In Table 4, a comparison is made among infants acquiring English as a first language, young bilingual children learning English as a second language, and young internationally adopted children learning English as a second first language. In the column related to infants, we can see that the consistency of their language input is total (English as first language—L1—all the way down the column), and although we know that some children receive more input than others in their first language, on the whole, there is a lot of support for these children to acquire English. Young bilingual children, in contrast, are learning two languages, the first or home language (L1) and English (L2). Life circumstances provide highly variable amounts of input in these two languages to these children. Decisions that parents make about which community to live in, which school situations their children are placed in, and which language is spoken at home all have an impact on how much these children maintain their first language and how rapidly they may acquire their second language (see Chapter 8).

Table 4.   Comparison of linguistic circumstances of infants learning English as a first language (L1), young bilingual children learning English as a second language (L2), and young internationally adopted children learning English as a second first language (2L1)

	Infants birth–30 months	Young bilingual children	Young internationally adopted children
Linguistic history	English = L1	Another language = L1 English = L2	Another language = L1 English = 2L1
Linguistic environment			
Home	L1	Various amounts of L1 and L2	2L1
Community	L1	Various amounts of L1 and L2	2L1
Societal	L1	L2	2L1
Result	L1 acquisition at expected rate	Maintenance, but perhaps lack of increase in L1; various rates of development of L2	Rapid loss of L1; rapid development of 2L1

Internationally adopted children, except in rare circumstances, will have heard a first language (L1) in their infancy but then will be exposed almost exclusively to English, their second first language (2L1), after adoption. For most of these children, this will mean a rapid loss of their first language and a rapid uptake of English. Unlike bilingual children, they do not need to spend time and cognitive effort moving back and forth between two languages. For the most part, they are also older than infants and therefore may move much more rapidly through the process of acquisition than infants. Clearly, if this is not happening, as was the case with Maya, then it is important to consider the need for intervention.

LANGUAGE ASSESSMENT OF INTERNATIONALLY ADOPTED CHILDREN

Once an early childhood educator has collected background information on an internationally adopted member of the classroom and has made the child feel welcome and comfortable, the next concern may be to think about how to assess that child's language development. Early childhood educators may well wonder: How quickly are young internationally adopted children able to acquire English, and what guidelines are available to signal the need for evaluation for language delay?

These are two of the questions that have been the focus of research on this population. Pioneering work on children adopted as infants and toddlers (Glennen, 2002; Glennen & Masters, 2002) and preschool-age children (Geren, Snedeker, & Ax, 2005; Snedeker, Geren, & Shafto, 2007) has begun to provide answers for professionals working with these children.

In a study of 130 internationally adopted infants and toddlers, predominantly from Russia, Glennen and Masters (2002) divided the sample into four groups based on age at adoption: 1) 12 months and younger, 2) 13–18 months, 3) 19–24 months, and 4) 25–30 months. Each group of children was followed longitudinally until they reached 37–40 months of chronological age. To evaluate vocabulary development in English, parents were periodically asked to check off all English words that their child was producing spontaneously from the list of words in the Language Development Survey (Rescorla, 1989). Figure 8, from Glennen and Masters's (2002) findings, indicates that typically developing infants whose first language is English (the solid thick line) can be expected to use more than 275 of the 310 words on the Language Development Survey by the time they are 37–40 months old. Of the internationally adopted children, the children who were adopted before they were 12 months old (the solid, thinner line) nearly matched

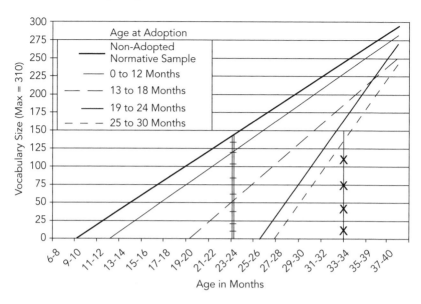

Figure 8. Vocabulary growth for four age-at-adoption groups on the Language Development Survey (Rescorla, 1989). Nonadopted normative data derived from Rescorla and Achenbach (2002). (From Glennen, S., & Masters, M.G. [2002]. Typical and atypical language development in infants and toddlers adopted from eastern Europe. *American Journal of Speech-Language Pathology, 11*, 420; adapted by permission.)

the achievement of children whose first language is English by the time they were 37–40 months old. The children in the older groups followed similar, or in the case of the slightly older children, even steeper, trajectories. However, these children acquired fewer words in English overall because of the shorter amount of time available to them before reaching the cutoff of 37–40 months of age.

What this means for children adopted before the age of 12 months is that they can be expected, for the most part, to develop English at the same rate as an infant born in the United States. What this means for children adopted as toddlers is that, for the most part, their English language development, although rapid, will still not have reached the level of their same-age peers who are first language speakers of English by the time they reach preschool age. For example, among the typically developing infants, it is expected that they will know an average of almost 150 words on the Language Development Survey by the time they are 24 months old (step-ladder vertical line), whereas children adopted at 25–30 months of age will not have reached that level, on average, until 10 months later (cross-hatched vertical line). The older the children are at time of adoption, the further they have to go before reaching the expected vocabulary level for their age. Glennen and Masters (2002) concluded, "What is apparent from the developmental data is that, for the majority of internationally adopted toddlers, acquisition of the English language begins soon after coming to their adopted home and progresses quickly" (p. 426). For internationally adopted children who are making good gains in English, no further evaluation is necessary at this time. However, Glennen and Masters recommended, "Any child who is not progressing rapidly should be referred immediately for speech and language services" (p. 426).

What of children who are adopted at preschool age? Do these children present the same picture as the infants and toddlers in the Glennen and Masters (2002) study, or are there different characteristics evident due to these children's more extensive experiences and greater cognitive abilities?

Snedeker and colleagues (Snedeker, Geren, & Shafto, 2007; Geren, Snedeker, & Ax, 2005) have studied young children adopted from China between the ages of 31 and 66 months. As in the previous study, parents of these children were asked to use a checklist to track their acquisition of English vocabulary, in this case for the first 18 months after adoption. Unlike the Language Development Survey, however, which has a maximum of 310 vocabulary items, the measure used by this research team was the MacArthur-Bates Communicative Development Inventory 2 (CDI-2) (Fenson et al., 1993), which contains a vocabulary checklist of 680 items. Consequently, the number of words indexed by this measure is considerably higher than that of the Language Development Survey. However, it is still possible to make comparisons based on the age-equivalent scores for the two measures.

Figure 9, from Snedeker, Geren, and Shafto (2007), shows the results for all of the 27 children as a single group. Again, vocabulary acquisition in English begins very soon after arrival. After 3 months, the preschool-age children in this sample, on average, had an expressive vocabulary that was equivalent to a 24-month-old native speaker of English (the hatched horizontal line). And by 12 months after adoption, many of the children had reached the ceiling of the CDI-2, scoring above the age equivalent of 30 months. In this group, older children acquired English vocabulary more rapidly than younger children, but only in the first 3 months. As with the toddlers studied by Glennen and Masters, these preschool-age internationally adopted children "hit the ground running, going through the same stages as infants but more quickly" (Snedeker, Geren, & Shafto, 2007, p. 85). Consequently, a preschool-age child who is not showing rapid English vocabulary acquisition and combining words to make longer utterances within a few months of adoption should be evaluated for speech-language intervention. However, it is definitely not appropriate to evaluate these children using the norms established for children who are native speakers of

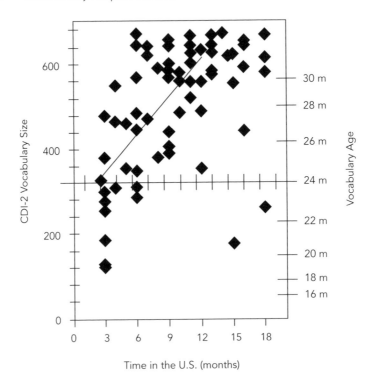

Figure 9.   Vocabulary growth for preschoolers, adopted between 30 and 66 months of age, on the Communicative Development Inventory 2 (CDI-2; Fenson et al., 1993). Nonadopted normative data from the CDI-2 appears on the secondary y-axis. (From Snedeker, J., Geren, J., & Shafto, C. [2007]. Starting over: International adoptions as a natural experiment in language development. *Psychological Science, 18*[1], 82; adapted by permission.)

English. As Geren, Snedeker, and Ax (2005) concluded about the internationally adopted preschoolers, "After about a year, the children in our study had lexical [*word*] knowledge and syntactic [*combining words*] abilities that surpassed those of the typical 30-month-old child. Yet they still appeared to have a long way to go before they would catch up with their monolingual peers" (p. 52; author's additions in italics).

Parents Can Help Collect Vocabulary Information

Given these results, then, early childhood educators should ask parents how their child is doing in terms of learning vocabulary in English, and then they should compare those answers with the information available from research. When asking parents about this area of development, it will be necessary to consider whether they are comparing their internationally adopted child with native English-speaking children of the same age. If this is the case and the child was adopted after

12 months of age, then they need to be helped to understand that that is not a useful comparison for young, internationally adopted children. What is important is that the child is acquiring English words readily and rapidly and is following the same trajectory as first-language learners in terms of combining words to form sentences.

To help parents see how their child is doing, it would be very useful to have parents fill out a checklist like the MacArthur-Bates Communicative Development Inventories (CDIs). This type of assessment is appropriate to use with English-speaking parents as they are in the best position to evaluate their child's English vocabulary knowledge. If the child is very young or is very newly adopted, the CDI: Words and Gestures form (Fenson et al., 2007) will probably be most appropriate. If the child is a toddler or has been learning English for 6 months or more, the CDI: Words and Sentences form (previously the CDI-2) (Fenson et al., 2007) will probably be the most helpful. If the child involved is a preschooler or has been learning English for more than 1 year, it might be necessary to use the CDI-III, which is normed for native English-speaking children up to age 37 months (Fenson et al., 2007). An initial administration of the checklist can be used to indicate which level the child is at in terms of age-equivalent native-born English speakers. Repeated administrations can be used as a dynamic assessment to see how much progress the child is making. Table 5 presents clinical guidelines developed by Glennen and Masters (2002) for children adopted from under 12 months to 30 months of age and guidelines suggested by the findings of Snedeker and colleagues (2007) for children adopted between 31 and 66 months of age. Using these guidelines, parents and teachers can see if an individual child's progress is or is not appropriate and can make decisions about whether an intervention for language delay should be considered.

Maya's Progress

When looking at these guidelines, it is obvious that Maya's parents' decision to seek early intervention was appropriate. Given that she was 11 months old at adoption, Maya should have been developing similarly to infants born in the United States. However, her parents felt that she was not making the language progress expected of a child her age, so they sought help.

Maya was assessed on a variety of measures at 15 months by the early intervention unit in her community. She scored at or above her age in social and emotional development, self-care, cognitive development, and fine and gross motor development. She was also found to be at age level for receptive language. However, her productive language was evaluated as being equivalent to that of a 10-month-old. For

Table 5. Guidelines for expected progress in language development in English for internationally adopted children birth to 66 months of age at the time of adoption

Child's age at time of adoption	When the child should start using English	When the child should start using 50 words/two-word phrases	Evaluation
Birth–12 months	At same rate as native-born English speakers	By age 18 months	Can be evaluated by assessment tools (e.g., CDIs) used as dynamic criterion references. After age 36 months, standardized tests normed for English-speaking children can be used.[a]
13–18 months	Within 3–6 months	By age 24 months	Can be evaluated by assessment tools (e.g., CDIs) used as dynamic criterion references. After age 37-40 months, standardized tests normed for English-speaking children can be used but will slightly underrepresent ability.[a]
19–24 months	Within 3–6 months	By age 28–30 months	Can be evaluated by assessment tools (e.g., CDIs) used as dynamic criterion references. After age 37–40 months, standardized tests normed for English-speaking children (EXCEPT those that index syntax and grammar) can be used but will slightly underrepresent ability.[a]
25–30 months	Within 3 months	By age 31–33 months	Can be evaluated by assessment tools (e.g., CDIs) used as dynamic criterion references. By 40 months, still cannot be evaluated using tests normed for English-speaking peers.[a]

Table 5. Guidelines for expected progress in language development in English for internationally adopted children birth to 66 months of age at the time of adoption

Child's age at time of adoption	When the child should start using English	When the child should start using 50 words/two-word phrases	Evaluation
31–66 months	Within 3 months	Within 3 months	Can be evaluated by assessment tools (e.g., CDIs) used as dynamic criterion references.

Sources: Glennen and Masters (2002) and Snedeker, Geren, and Shafto (2007).
[a]Guidelines for the use of standardized tests are from Glennen and Masters (2002, pp. 428–429).
Key: CDIs = MacArthur Communicative Development Inventories (Fenson et al., 2007).

the next 5 months, a speech-language pathologist visited Maya and her mother at home on a weekly basis. Maya made such good progress that these visits were reduced to twice monthly at 20 months and were discontinued at 24 months.

In the sessions, the speech-language pathologist played games with Maya that required a verbal response for her to participate. Whenever Maya made an attempt to use her language, the pathologist would respond very enthusiastically. By 17 months, Maya had 10 words; by 20 months, she had 25 words and had begun to use two-word phrases (*"baba no"*); by 24 months, she had a lot of two-word phrases; and by 25 months, she had begun to use three-word phrases.

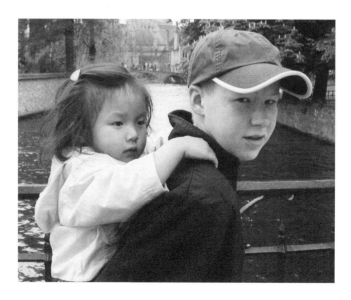

At her final evaluation with the early intervention unit at 27 months, Maya was again found to be at or above her age in social and emotional development (27 months), self-care (27 months), cognitive development (30 months), fine motor skills (28 months), and slightly below her age in gross motor skills (26 months). The best news was her language scores: 28 months for receptive language and 27 months for productive language. Maya was rated as having good articulation and speech sounds, as using primarily one- to three-word combinations, and as having an appropriate range of vocabulary words for her age. When she started attending a preschool classroom the following month, the teachers were impressed by her excellent language abilities and her use of social language (e.g., "Thank you," "Excuse me"). Throughout preschool, kindergarten, and first grade, Maya continued to do well in all aspects of school, becoming an avid reader and writer (see Figure 10).

EARLY CHILDHOOD CLASSROOMS FOR INTERNATIONALLY ADOPTED CHILDREN

As mentioned previously, most internationally adopted children will spend a considerable amount of time in the family context before they are introduced to a group setting like an early childhood classroom. During that time, they will most likely have acquired considerable conversational or communicative English, the type of vocabulary and language abilities that make day-to-day communication possible. But, as we have seen from the previously mentioned research, unless these children were adopted at a very young age, there is a good chance that their level of vocabulary and syntax will not be as advanced as those of a child who has grown up speaking English. Furthermore, these children will be a long way from beginning to acquire more school-relevant language, which is also called extended discourse or academic, decontextualized, or cognitive language—that is, language that is related to literacy development. The role of the teacher in these circumstances, then, should be to provide a highly enriched language context to help with vocabulary and syntactic development and to begin the introduction of higher-level, cognitively challenging language when appropriate (see Chapter 7). Maya's mother mentioned how she wished teachers to approach Maya's learning: teaching to her age level (i.e., her cognitive level), not to her language level, which might be less advanced.

This distinction between communicative and cognitive language has been made particularly forcefully by Boris Gindis, a child psycholo-

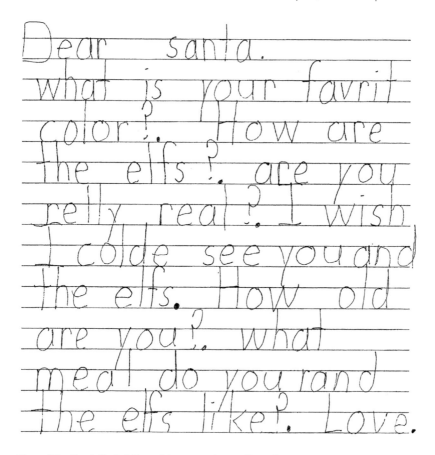

Figure 10. Maya's Santa letter, written at age 6 years, 8 months.

gist who specializes in the psychoeducational issues of internationally adopted children. He commented,

> While a native speaker has 4 to 5 years of intense language development (as a foundation for) her academic language . . ., an international adoptee has hardly half this time. Fully functional communicative fluency in the new language is usually achieved by international adoptees within the first year in the country. However, the speedy learning of basic communicative skills in the English language and speaking without accent with the age-appropriate lingo do not mean that international adoptees will master the cognitive aspect of the English language equally well. . . . Unfortunately, neither adoptive parents nor school personnel realize that a child's conversational proficiency in English is not enough to ensure the mastery of the English language needed for age-appropriate academic functioning. (Gindis, 2006)

Consequently, "internationally adopted children are at increased risk of reading failure" (Gindis, n.d.; see also http://www.bgcenterschool.org for materials for early childhood educators and parents of internationally adopted children). This point is reinforced by a study of 193 Norwegian children (11–16 years old) who had been adopted from Korea and Colombia as young children (Dalen, 2001). These children were matched with Norwegian-born children, and all children were rated with regard to educational skills; language skills divided into two subscales, day-to-day language and school language; school behavior; problem behavior; and parental support. The results showed that, as a group, the adopted children had lower school performance than the Norwegian-born children. However, there was also a considerable range within the adopted children's performance. This range was explained by two factors: how well the children could use language at a higher cognitive level and their level of hyperactive behavior. In discussing these results, Dalen commented,

> The (adoptive) children's language problems seemed to be particularly linked to using language at a higher cognitive level (the school language). The present study showed that there was no link between the adopted children's day-to-day language skills and their school results. On the other hand, there was a significant link between their school language skills and their school performances. Mastery of de-contextualized language seemed to be more important for performing well in school than having a good command of day-to-day language. Parents and teachers should therefore be aware that adopted children's good daily language skills can conceal some deeper language difficulties. (2001, p. 52)

CONCLUSION

For early childhood educators, several important points should be kept in mind when working with internationally adopted children and their parents:

1. Internationally adopted children will have had a variety of early experiences that will have an impact on their adjustment to their new circumstances. It will be important for early childhood educators to collect relevant information about those experiences to help in evaluating these children in the early childhood setting.

2. Internationally adopted children, unlike bilingual children, are not likely to have a prolonged nonverbal period. If a child who was older than 1 year of age at the time of adoption is not making progress understanding and then using English within the first 3–6 months, a referral for early intervention could well be necessary.

3. Internationally adopted children may quickly begin to use an impressive amount of conversational English. However, early childhood educators need to be aware that their vocabulary and syntax will not be as proficient as that of native-born speakers of English for quite a while. It will therefore be particularly useful for these children to be in a language-rich classroom environment.

4. Internationally adopted children may find extended discourse and literacy uses of English particularly challenging. Early childhood educators should continue to be aware that these children may be at risk for literacy development because of the time necessary to develop these aspects of a new language and should therefore provide many opportunities for these children to develop discourse level skills in English.

References

Bailey, A. (2008). Assessing the language of young learners. In N.H. Hornberger, P. Clapham, & C. Corson (Eds.), *Encyclopedia of language and education: Volume 7. Language testing and assessment* (2nd ed.). New York: Springer Science + Business Media.

Beals, D., & Snow, C. (1994). "Thunder is when the angels are upstairs bowling": Narratives and explanations at the dinner table. *Journal of Narrative and Life History, 4*(4), 331–352.

BG Center Online School for Internationally Adopting Parents and Professionals: Post-Adoption Learning (PAL) Center, Inc. (2007). *Home page.* Retrieved July 1, 2007, from http://www.bgcenterschool.org

Bowman, B., & Stott, F. (1994). Understanding development in a cultural context: The challenge for teachers. In B.L. Mallory & R.S. New (Eds.), *Diversity and developmentally appropriate practices: Challenges for early childhood education* (pp. 119–133). New York: Teachers College Press.

Bredekamp, S., & Rosegrant, T. (1992). Reaching potentials: Introduction. In S. Bredekamp & T. Rosegrant (Eds.), *Reaching potentials: Vol. 1. Appropriate curriculum and assessment for young children* (pp. 2–8). Washington, DC: National Association for the Education of Young Children.

Bredekamp, S., & Rosegrant, T. (Eds.). (1995). *Reaching potentials: Vol. 2. Transforming early childhood curriculum and assessment.* Washington, DC: National Association for the Education of Young Children.

Bunce, B.H. (1995). *Building a language-focused curriculum for the preschool classroom: Vol. II. A planning guide.* Baltimore: Paul H. Brookes Publishing Co.

Bunce, B.H., & Watkins, R.V. (1995). Language intervention in a preschool classroom: Implementing a language-focused curriculum. In M.L. Rice & K.A. Wilcox (Eds.), *Building a language-focused curriculum for the preschool classroom: Vol. I. A foundation for lifelong communication* (pp. 39–71). Baltimore: Paul H. Brookes Publishing Co.

Cambridge Public Schools. (1995). *Preschool Language Interview for the Child (PLIC).* Cambridge, MA: Author.

Christian, D., & Whitcher, A. (1995). *Directory of two-way bilingual programs in the United States* (Rev. ed.) (SuDoc ED 1.310/2:384242). Washington, DC: National Center for Research in Cultural Diversity and Second Language Learning, Center for Applied Linguistics.

Cocking, R., & McHale, S. (1981). A comparative study of the use of pictures and objects in assessing children's receptive and productive language. *Journal of Child Language, 8,* 1–13.

Collier, V. (1987). Age and rate of acquisition of second language for academic purposes. *TESOL Quarterly, 21*(4), 617–641.

Collier, V. (1989, September). How long? A synthesis of research on academic achievement in second language. *TESOL Quarterly, 23*(3), 509–531.

Cummins, J. (1984). *Bilingualism and special education: Issues in assessment and pedagogy.* San Diego: College-Hill Press.

Dalen, M. (2001). School performances among internationally adopted children in Norway. *Adoption Quarterly, 5*(2), 39–57.

Dickinson, D., & Tabors, P. (2001). *Beginning literacy with language: Young children learning at home and school.* Baltimore: Paul H. Brookes Publishing Co.

Ervin-Tripp, S. (1974, June). Is second language learning like the first? *TESOL Quarterly, 8*(2), 111–127.

Espinosa, L. (2005). Curriculum and assessment considerations for young children from culturally, linguistically, and economically diverse backgrounds. *Psychology in the Schools, 42*(8), 837–853.

Fantini, A. (1985). *Language acquisition of a bilingual child.* San Diego: College-Hill Press.

Fenson, L., Dale, P.S., Reznick, J.S., Thal, D., Bates, E., Hartung, J.P., Pethick, S., & Reilly, J.S. (1991). *Technical manual for the MacArthur Communicative Development Inventories.* San Diego: San Diego State University.

Fenson, L., Dale, P.S., Reznick, J.S., Thal, D., Bates, E., Hartung, J.P., Pethick, S., & Reilly, J.S. (1993). *MacArthur Communicative Development Inventories: User's guide and technical manual.* Baltimore: Paul H. Brookes Publishing Co.

Fenson, L., Marchman, V.A., Thal, D.J., Dale, P.S., Reznick, J.S., & Bates, E. (2007). *MacArthur-Bates Communicative Development Inventories: User's guide and technical manual, second edition.* Baltimore: Paul H. Brookes Publishing Co.

Garnica, O. (1983). Social dominance and conversational interaction: The omega child in the classroom. In J.L. Green & C. Wallat (Eds.), *Ethnography and language in educational settings* (pp. 229–252). Norwood, NJ: Ablex Publishing.

Garvey, C. (1977). *Play.* Cambridge, MA: Harvard University Press.

Genishi, C., & Brainard, M. (1995). Assessment of bilingual children: A dilemma seeking solutions. In E.E. García & B. McLaughlin (Eds.), *Meeting the challenge of linguistic and cultural diversity in early childhood education* (pp. 49–63). New York: Teachers College Press.

Geren, J., Snedeker, J., & Ax, L. (2005). Starting over: A preliminary study of early lexical and syntactic development in internationally adopted preschoolers. *Seminars in Speech and Language, 26*(1), 44–53.

Gindis, B. (n.d.). *What should adoptive parents know about their children's language-based difficulties?* International Adoption Articles Directory, Post-Adoption Learning (PAL) Center, Inc. Retrieved August 16, 2007, from http://www.adoptionarticlesdirectory.com/Article/What-should-adoptive-parents-know-about-their-children-s-language-based-school-difficulties—Part-3-/7

Glennen, S. (2002). Language development and delay in internationally adopted infants and toddlers: A review. *American Journal of Speech-Language Pathology*, *11*, 333–339.

Glennen, S. (2006). *Orphanage care and language*. Retrieved July 1, 2007, from http://pages.towson.edu/sglennen/OrphanageCareandLanguage.htm

Glennen, S., & Masters, M. G. (2002). Typical and atypical language development in infants and toddlers adopted from eastern Europe. *American Journal of Speech-Language Pathology*, *11*, 417–433.

Gonzalez, V., Bauerle, P., & Felix-Holt, M. (1996). Theoretical and practical implications of assessing cognitive and language development in bilingual children with qualitative methods. *Bilingual Research Journal*, *20*(1), 93–131.

Goodwin, W.L., & Goodwin, L.D. (1982). Measuring young children. In B. Spodek (Ed.), *Handbook of research in early childhood education* (pp. 523–563). New York: Free Press.

Groze, V., & Ileana, D. (1996). A follow-up study of adopted children from Romania. *Child and Adolescent Social Work Journal*, *13*(6), 541–565.

Hakuta, K. (1978). A report on the development of grammatical morphemes in a Japanese girl learning English as a second language. In E.M. Hatch (Ed.), *Second language acquisition: A book of readings* (pp. 132–147). Rowley, MA: Newbury House Publishers.

Hakuta, K. (1986). *Mirror of language: The debate on bilingualism.* New York: Basic Books.

Half the Sky Foundation. (n.d.). *Home page.* Retrieved July 3, 2007, from http://www.halfthesky.org

Head Start Bureau. (2002, April 8–9). English Language Learners Focus Group Report. *Identifying strategies to support English language learners in Head Start and Early Head Start programs.* Washington, DC: Head Start Bureau.

Heise-Baigorria, C. & Tabors, P. (2004). *Bilingual Early Language and Literacy Assessment (BELA).* Cambridge, MA: Cambridge 0–8 Council/Cambridge Public Schools. Retrieved July 2, 2007, from http://www.cpsd.us/bela

Hill, E. (1980). *Where's Spot?* New York: G.P. Putnam's Sons.

Hirschler, J. (1991). *Preschool children's help to second language learners.* Unpublished doctoral dissertation, Harvard Graduate School of Education, Cambridge, MA.

Hirschler, J. (1994, Winter). Preschool children's help to second language learners. *Journal of Educational Issues of Language Minority Students*, *14*, 227–240.

Huang, J., & Hatch, E.M. (1978). A Chinese child's acquisition of English. In E.M. Hatch (Ed.), *Second language acquisition: A book of readings* (pp. 118–131). Rowley, MA: Newbury House Publishers.

Itoh, H., & Hatch, E.M. (1978). Second language acquisition: A case study. In E.M. Hatch (Ed.), *Second language acquisition: A book of readings* (pp. 76–88). Rowley, MA: Newbury House Publishers.

Jackson-Maldonado, D., & Bates, E. (1988). *Inventario del Desarrollo de las Habilidades Communicativos.* San Diego: University of California, Center for Research in Language.

Johnson, D., & Dole, K. (1999). International adoptions: Implications for early intervention. *Infants and Children*, *11*(4), 34–45.

Krashen, S. (1980). The input hypothesis. In J.E. Alatis (Ed.), *Current issues in bilingual education: Georgetown University Roundtable on Languages and Linguistics* (pp. 168–180). Washington, DC: Georgetown University Press. (ERIC Document ED 219969)

Mallory, B.L., & New, R.S. (Eds.). (1994). *Diversity and developmentally appropriate practices: Challenges for early childhood education.* New York: Teachers College Press.

McAfee, O., Leong, D.J., & Bodrova, E. (2004). *Basics of assessment: A primer for early childhood educators.* Washington, DC: National Association for the Education of Young Children.

McKay, P. (2006). *Assessing young language learners.* New York: Cambridge University Press.

McLaughlin, B., Blanchard, A., & Osanai, Y. (1995, June). *Assessing language development in bilingual preschool children* [National Clearinghouse for Bilingual Education Rep. No. 22]. Washington, DC: George Washington University. Retrieved August 16, 2007, from http://www.ncela.gwu.edu/pubs/pigs/pig22.htm

Meese, R. (2005). A few new children: Postinstitutionalized children of intercountry adoption. *Journal of Special Education, 39*(3), 157–167.

Meisel, J. (1989). Early differentiation of languages in bilingual children. In K. Hylterstam & L. Obler (Eds.), *Bilingualism across the lifespan: Aspects of acquisition, maturity, and loss* (pp. 13–54). Cambridge, England: Cambridge University Press.

Meisels, S. (1994). Designing meaningful measurements for early childhood. In B.L. Mallory & R.S. New (Eds.), *Diversity and developmentally appropriate practices: Challenges for early childhood education* (pp. 202–222). New York: Teachers College Press.

Meyer, C. (1989). *The role of peer relationships in the socialization of children to preschool: A Korean example.* Unpublished doctoral dissertation, Ohio State University, Columbus.

Miller, L.C., & Hendrie, N.W. (2000). Health of children adopted from China. *Pediatrics, 105*(6), 76.

National Association for the Education of Young Children. (1996). *Developmentally appropriate practice in early childhood programs serving children from birth through age 8: A position statement of the National Association for the Education of Young Children.* Retrieved May 23, 2007, from http://www.naeyc.org/about/positions/pdf/PSDAP98.PDF

National Association for the Education of Young Children. (1996, January). NAEYC position statement: Responding to linguistic and cultural diversity—Recommendations for effective early childhood education. *Young Children,* 4–12.

National Association for the Education of Young Children. (1998). *Learning to read and write: Developmentally appropriate practices for young children: A joint position statement of the International Reading Association and the National Association for the Education of Young Children.* Retrieved May 23, 2007, from http://www.naeyc.org/about/positions/pdf/PSREAD98.PDF.

National Association for the Education of Young Children. (2003). *Early childhood curriculum, assessment, and program evaluation: Building an effective, accountable system in programs for children birth to age 8: A joint position statement of the National Association for the Education of Young Children (NAEYC) and the National Association of Early Childhood Specialists in State Departments of Education (NAECS/SDE).* Retrieved May 23, 2007, from http://www.naeyc.org/about/positions/pdf/pscape.pdf

National Association for the Education of Young Children. (2005a). *Screening and assessment of young English-language learners: Supplement to the NAEYC position statement on early childhood curriculum, assessment, and program evaluation.* Washington, DC: Author.

National Association for the Education of Young Children. (2005b). *Where we stand on the screening and assessment of young English-language learners.* Washington, DC: Author.

Páez, M.M., Tabors, P.O., & López, L.M. (2007). Dual language and literacy development of Spanish-speaking preschool children. *Journal of Applied Developmental Psychology, 28*(2), 85–102.

Pearson, B., & Fernández, S. (1994). Patterns of interaction in the lexical growth in two languages of bilingual infants and toddlers. *Language Learning, 44*(4), 617–653.

Pearson, B., Fernández, S., Lewedeg, V., & Oller, D.K. (1997). The relation of input factors to lexical learning by bilingual infants. *Applied Psycholinguistics, 18*, 41–58.

Rescorla, L. (1989). The Language Development Survey: A screening tool for delayed language in toddlers. *Journal of Speech and Hearing Disorders, 54*, 587–599.

Rescorla, L., & Achenbach, T. (2002). Use of the Language Development Survey (LDS) in a national probability sample of children 18 to 35 months old. *Journal of Speech, Language, and Hearing Research, 45*, 434–445.

Rice, M.L. (1991). Children with specific language impairment: Toward a model of teachability. In N.A. Krasnegor, D. Rumbaugh, R. Schiefelbusch, & M. Studdert-Kennedy (Eds.), *Biological and behavioral determinants of language development* (pp. 447–480). Hillsdale, NJ: Lawrence Erlbaum Associates.

Rice, M.L., & Wilcox, K.A. (1990). *Language acquisition preschool: A model preschool for language disordered and ESL children* (Grant No. G008630279). Washington, DC: U.S. Department of Education, Office of Special Education Programs.

Rice, M.L., & Wilcox, K.A. (Eds.). (1995). *Building a language-focused curriculum for the preschool classroom: Vol. 1. A foundation for lifelong communication.* Baltimore: Paul H. Brookes Publishing Co.

Rodriguez, R. (1983). *Hunger of memory: The education of Richard Rodriguez.* New York: Bantam Books.

Rogoff, B., Gauvain, M., & Ellis, S. (1984). Development viewed in its cultural context. In M. Bornstein & M. Lamb (Eds.), *Developmental psychology* (pp. 533–571). Hillsdale, NJ: Lawrence Erlbaum Associates.

Saunders, G. (1988). *Bilingual children: From birth to teens.* Philadelphia: Multilingual Matters.

Saville-Troike, M. (1987). Dilingual discourse: The negotiation of meaning without a common code. *Linguistics, 25*, 81–106.

Saville-Troike, M. (1988). Private speech: Evidence for second language learning strategies during the "silent period." *Journal of Child Language, 15*, 567–590.

Shatz, M., & Gelman, R. (1977). Beyond syntax: The influence of conversational constraints on speech modifications. In C.E. Snow & C.A. Ferguson (Eds.), *Talking to children: Language input and acquisition* (pp. 189–198). New York: Cambridge University Press.

Smith, H., & Heckman, P. (1995). The Mexican-American war. In E. García & B. McLaughlin (Eds.), *Meeting the challenge of linguistic and cultural diversity in early childhood education* (pp. 64–84). New York: Teachers College Press.

Smith, M. (1996). *Teacher-child interaction in early childhood education classrooms: Theoretical and practical perspectives.* Unpublished doctoral dissertation, Clark University, Worcester, MA.

Snedeker, J., Geren, J., & Shafto, C. (2007). Starting over: International adoptions as a natural experiment in language development. *Psychological Science, 18*(1), 79–87.

Snow, C. (1983). Age differences in second language acquisition: Research findings and folk psychology. In K. Bailey, M. Long, & S. Peck (Eds.), *Second language acquisition studies* (pp. 141–150). Rowley, MA: Newbury House.

Snow, C., & Hoefnagel-Hohle, M. (1977). Age differences in the pronunciation of foreign sounds. *Language and Speech, 20,* 357–365.

Snow, C.E., Burns, M.S., & Griffin, M. (Eds.) (1998). *Preventing reading difficulties in young children.* Washington, DC: National Academies Press.

Snow, C.E., Porche, M.V., Tabors, P.O., & Harris, S.R. (2007). *Is literacy enough? Pathways to academic success for adolescents.* Baltimore: Paul H. Brookes Publishing Co.

Sutherland, Z., & Arbuthnot, M. (1991). *Children and books* (8th ed.). New York: HarperCollins.

Tabors, P. (1982). *Panos: A case study of a bilingual child.* Unpublished manuscript, Harvard Graduate School of Education, Cambridge, MA.

Tabors, P. (1984). *The identification of categories of environmental support available for second language acquisition in a nursery school classroom.* Unpublished qualifying paper, Harvard Graduate School of Education, Cambridge, MA.

Tabors, P. (1987). *The development of communicative competence by second language learners in a nursery school classroom: An ethnolinguistic study.* Unpublished doctoral dissertation, Harvard Graduate School of Education, Cambridge, MA.

Tabors, P. (1988). *The plan for the Demonstration School.* Unpublished manuscript, University of Lowell, Lowell, MA.

Tabors, P. (1998, November). What early childhood educators need to know: Developing effective programs for linguistically and culturally diverse children and families. *Young Children,* 20–26.

Tabors, P. (2002). Language and literacy for *all* children. *Head Start Bulletin, 74,* 10–14.

Tabors, P., Aceves, C., Bartolomé, L., Páez, M., & Wolf, A. (2000). Language development of linguistically diverse children in Head Start classrooms: Three ethnographic portraits. *NHSA Dialog, 3*(3), 409–440.

Tabors, P., & López, L.M. (2005). How can teachers and parents help young children become (and stay) bilingual? *Head Start Bulletin, 78,* 14–17.

Tabors, P., Páez, M., & López, L. (2003). Dual language abilities of bilingual four-year olds: Initial findings from the Early Childhood Study of Language and Literacy Development of Spanish-speaking Children. *NABE Journal of Research and Practice, 1*(1), 70–91. Retrieved August 16, 2007, from http://www.uc.edu/njrp/pdfs/Tabors.pdf

Tabors, P., & Snow, C. (1994). English as a second language in preschools. In F. Genesee (Ed.), *Educating second language children: The whole child, the whole curriculum, the whole community* (pp. 103–125). New York: Cambridge University Press.

Taeschner, T. (1983). *The sun is feminine: A study of language acquisition in bilingual children.* New York: Springer-Verlag.

The University of Kansas, Department of Speech-Language-Hearing: Sciences and Disorders. (2006). *Language Acquisition Preschool.* Retrieved June 30, 2007, from http://www2.ku.edu/~splh/Clinics/LAP.html

U.S. Census Bureau. (2005). *2005 American Community Survey.* Washington, DC: Author.

U.S. Department of State, Bureau of Consular Affairs. (2007). *Immigrant visas issued to orphans coming to the United States.* Retrieved May 23, 2007, from http://travel.state.gov/family/adoption/stats/stats_451.html.

Williams, L.R., & De Gaetano, Y. (1985). *ALERTA: A multicultural, bilingual approach to teaching young children.* Menlo Park, CA: Addison-Wesley.

Wong Fillmore, L. (1976). *The second time around: Cognitive and social strategies in second language acquisition.* Unpublished doctoral dissertation, Stanford University, Palo Alto, CA.

Wong Fillmore, L. (1979). Individual differences in second language acquisition. In C.J. Fillmore, D. Kempler, & W.S-Y. Wang (Eds.), *Individual differences in language ability and language behavior* (pp. 203–228). New York: Academic Press.

Wong Fillmore, L. (1985). *Second language learning in children: A proposed model—Proceedings of a conference on issues in English language development.* Washington, DC: ERIC Clearinghouse. (ERIC Document ED273149)

Wong Fillmore, L. (1991a). Language and cultural issues in the early education of language minority children. In S. Kagan (Ed.), *The care and education of America's young children: Obstacles and opportunities. 90th yearbook of the National Society for the Study of Education, Part I* (pp. 30–49). Chicago: University of Chicago Press.

Wong Fillmore, L. (1991b). When learning a second language means losing the first. *Early Childhood Research Quarterly, 6*(3), 323–346.

Woodcock, R. (1991). *Woodcock Language Proficiency Battery–Revised.* Itasca, IL: Riverside Publishing.

Woodcock, R., & Muñoz-Sandoval, A. (1995). *Woodcock Language Proficiency Battery–Revised Spanish Form.* Itasca, IL: Riverside Publishing.

Yim, M.K. (1984). *Turn the page please: Learning a second language through picture book reading.* Unpublished qualifying paper, Harvard Graduate School of Education, Cambridge, MA.

Appendix A

Parent Questionnaire

Parent Questionnaire

Instructions: Please fill out as much as you can. Do not feel you must answer every question. These questions are meant to make your child's experience in our classroom more enjoyable.

1. Child's name _____

2. Father's name _____

3. Father's country of origin _____

4. Mother's name _____

5. Mother's country of origin _____

6. What name do you use for your child? _____

7. How did you decide to give your child this name? _____

   _____

   _____

8. Does this name have a particular meaning or translation? _____

   _____

   _____

9. Where was your child born? _____

   _____

10. Where else has your child lived and when? _____

    _____

    _____

11. How long has your family lived in _____? _____
                                       [name of city/town/community]

(continued)

12. What language or languages do you use to talk to your child?

    Father: _____

    Mother: _____

13. Do you speak any other languages?

    Father: _____

    Mother: _____

14. Who else does your child spend time with besides you? (Please include sisters and brothers, aunts and uncles, cousins, grandparents, family friends, and child care providers.)

Name	Relation to child	Age	Language used with child

15. Please estimate how many English words your child knows (circle one):

    less than 10   10–50   51–100   101–200   more than 200

16. Do you belong to a particular religious group?   Yes   No

    If yes, which one? _____

17. List the food that your child likes to eat. _____
    _____
    _____

18. List the food that your child does not like to eat. _____
    _____
    _____

(continued)

19. What does your child usually use when eating?

    fingers   chopsticks   fork and spoon

20. How does your child let you know he or she needs to use the toilet?_____

    _____

    _____

Please complete the following sentences.

21. When my child is with a group of children, I would expect my child to _____

    _____

    _____

22. When my child needs help from an adult, I would expect my child to _____

    _____

    _____

23. If my child is misbehaving in class, I would expect the teacher to _____

    _____

    _____

24. If my child is unhappy in class, I would expect the teacher to _____

    _____

    _____

25. The most important thing my child can learn in class this year would be _____

    _____

    _____

(continued)

26. Is there any other information you would like to give us about your family or your child?

_____

_____

_____

_____

_____

Observing Children Learning English (OCLE)

Observing Children Learning English (OCLE)

This checklist is a tool for keeping track of the progress of young children learning English as a second language **over time**. In the checklist, *understands* means that the child responds nonverbally to a word or phrase, *repeats* means that the child repeats a word or phrase used by another person, and *uses* means that the child produces a word or phrase without anyone having recently used the same word or phrase. To collect accurate information, particularly concerning what a child understands, it is important to make sure that the child isn't responding to other cues in the context (e.g., gestures, eye gaze, what other children are doing, what is expected in a given situation). For example, a child who sees other children sitting down at a table and complies when asked to sit down may be demonstrating a reading of the situation rather than actual word comprehension. Items may be completed when observed in naturally occurring communication or may be elicited. Place the date and any other notes in the blank space provided after each item.

Child's name _____ Teacher's name _____
Start date _____ Completion date _____

Vocabulary	UNDERSTANDS	REPEATS	USES
Names			
Own			
Teacher:			
Teacher:			
Other adult:			
Other adult:			
Child:			
Child:			
Child:			
Child:			
Other:			
Body parts			
Hand(s)			
Eye(s)			
Nose			
Mouth			

(continued)

Vocabulary	UNDERSTANDS	REPEATS	USES
Arm(s)			
Leg(s)			
Foot/feet			
Clothing			
Coat/jacket			
Shoe(s)			
Hat			
Mitten(s)			
Boot(s)			
Smock			
Other:			
Other:			
Toys			
LEGOs			
Blocks			
Puzzles			
Playdough			
Book(s)			
Other:			
Locations			
Here			
There			
In(side)			
Out(side)			
Under			
Above			
Art or writing			
Paper			
Crayon			
Marker			
Paint			
(Paint)brush			
Other:			
Social relations			
Mom(my)			
Dad(dy)			

(continued)

Vocabulary	UNDERSTANDS	REPEATS	USES
Sister			
Brother			
Friend			
Other:			
Areas			
Bathroom			
House			
Rug/circle			
Mealtimes			
Milk			
Juice			
Cup			
Plate			
Napkin			
Eat			
Drink			
Fork			
Spoon			
Garbage			
Other:			
Other:			
Colors (list 4)			
Shapes (list 2)			
Numbers 1–10			

Formulaic/social interactive	REPEATS	USES
Yes		
No		
Hi		

(continued)

Formulaic/social interactive	REPEATS	USES
Good (bye) bye		
Okay		
Hey		
Uh-oh		
Stop		
My turn		
Me too		
Excuse me		
I don't know		
Please		
Thank you		
More		
Mine		
I want (it) (that) (this) (some)		
Give me (it) (that) (this) (some)		
Look at (this) (it)		
Other:		
Other:		
Other:		
Other:		
Other:		
Other:		
Other:		

Productive language	USES
"Frames and slots"	
I want/wanna + (noun) or (verb)	
I'(ve) got(ta) + (noun) or (verb)	
I need + (noun) or (verb)	
Let's do (noun) or (verb)	
Give me (a) (the) + (noun)	
Other:	
Other:	
Other:	
Other:	

(continued)

	USES
Negatives	
(Pronoun/noun) no (verb)	
(Pronoun/noun) don't (doesn't) (verb)	
Questions	
Pronoun/noun (auxiliary) verb (? word)*?[+]	
(? word) pronoun/noun (auxiliary) verb?[++]	
(? word) auxiliary pronoun/noun verb?[+++]	
Other original phrases (list)	

Key:* = *what, why, who, when, where,* or *how;* + example: I do what?; ++ example: What I do?; +++ example: What do I do?

Other notes concerning these observations

Date	Notes

One Child, Two Languages
SECOND EDITION

Study Guide
Patton O. Tabors and Mariela M. Páez

Introduction

Guided Activities

Forms

    Language and Culture Questionnaire

    Classroom Practices Questionnaire

    Home Language Inventory

    Literacy Activities Checklist, Part 1

    Literacy Activities Checklist, Part 2

    Goals Chart

Introduction

In the 11 years since *One Child, Two Languages* was first published, it has been used extensively as the basis for professional development workshops for in-service teachers and as a textbook in academic classes for preservice teachers. Having participated in both of these settings, we understand that in-service and preservice teachers may well approach this material differently. Consequently, this study guide has been written with both of these audiences in mind.

For in-service teachers, the questions and suggested activities are meant to provide an opportunity to reflect on your practice and integrate this information into what you are already doing. If, however, some of the study questions meant for preservice teachers look intriguing, then those can be included in your discussions as well.

For preservice teachers, this study guide is meant to provide an opportunity to think about how you might go about setting up your practice so that all children will benefit from your teaching. If preservice teachers have access to a classroom with second-language–learning children, some of the study questions labeled "in-service" may be appropriate as well.

How should the study guide be used? If the book is being used as a textbook, the study guide can be the basis for directed reading and for discussion among the members of a class. Small group or pair discussions are often the most effective way to allow all of the members of a class to be heard.

If the book is being used in a professional development setting, there are various options, everything from forming a book club to developing presentations to deliver to other professionals. In these instances, the study guide can be used to structure the material for discussion or for presentation. Of course, it is meant only as a set of suggestions to get the process started. After that, it should act as a springboard for other ideas.

For the past 11 years, there has been no study guide for this book. This has not meant, however, that teachers have not found their own ways of absorbing the information and making it relevant to their everyday practice with children. My (Patton's) favorite experience occurred a number of years ago in Maryland. I was visiting a Head Start program and a teacher wanted me to autograph her copy of *One Child, Two Languages*. "I'll be right back," she said as she headed off to her classroom. When she came back, she looked a little embarrassed as she held out her copy of the book to me. "It's a little worn out," she apologized. I was thrilled to see that there were notes written between the lines of text, that there were little yellow sticky tags attached to many of the pages, and that there was quite a bit of finger paint evident throughout. "It's just like my favorite recipe book," I told her. "That means you have really *used* it!" Hopefully this study guide will help more teachers wear out this book.

Guided Activities

BEFORE AND AFTER

Gauging attitudes and beliefs

Preservice and in-service: Before starting to read *One Child, Two Languages*, it would be very useful to think about your personal attitudes about some of the issues that will be addressed in the book. Then after you have read and discussed the book, it would be interesting to return to those attitudes and find out what has changed. In order to do this, print from the CD-ROM or photocopy from this study guide the Language and Culture Questionnaire, fill it out, and put it away until later; then, complete it a second time (without looking back at the first one) and compare your answers. Reflect on how and why your attitudes have or have not changed.

Documenting classroom practices

In-service: For teachers who are already in classrooms, it would also be useful to examine your practices before beginning to read and discuss the book. To do this, print from the CD-ROM or photocopy from this study guide the Classroom Practices Questionnaire, fill it out, and put it away until later; then, complete it a second time (without looking back at the first one) and compare your answers. Reflect on how and why your practices have or have not changed.

CHAPTER ONE

Identifying early childhood program types

In-service: Check Table 1 on page 3 and locate which of the three types of programs serving bilingual children is closest to the situation that you are involved in. How is your program similar to the description of that type? How is it different? If there are differences, what effect do you think they have on the language environment of your program?

Noting changes in language backgrounds of children

In-service: Has the make-up of the language backgrounds of the children in your classroom/program changed over the past few years? If so, how? What impact has that had on your classroom/program? Give three examples of changes.

Interviewing a second-language learner

Preservice: Locate someone who had to learn a second language after moving from one place to another as a child. Interview that person about what that experience was like. You might want to include questions about how old the person was when he or she moved, what type of school experiences the individual had, what type of social experiences this person had, and what he or she thinks the long-term life impact has been of these experiences. After the interview, reflect on what you have learned. Share a summary of the interview with your classmates and compare the experiences of the person you interviewed with those that others have interviewed.

Exploring the effect of different circumstances on children's second-language development

Preservice and in-service: Speculate on how different you think first- *and* second-language acquisition might be for the children described below. Consider maintenance and/or development of the children's first language, sources of input for the second language, likely development of the second language, and possible first language loss in the first year after their arrival.

- A 2-year-old girl who comes to the United States with her parents and two older siblings from Guatemala and lives in a predominantly Spanish-speaking community. Soon after her arrival, she begins attending the Early Head Start program in her community.

- A 7-year-old boy who comes to the United States with his parents and a younger sibling from Russia and moves into a predominantly English-speaking neighborhood. Soon after his arrival, he begins attending first grade at his neighborhood school.

CHAPTER TWO

Thinking about social competence

In-service: Have you ever worked with a child with the characteristics of an "omega" child? If so, what were those characteristics? Were they resolved? If so, how?

Giving advice about social and linguistic constraints

Preservice: One day when I (Patton) was visiting an early childhood program, the director pulled me aside and asked me to observe one of the children in the classroom, a young girl who had recently arrived from Latvia. When the girl entered the classroom she went to a table and sat down without any problems. However, after settling at the table, she did not move and she did not interact in any way with the children or adults around her. In fact, when the teachers wanted her to join the group at circle time or get ready to go outside, they had to physically move her from one location to another. The girl did not protest, but she made no effort to move around the room on her own or to participate in the activities. The director was clearly concerned. Given the information about social and linguistic constraints outlined in this chapter, what type of advice would you give this director?

Charting social and linguistic constraints

Preservice and in-service: Develop an observational chart that will help you observe social constraints (e.g., isolation, invisibility, being treated like much younger children) and linguistic constraints (e.g., not being able to respond, use of nonverbal communication, being misunderstood) that young second-language–learning children face. Spend 15 minutes observing a young second-language–learning child in a group situation. Record any instances of this child's social and/or linguistic constraints. Share your observations with classmates or colleagues and compare what you observed.

CHAPTERS THREE, FOUR, AND FIVE

Checking on children's development in English

In-service: Print from the CD-ROM or photocopy from Appendix B two copies of the checklist called Observing Children Learning English (OCLE). Choose two children from your classroom who are at different stages of learning English, one who is just getting started and one who has more advanced skills. Spend a week watching each of the children whenever possible, filling out the checklist as you do. Remember that you can elicit responses as well as merely observing the child's language. For example, you can show the child various objects from the checklist and see which names the child knows. If the child does not respond, you can give the name and see if he or she repeats it. After filling out both checklists, compare what you know about each child's skills and identify areas that you might want to work on with each child.

Writing case studies of children displaying different second-language abilities

In-service or preservice: Review the four periods along the developmental pathway for young children learning English as a second language (see Chapters 3 and 4). Choose one of the periods and, without disclosing which period it is, write a one page hypothetical case study focusing in on a child who is displaying the characteristics of that period. Give some family background details, information about the age of the child and his or her length of stay in the United States, and the group context that the child is in. Then present an observation that demonstrates where the child is in the development of his or her new language. Finally, include some details about this child's individual approach to this cognitive task (see Chapter 5). Compare case studies with classmates or colleagues and see if you can tell where each child is along the developmental pathway. Brainstorm possible strategies for supporting each child's development.

CHAPTER SIX

Interviewing parents

In-service: Print from the CD-ROM or photocopy from Appendix A the Parent Questionnaire and copy it for all of the parents (not just the parents of second-language–learning children) in your classroom. Ask parents to complete the questionnaire at home, or ask the questions yourself during a conference or home visit. By using the questionnaire, did you discover important information that you did not have before? If so, how do you plan on using that information in your curriculum planning and in talking with parents?

Getting information about family language use

In-service: Print from the CD-ROM or photocopy from this study guide the Home Language Inventory and make several copies to use with the families of the second-language–learning children in your classroom. By asking the simple question "What language or languages does each of these people use with your child?" you can get a good idea of the languages the child has been exposed to. Just place an "X" in the column that matches the response for each person. For example, if the mother tells you that she speaks both the home language and English about equally with her child, you would place an "X" in the intersecting box for Mother and Both Equally. Administer the inventory to the parents of a number of second-language–learning children and notice that children are receiving different levels of home language and English. Speculate on what this might mean for each child's bilingualism. Use the inventory at the beginning of the school year and then again in the spring. Notice any changes in the answers. How do you think those changes might affect the child's bilingualism?

Developing a bilingual tape

In-service: First decide what words you would like to be able to say in another language. Then find a parent or community person who is willing to translate those words and participate in making the tape.

When you have the list of words in both languages, make the tape by alternately recording the English word (spoken by you) and the word in the second language (spoken by the parent or community person). Use the tape in your classroom with the children, giving all of the children a chance to pronounce the words. Have the tape available for the children to listen to on their own. Encourage the children to make a similar tape. For literacy purposes, make a poster that includes the written form of the same words in each language (in different colors) and an illustration of each word.

Discovering cultural information

In-service and preservice: Choose an ethnic/cultural group, either one that is represented in your classroom or one that interests you particularly, and find a cultural representative who is willing to be interviewed. Plan in advance the types of cultural information that you want to know about, including such issues as how and why young children should be disciplined, what the expectations are concerning separation from parents/family, whose job it is to provide socialization, and what the beliefs are about how young children develop and learn. Keep in mind that you are collecting one person's perspective on these issues. Reflect on how these cultural practices may be different from your own and what those differences might mean for the children in your care. Compare your results with those of classmates and colleagues.

Using techniques to communicate with second-language–learning children

In-service and preservice: Select a young second-language–learning child to work with. Think about what you know about the child's English language ability and which of the following techniques—buttressing, repetition, talking about the here and now, or expansion and extension—might be most appropriate for communicating with the child. Choose one of the techniques and spend 15–20 minutes playing with the child, stressing that particular technique as you talk. Note how the child reacts. Tape record the session with parental permission so you can go back and analyze your use of the technique and the child's responses. Was this an effective strategy? How would you change what you did if your approach was not effective?

Identifying aspects of classroom organization that support second-language–learning children

In-service and preservice: Read the following observation of the organization of a classroom serving second-language–learning children.

What aspects will be particularly helpful for these children and how will they help? What else could be added to this classroom?

> Ana's and Lilian's classroom is bright and cheerful with many colorful posters of scenes from all over the world on the walls and children's artwork hanging from lines strung across the room from wall to wall. Labels are attached to several of the objects in the room—a table, a chair, the bookcase, the water table—with the name of the object written in English (in blue), in Spanish (in red), and in Chinese (in green). One of the work tables available to the children is slightly off in a quiet part of the room. LEGO toys are spread out on the table, and a bookcase nearby has puzzles, multicultural books, and children's photos from home. At another table, a group of children, selected by the teacher, is working on a project to make muffins for the whole class. Right next to the door there is a large poster with the schedule for the day. Another poster—with the word *BUDDIES* at the top—has two parallel lists of children's names. The names are detachable so they can be moved around the poster.

CHAPTER SEVEN

Facilitating oral language development

In-service or preservice: Choose one or two of the suggestions for facilitating oral language development for second-language–learners in your classroom. Plan a series of lessons that use these techniques over the course of a week. Keep a journal detailing the lessons and the reactions of the second-language learners. At the end of the week, write a summary of what you feel was the most effective technique and why. Make an effort to incorporate the effective methods in your practice.

Constructing a dictionary

In-service: Develop one or more dictionaries in which common words in English are translated into another language or languages. Write each word and the translation on a piece of paper that can be placed alphabetically in a three-ring binder. Leave room for children to illustrate the entry. Build the dictionary throughout the school year. When a new word is introduced in English, be sure to translate it and include it in the dictionary. Enlist the help of parents in this ongoing activity.

Checking on literacy activities

In-service: Print from the CD-ROM or photocopy from this study guide the Literacy Activities Checklist, Part 1. Spend a week filling in examples of activities and children's learning in each of the categories (alphabet knowledge, phonological awareness, book and print concepts, vocabulary, and discourse skills). Are you covering all of these categories? Are you concentrating on some more than others? If so, why? Are there areas that you feel you should include more often?

Checking on literacy activities in a language other than English

In-service: Print from the CD-ROM or photocopy from this study guide the Literacy Activities Checklist, Part 2. Plan a week of activities that will cover the same categories as the Literacy Activities Checklist, Part 1 (alphabet knowledge, phonological awareness, book and print concepts, vocabulary, and discourse skills) but *in a language other than English.* Fill in examples of the activities and children's learning in each of the categories. Reflect on how easy or difficult it was to organize this week's activities and on the types of learning that different children in the classroom were able to display. Does this experience encourage you to integrate this type of learning more extensively into your classroom?

Inventing a game

Preservice: Invent a game that a group of children can play outside. Make the game accessible to second-language learners as well as English speakers. Outline how the game will be played, how you will explain the game to the children, and how you think the game will support children's second-language learning. If you can get a group of children together, including second-language–learning children, try out the game. Did it meet your goals?

Planning literacy activities

Preservice: Print from the CD-ROM or photocopy from this study guide the Literacy Activities Checklist, Part 1. Plan a week of activities to cover the categories on the checklist (alphabet knowledge, phonological awareness, book and print concepts, vocabulary, and discourse skills). Fill in the checklist with examples of these activities and the types of learning you would expect children to display in each of the categories. How do you think these activities would particularly benefit second-language–learning children?

Planning literacy activities in a language other than English

Preservice: Print from the CD-ROM or photocopy from this study guide the Literacy Activities Checklist, Part 2. Plan a week of activities to cover the categories on the checklist (alphabet knowledge, phonological awareness, book and print concepts, vocabulary, and discourse skills) *in a language other than English.* Fill in the checklist with examples of these activities and the types of learning you would expect children to display in each of the categories. How do you think these activities would particularly benefit second-language–learning children? Reflect on how easy or difficult it was to organize this week's activities. Do you think you would want to integrate this type of learning into your classroom?

CHAPTER EIGHT

Planning activities for use with parents

Preservice or in-service: Design an activity for each of the categories for involving parents of second-language–learning parents in a classroom (lending a hand, demonstrating a talent or skill, working with parents around cultural issues, and maintaining home-language development in the classroom). For each activity discuss what your goal is, what the activity would involve, how you would recruit parent involvement, and what the likely results might be for the children in the class.

Planning and delivering a presentation to parents

In-service: Prepare a 10-minute presentation for a parent meeting on the topic of bilingualism that would answer the following questions:

- What language should families whose first language is not English be speaking at home? Why?

- How can these families encourage their children to use their home language?

- What if the child or children in the family don't want to use the home language? What can families do then?

What reaction did you receive about this presentation?

Talking with parents

Preservice: Pair up with another class member and designate one person as a teacher and the other as a parent who speaks a home language that is not English. Have the parent ask the teacher the following questions:

- What language should we be speaking at home? Why?

- How can we encourage our children to use our home language?

- What if our child or children don't want to use our home language? What can we do then?

Switch roles after the first session and play out the same questions a second time. How easy or difficult was it to play each role? Why?

Finding out about educational programs

In-service or preservice: Research the educational programs in your community that serve second-language–learning children. If you are working with a group of classmates or colleagues, divide up the programs, visit them, and then compare notes after your visits. Find the answers to the following questions for each program:

- How does the program characterize its program in terms of language (first language program? transitional bilingual program? two-way bilingual program? general education with or without ESL support?)?

- What home languages are represented in the program?

- What languages are *used* in the classrooms?

- What language is used for each of the following:
Group times/circle time
Instructional activities
Small group activities
Personal communications between teachers and children

- Are there efforts to maintain the children's first languages? How?

- Are there English-speaking children included in the classroom? What role do they play with second-language–learning children?

- How are assessments made concerning children moving into the general education program?

Think about how this information could be important when conferencing with parents of second-language learning children.

CHAPTER NINE

Describing how your program assesses second-language learners

In-service: Think about the ways that you have available to you to assess second language learners in your classroom. How closely do they match the recommendations of the National Association for the Education of Young Children (NAEYC) 2005 position statement on the screening and assessment of young English-language learners (available on the included CD-ROM)? Consider if you 1) rely on systematic observational tools as the primary source of guidance to inform instruction and to improve outcomes for English-language learners, 2) use assessments for young English-language learners that are based on multiple methods and measures, and 3) use assessments of young English-language learners that are ongoing with special attention to repeated assessments of language development over time.

Using the Observing Children Learning English (OCLE) checklist to assess second-language learners' English language progress

In-service: Print from the CD-ROM or photocopy from Appendix B the checklist called Observing Children Learning English (OCLE). Make as many copies as you will need to keep a running assessment of all of the second-language–learning children's progress in English. Place the assessments on individual clipboards and keep them handy in the classroom. Fill in the checklist whenever you can for any individual child. Keep in mind what each child's progress means in terms of your curriculum activities. Use the checklists in conference with parents to help them understand how their child is doing in learning English. Discontinue use when a child's productive use of English has progressed so far that the checklist is no longer relevant.

Using the Bilingual Early Language Assessment (BELA) to assess second-language learners' dual language progress

In-service and preservice: Go to the web site for the BELA (http://www.cpsd.us/bela) and download the materials and the instructions for assembling the toolkit free of charge. Put together an assessment team of one speaker of English and one speaker of the home language of a child to be assessed. If the home language is not one of the languages already available for the BELA, you will need to have the instrument translated into that language. After you have prepared all of the materials and the toolkit, practice administering the assessment before the actual administration. Follow the instructions in the administration manual. With your team member, administer the assessment in each language, fill out the score sheets, and complete the Dual Language Record. Compare your findings in the child's two languages. What conclusions can you draw from this assessment? What further information would you receive if you continued to use this assessment over time? How would you use this assessment information when planning activities involving this child? What information could you share with this child's parents?

Using field notes to clarify thinking about an individual child

In-service or preservice: Select a second-language–learning child to observe over the course of a week. Write down what you observe about the child's behavior and communication whenever you can. Develop field notes like those in the case study of Taro at the end of Chapter 9, first detailing what you have observed and then commenting on what your thoughts, ideas, or reflections are about what you observed. Write a summary of your conclusions at the end of the week. How could you use this information?

CHAPTER TEN

Planning for improving practice

In-service: Print from the CD-ROM or photocopy from this study guide the Goals Chart. Choose three aspects of your practice with second-language–learning children that you would like to work on. Make a plan for each of these aspects in terms of these categories: action (What do you want to do?), resources (What will you need?), people (Who will you involve?), duration (How long will it take?), goal (What do you want to achieve?), and outcomes (What did you achieve?). Fill in the categories on the Goals Chart as you implement the plan. Were the outcomes what you had hoped for? Why or why not? Could the plan be modified to achieve those outcomes?

Writing position statements

In-service: Write out a position statement that details the policy that you have in your classroom for second-language–learning children and their families. Write a position statement that details the policy that your program or educational unit has for second-language–learning children and their families. How similar or different are the statements? What does that mean? If it is difficult to develop such a statement for either your classroom or your program or educational unit, what does that tell you? Get together with other teachers and see if you can come up with a position statement that can be implemented in your classrooms.

Developing lesson plans for a classroom serving both second-language–learning children and children from English-speaking homes

Preservice: Develop a day-long series of lesson plans of activities that you would use in a classroom serving both second-language–learning children and children from English-speaking homes. For each activity include how it would work for both groups of children. Include as many aspects of communication, classroom organization, and curriculum support as you can. What would you expect the children to know at the end of the day that they did not know when they arrived in the classroom in the morning?

CHAPTER ELEVEN

In-service and preservice: Locate a young child who has been adopted internationally. Collect information concerning the child's background, experiences since adoption, and present linguistic abilities. Consider having the parents complete the appropriate CDI (Fenson et al., 2007; see Chapter 11, p. 195) to check the child's vocabulary level in English. Or, ask parents to keep a journal of all of the English words that their child uses in the course of a week. Compare these results with the guidelines for expected progress that are presented in Table 5 (pp. 196–197). Consider what you might tell the parents about how their child is doing and what recommendations you might have for curriculum activities targeted for this child.

Language and Culture Questionnaire

In this questionnaire, the term *bilingual* means "a child who is being exposed to at least two languages on a daily basis."

Read each statement carefully and then circle the *one* response that most closely fits your level of agreement with the statement.

1. It is easy for children to learn a second language.

   strongly disagree   disagree   agree   strongly agree

2. The most appropriate educational program for all children is one that is based entirely on American values and ways of doing things.

   strongly disagree   disagree   agree   strongly agree

3. It is important that all educational personnel know how children learn a new language.

   strongly disagree   disagree   agree   strongly agree

4. The same educational program will work for all children, bilingual or not.

   strongly disagree   disagree   agree   strongly agree

5. English should be the only language spoken during school-sponsored activities.

   strongly disagree   disagree   agree   strongly agree

6. Parents whose first language is *not* English should speak English at home to help their children learn it as quickly as possible.

   strongly disagree   disagree   agree   strongly agree

7. It takes a long time for young children to become proficient in a second language.

   strongly disagree   disagree   agree   strongly agree

(continued)

8. Educational personnel can help children from other cultures become bicultural by respecting their home culture and introducing aspects of American culture.

strongly disagree   disagree   agree   strongly agree

9. It is important for teachers to share information about home languages with all of the children in the classroom.

strongly disagree   disagree   agree   strongly agree

10. There's no point in educational personnel trying to communicate with parents who speak a different language.

strongly disagree   disagree   agree   strongly agree

11. Parents should continue to speak their home language with their children.

strongly disagree   disagree   agree   strongly agree

12. The process of learning English is remarkably similar for all children no matter what other language they speak.

strongly disagree   disagree   agree   strongly agree

13. All children should be exposed to materials from other languages and cultures.

strongly disagree   disagree   agree   strongly agree

14. The more bilingual children there are in an educational program, the more need there will be for special education services.

strongly disagree   disagree   agree   strongly agree

Classroom Practices Questionnaire

Read each statement and then circle the *one* response that most closely fits your practice.

1. I collect information about all of the families whose children are in my class, including where the families come from and what languages are spoken at home.

   always   often   sometimes   never

2. I use pictures, objects, gestures, and other forms of nonverbal communication to help bilingual children understand what I am saying.

   always   often   sometimes   never

3. I ask bilingual parents to provide a few key words in their home language so I can use them with their children in my class.

   always   often   sometimes   never

4. I include materials, such as books, pictures, toys, and labels, that reflect the cultures and languages of all the children in the classroom.

   always   often   sometimes   never

5. I make sure that bilingual children have opportunities to interact with English-speaking children in my classroom.

   always   often   sometimes   never

6. I keep careful notes about the language skills of the bilingual children in my classroom.

   always   often   sometimes   never

7. I talk with parents of bilingual children about their language goals for their children.

   always   often   sometimes   never

(continued)

8. I make a special effort to find out all I can about how young children learn a second language.

   always   often   sometimes   never

9. I spend time thinking of ways to make bilingual parents feel welcome in my classroom.

   always   often   sometimes   never

10. I attend cultural festivals and community activities related to the cultures of the children in my classroom.

   always   often   sometimes   never

11. I encourage parents of bilingual children to continue to speak their first language at home.

   always   often   sometimes   never

12. I plan specific activities in the classroom, like story time or circle time, as opportunities for language development for both English-speaking and bilingual children.

   always   often   sometimes   never

13. I invite parents and others who speak the languages of the children to come to class and use those languages to do activities with all of the children.

   always   often   sometimes   never

Home Language Inventory

Ask the parent(s), "What language does each of these people speak with your child?"

	Only Home Language[1]	Mostly Home Language	Both Equally	Mostly English	Only English
Mother					
Father					
Older Sibling(s)					
Younger Sibling(s)					
Grandparent(s)					
Caregiver(s)					

[1]What is the home language? _____

This form can be modified if there is more than one home language.

Literacy Activities Checklist, Part 1

Enter examples of activities that support the categories in Column I, and enter examples of what children have learned in Column II.

I	II
What Teachers Do	What Children Learn
Alphabet Knowledge Activities that target letter recognition:	To identify the letters of the alphabet:
Phonological Awareness Activities that emphasize the sounds that make up words:	To identify the sounds that make up words:
Book and Print Concepts Activities that show how books look and how they work:	What the contents of a book are, including where the print is and where the book starts and ends:
Vocabulary Knowledge Activities that emphasize words and their meanings:	That there are lots and lots of words that are used for talking, writing, and reading:
Discourse Skills Activities that encourage telling stories, explaining how the world works, or building a fantasy world:	To use these more sophisticated oral language forms:

From Office of Head Start, "Language and Literacy for All Children," *Head Start Bulletin*, No. 74, Washington. Department of Health and Human Services, Administration for Children and Families, 2002; adapted by permission. In *One Child, Two Languages: A Guide for Early Childhood Educators of Children Learning English as a Second Language, Second Edition*, by Patton O. Tabors (2008, Paul H. Brookes Publishing Co., Inc.).

Literacy Activities Checklist, Part 2

Enter examples of activities that support the categories in Column I, and enter examples of what children have learned in Column II.

I	II
What Teachers Do	What Children Learn
Alphabet Knowledge Activities that target comparing alphabets or writing systems in other languages:	That other languages have different alphabets or writing systems:
Phonological Awareness Activities that present the sounds of other languages:	That other languages have different sounds but all languages use sounds to make words:
Book and Print Concepts Activities that show how books written in other languages look and how they work:	That books may look quite different and even be read in a different way if they are written in other languages:
Vocabulary Knowledge Activities that emphasize that there are words in other languages that mean the same thing as words in English:	That other languages use different words for the same object or concept:
Discourse Skills Activities that demonstrate that other languages have similar forms, although they may seem a bit different:	That these or similar forms exist in other languages as well:

From Office of Head Start, "Language and Literacy for All Children," *Head Start Bulletin*, No. 74, Washington. Department of Health and Human Services, Administration for Children and Families, 2002; adapted by permission. In *One Child, Two Languages: A Guide for Early Childhood Educators of Children Learning English as a Second Language, Second Edition*, by Patton O. Tabors (2008, Paul H. Brookes Publishing Co., Inc.).

Goals Chart

Choose three aspects of your practice with second-language–learning children that you would like to work on. Make a plan for each of these aspects in terms of the categories below. Fill in the categories as you implement the plan.

	Action What do you want to do?	**Resources** What will you need?	**People** Who will you involve?	**Duration** How long will it take?	**Goal** What do you want to achieve?	**Outcome** What did you achieve?
Project #1						
Project #2						
Project #3						

One Child, Two Languages: A Guide for Early Childhood Educators of Children Learning English as a Second Language, Second Edition, by Patton O. Tabors.

Index

Tables, figures, and footnotes are indicated by *t*, *f*, and *n*, respectively.

Permissions

This book is an expansion of an earlier chapter by Tabors, P., & Snow, C.E. (1994). English as a second language in preschools. In F. Genesee (Ed.), *Educating second language children: The whole child, the whole curriculum, the whole community* (pp. 130–125). New York: Cambridge University Press. Portions of the chapter have been reprinted throughout the book with the permission of Cambridge University Press.

The cartoon ROSE IS ROSE by Pat Brady, which appears on page 9, is reprinted by permission of United Feature Syndicate, Inc.; ROSE IS ROSE © United Feature Syndicate, Inc.

The extracts on pages 34 and 35 are from Garnica, O. (1983). Social dominance and conversational interaction: The omega child in the classroom. In C. Wallat & J. Green (Eds.), *Ethnography and language in educational settings* (pp. 229–252). Norwood, NJ: Ablex Publishing; reprinted by permission.

The quotations on pages 58, 61, 71–72, 72, 80, and 80–81 and the social and cognitive strategies that appear on pages 72–74 are reprinted from Wong Fillmore, L. (1979). Individual differences in second language acquisition. In C.J. Fillmore, D. Kempler, & W.S-Y. Wang (Eds.), *Individual differences in language ability and language behavior* (pp. 209–218). New York: Academic Press; reprinted by permission.

The position statement quotations that appear on pages 106, 107, 144, 145, 145–146, 152–153, 174, 175, 176, 177, 178, and 181 are copyright © National Association for the Education of Young Children.